It's Been Beautiful

A production of the Console-ing Passions book series
Edited by Lynn Spigel

D1453330

It's Been Beautiful

Soul! and Black Power Television

GAYLE WALD

WITH PHOTOGRAPHS BY CHESTER HIGGINS

DUKE UNIVERSITY PRESS   *Durham and London*   2015

Library of Congress Cataloging-

in-Publication Data

Wald, Gayle, 1965–

It's been beautiful : Soul! and black power television /

Gayle Wald ; with photographs by Chester Higgins.

pages cm—(Spin offs)

Includes bibliographical references and index.

ISBN 978-0-8223-5825-1 (hardcover : alk. paper)

ISBN 978-0-8223-5837-4 (pbk. : alk. paper)

ISBN 978-0-8223-7580-7 (e-book)

1. Soul! (Television program) 2. Soul music. 3. African Americans

in television broadcasting—United States—History. I. Higgins, Chester.

II. Title. III. Series: Console-ing passions book series. Spin offs.

PN1992.77.S663W35 2015

791.45'72—dc23   2014043821

Contents

illustrations   vii

Photographer's Note. A Vision of *Soul!*, by Chester Higgins   ix

Introduction. "It's Been Beautiful"   1

1   *Soul!* and the 1960s   36

2   The Black Community and the Affective Compact   70

3   "More Meaningful Than a Three-Hour Lecture": Music on *Soul!*   104

4   Freaks Like Us: Black Misfit Performance on *Soul!*   145

5   The Racial State and the "Disappearance" of *Soul!*   181

Conclusion. *Soul!* at the Center   213

acknowledgments   221

notes   225

bibliography   253

index   265

Illustrations

PHOTOGRAPHS BY CHESTER HIGGINS

I.1   Ellis Haizlip and Kathleen Cleaver 2
I.2   Toni Morrison 3
I.3   Gladys Knight 7
I.4   Roberta Flack 10
I.5   Odetta 11
I.6   Arsenio Hall 12
I.7   Anna Horsford 17
I.8   The New York Community Choir 24
1.1   Novella Nelson 37
1.2   Anna Horsford 53
2.1   Novella Nelson 78
2.2   Ellis Haizlip and Georgia Jackson 85
2.3   Alice Hille 93
2.4   Ellis Haizlip, Melvin Van Peebles, and Stan Lathan 94
3.1   Nick Ashford and Valerie Simpson 105
3.2   The Staple Singers 108
3.3   Nikki Giovanni and Miriam Makeba 111
3.4   Thelonious Monk 119
3.5   Max Roach 120
3.6   Rahsaan Roland Kirk 121
3.7   Felipe Luciano 129
3.8   Mongo Santamaría 137

3.9   Labelle 138

3.10   Al Green 143

4.1   Betty Shabazz 146

4.2   Sidney Poitier, Novella Nelson, and Harry Belafonte 148

4.3   Jackie Early, Nikki Giovanni, Sonia Sanchez, and Saundra
        Sharp 149

4.4   Nikki Giovanni and James Baldwin 157

4.5–4.8 James Baldwin 158

4.9   Amiri Baraka 170

4.10   Children in the *Soul!* studio audience 174

5.1   Esther Phillips 207

5.2   Woody King and Vertamae Grosvenor 210

5.3   Ellis Haizlip 212

C.1   Ellis Haizlip 219

Photographer's Note

Coming to New York from Tuskegee Institute gave me the chance to share in the cultural wellspring that was bubbling up in 1970s Harlem. Where else could I hear poetry slams by Amiri Baraka at the Schomburg Center, listen to Minister Louis Farrakhan's rallies at Malcolm Shabazz Mosque or Olatunji playing his drums in Mount Morris Park, browse Michaux's African National Memorial Bookstore at the corner of 125th Street and Seventh Avenue, or watch Black Panthers protest against the displacement of black-owned businesses? Although I lived in Brooklyn, I ventured to Harlem almost daily to experience the street life there that brimmed with new confidence in being black, embracing Africanness, and giving voice to visions of a new world where the black point of view had a seat at the policy-making table.

I focused my work on giving visual imagery to the black consciousness that arose out of the civil rights era and African studies. I made the rounds of exhibits and literary festivals looking for opportunities to make publicity portraits, and my images began to appear in a few books and on a book cover for the poet Nikki Giovanni.

To support my family and my work, I sought out freelance opportunities at the *New York Times* Arts and Leisure section and Channel 13. Nikki Giovanni introduced me to Ellis Haizlip, her friend and the producer of *Soul!* Recognizing that I had skills that could serve him well, he hired me to shoot the publicity stills for the show.

Producing publicity images for *Soul!* gave me a privileged window into the black arts movement of the 1970s and a unique opportunity to observe how lighting directors and studio directors manage in a television setting. *Soul!* was a very political show of music and jazz interspersed with in-depth, informative interviews. Each session began with the director working with the stage manager, technicians, camera operators, and audio staff to set up different areas of performance. When the talent arrived, they went to their dressing rooms, where stylists awaited to work their hair and apply makeup.

Each hour-long show was edited down from eight to ten hours of setups, rehearsals, and actual tapings. We always had to be ready for however long it took to finish the show; to appease hunger and thirst, a buffet was provided for the staff and talent during the setup period. The audience poured in closer to taping time.

I learned so much from my days with *Soul!*, overhearing the banter and rich conversations about issues of the day. For me, the weekly productions were more like creative workshops and helped verify my own struggles with my personal work.

As a twenty-six-year-old from Alabama who had been introduced to jazz for the first time at the Tuskegee Institute, I was immensely fortunate to find myself in a television studio where live performances of the great jazz and R&B musicians and discussions with the celebrated poets, essayists, novelists, filmmakers, and political theorists of our time brought the new wave of black culture to a national television audience. I can best describe my time there as being in *Soul!* heaven.

CHESTER HIGGINS

Introduction

There's no precise term that can convey the essence of the
show; black culture is not inexact for it, but that's too pompous a
term; it's a program that combines entertainment and talk, and it
is a soul show. Once the culture of soul is fully documented,
a new word may spring up in its place.
—Ellis Haizlip

It's Been Beautiful tells the story of *Soul!*, an understudied landmark in
the history of American television. One of the earliest black-produced
shows on TV, *Soul!* was the only nationally televised program dedicated to cultural expressions of the black freedom movement of the
late 1960s and early 1970s. For five seasons beginning in 1968—first locally on WNDT (later WNET; Channel 13, New York City's main public
broadcasting outlet), and then nationally via PBS distribution—*Soul!*
offered viewers a weekly platform for music, poetry, dance, politics,
style, and fashion.[1] It provided an intimate stage for mainstream black
culture heroes such as Sidney Poitier and Harry Belafonte and a rare
friendly forum for figures like Louis Farrakhan, Stokely Carmichael,
and Kathleen Cleaver (figure I.1), who were regarded by mainstream
media outlets as beyond the pale. On *Soul!*, Sonia Sanchez and Amiri
Baraka recited their poems; Toni Morrison read from her debut novel
The Bluest Eye (figure I.2); Nick Ashford and Valerie Simpson brought
the studio audience to its feet with the performance of their soulful

I.1. On the *Soul!* set: Ellis Haizlip takes a break from interviewing Kathleen Cleaver while a sound engineer checks the mic.

anthem, "Reach Out and Touch (Somebody's Hand)"; Vertamae Grosvenor demonstrated "vibration cooking"; Earth, Wind and Fire (in an early incarnation with the singer Jessica Cleaves) played a funky set that included a cover of James Taylor's "Don't Let Me Be Lonely Tonight"; Wilson Pickett joined the legendary Marion Williams in the popular gospel number "Oh Happy Day"; and George Faison's modern dance troupe performed *Poppy*, a ballet about drug addiction set to music by Miles Davis. *Soul!* was where the Last Poets performed their politically explosive works, Nikki Giovanni and James Baldwin talked frankly about sex and Black Power, and the musicians Mongo Santamaría, Letta Mbulu, Miriam Makeba, and Hugh Masekela, and poet Keorapetse Kgositsile explored black consciousness and identity transnationally. U.S. audiences watched *Soul!* on their local public television outlets in places like Tulsa and Miami, but viewers included Canadians picking up the signal from Buffalo and Jamaicans who watched tapes of *Soul!* in Kingston.[2]

I.2. Toni Morrison reads from her debut novel, *The Bluest Eye*.

Behind this eclecticism and cultural edginess was Ellis B. Haizlip (1930–91), a New York–based producer whose immersion in African American performing, literary, and visual arts traditions and "debonairly Afrocentric" persona earned him the affectionate nickname "Mr. Soul."[3] Under Haizlip's leadership as the show's producer and regular host, *Soul!* televised a richly heterogeneous cast of artists and public figures, expanding opportunities for black performing artists and intellectuals on television while critiquing the notion that a TV show—let alone a weekly one-hour broadcast produced on a shoestring budget—could adequately or fully represent the black collective. No prime-time U.S. television show has ever addressed itself so unequivocally to black viewers as a culturally distinct audience or employed a greater percentage of black people, particularly black women, in significant creative positions.[4] None has been so committed to decentering heterosexual masculinity within black politics and culture. Likewise, none has been so intent on exploring the variety and vitality of black culture, and on understanding cultural expressions of the U.S. black freedom movement in the context of the affiliated cultural expressions of African-descended U.S. Latinos and black South Africans.

At the most basic level, *It's Been Beautiful* seeks to insert *Soul!* into the annals of television, where for the most part it has been overlooked. With the exception of discussions in Laurie Ouellette's indispensable *Viewers Like You?* and Devorah Heitner's recent *Black Power TV* and related investigations in works by James Ledbetter, Tommy Lee Lott, and a few others, we have no extended written accounts of *Soul!* as a key TV text of the era or as a cultural project joined by common cause to 1960s and 1970s political struggles.[5] *Soul!* receives scant mention in histories of public broadcasting, which, when they discuss programs aimed at minority audiences, tend to focus on public affairs shows such as *Black Journal*. And it is glaringly absent from the vast majority of histories of African Americans and television, where commercial broadcasting, because of its larger audience and association with popular genres like the situation comedy, has received the lion's share of attention. As authoritatively titled a text as the *Historical Dictionary of African-American Television*, for example, contains no entries on *Soul!* or Haizlip.[6]

These scholarly omissions are all the more noteworthy given *Soul!*'s documented popularity and favorable critical reception. Journalists praised the show for its fresh take on soul culture and its promotion of artists who could not be seen anywhere else on television. Viewers thrilled at seeing well-known talents who had not "crossed over" getting their proper due. Although observers occasionally registered discontent with the program's emphasis on performance, fearing it would reinforce notions that black people were only fit subjects of television representation if they were offering musical entertainment, much more common were advocates like Charles Hobson and Sheila Smith, who defended the show after attending the taping of a February 1970 episode with Curtis Mayfield as the guest host. "We don't know many people who would accuse Mayfield of being a stereotype of anything," Hobson and Smith wrote in *Tuesday*, a weekly insert aimed at black readers that was included in various Sunday newspapers in the 1960s and 1970s. Moreover, "if it is stereotyped to dig the Impressions, B. B. King and Eddie Floyd, the brothers and sisters who were on hand were certainly a group of beautiful, together stereotypes."[7]

Soul! never enjoyed the visibility of the era's commercial black programs, such as *Julia* and *Sanford and Son*. Yet despite competition from the three major networks and technological challenges associated with public television, which tended to broadcast on UHF channels inaccessible to all but state-of-the-art television sets, Haizlip's show attracted a substantial and loyal audience. A remarkable 1969 Harris poll—which may well be the first detailed study of the television viewing habits of urban African Americans as a distinct demographic group—found that more than 65 percent of black New York City households with access to *Soul!* watched it on a regular basis. A similar 1972 poll found the show competing favorably with commercial network fare among black audiences in Chicago, Cleveland, Detroit, Los Angeles, Philadelphia, and Washington, D.C. Evidence collected in the early 1970s found *Soul!* unique among nationally broadcast programs in being watched by black viewers across age groups.[8]

Interviews with *Soul!* fans conducted for this book attest to the program's enduring power. "I literally jumped out of my seat," recalls the jazz musician Bobby Sanabria, who happened upon the "Shades of Soul" episode featuring the New York Puerto Rican musicians Tito Puente and Willie Colón when flipping through the channels one night in November 1972. "Because there was nothing about us on TV. Nothing. Absolutely nothing."[9] Roland Washington, who had been part of the 1967 mass walkout by high-school students in Newark, was nineteen when his soul-funk cover band Soul Excitement! appeared on the program in March 1969. *Soul!* episodes featuring Gladys Knight (figure I.3), the Unifics, and the Delfonics brought everyone in Washington's multigenerational household together. "*Soul!* was a unifying force," he recalls, adding: "You didn't want to be walking in front of the TV or getting something to eat when *Soul!* was on."[10] Like Washington, Valerie Patterson, who watched *Soul!* on WPBT in Miami, remembers being deeply impressed by Haizlip. (So was her boyfriend, who with his fraternity brothers envisioned a Miami version of the show that never made it off the drafting table.) It was not just the way Haizlip conducted interviews, with an erudition that impressed her, but also the way he wore his thick glasses, his "huge" Afro, and his "regal," "erect" bearing.[11] Walter Fields, who watched as a child in his parents' home in Hackensack, New Jersey, says his family had a standing weekly "appointment" with *Soul!*, only one of two programs (the other was *The David Susskind Show*) that he was allowed to stay up for.[12]

As these reminiscences about the program suggest, *Soul!* is not just an overlooked cultural achievement of the 1960s and 1970s; it is also a television archive that offers new windows into black political and cultural expression in the Black Power era and the powerful feelings these expressions stirred in viewers in an era when black people had very circumscribed access to the televisual public sphere. In other words, it is not merely a noteworthy historical achievement or an archive of great performances (made all the more precious now that *Soul!* favorites such as Marion Williams, Nick Ashford, and Amiri Baraka are no longer among us), but an archive of what Raymond Williams calls "structures of feeling," expressive both of a particular time and place and of yet-to-be-realized formations, some of which retain their utopian allure after more than forty years. Mining this archive, *It's Been Beautiful* looks and listens for how episodes registered contemporary sociopolitical realities—what Williams calls the "temporal present"—as

I.3. Gladys Knight on the Club Soul set meant to evoke an intimate nightclub, February 1972.

well as future-facing "affective elements of consciousness," exemplified in the resonant slogan, "Black is beautiful."[13]

Soul! "imagined the dawn of a new world," observed the cultural critic Lisa Jones in a tribute to Haizlip written on the occasion of his death from lung cancer in 1991. Not only in its gathering of diverse black artists and intellectuals, but also in its visual aesthetic, the show represented the collective dream of black Americans for transport to an imagined place that promised a radically different social order. "Abstract sculpture served as scenery," Jones writes. "Interviews were shot from unexpected angles and the editing style was up-to-date psychedelic—lots of dissolves and superimpositions."[14] Performers' outfits and hairstyles were equally expressive of new modes of looking and being. Opulent red velvet jumpsuits, Afros, African-inspired head wraps and jewelry, plunging necklines, and billowing bell-bottoms pushed the frontiers of fashion and signified a new expressive freedom, claimed by men and women alike, to break with earlier traditions of black bourgeois respectability.[15] As Haizlip, anticipating Jones, told a Corporation for Public Broadcasting (CPB) reporter in 1970, the very name "Soul!" gestured toward a dreamed-of future. "Soul!," he noted, was the placeholder for an as-yet-unknown word—and world—that the television program, in its own small way, would attempt to envision.[16]

In foregrounding *Soul!* as an archive of affect as well as performance, this book reflects a shift in humanities scholarship toward the felt dimensions of cultural production and reception and the emotional saturation of the political imagination.[17] *It's Been Beautiful* is part of this shift, but it is also a specific attempt to bring such an orientation to bear on the study of African Americans and television, which has been marked by a preoccupation with questions of authenticity, realism, and positive images. In contrast, I attempt to use *Soul!* as an opportunity "to go beyond accounts of representation" and focus instead on cultural performance in the televisual construction and negotiation of blackness.[18] *Soul!* was indeed a pioneering outlet for collective black American self-exploration and self-affirmation in a medium that was only just integrating its representations of the U.S. family and polity and allowing racial minorities and women access to the means of production. When Newton N. Minow, chairman of the Federal Communications Commission, called television a "vast wasteland" in an oft-cited 1961 speech before the National Association of Broadcasters, he was referring principally to the vapidity and lack of intellectual substance of commercial broadcasting.[19] But Minow's appropriation of T. S. Eliot's metaphor for the sterility of modernity aptly captured many African Americans' sense of television, including noncommercial outlets, as an alternately neglectful and hostile place.

Within this sterile landscape, *Soul!* staffers, many of them the first African Americans to hold certain staff positions at New York's Channel 13, imagined themselves to be using the tools of television broadcasting to plant "black seeds"—a metaphor that reflects their eagerness for opportunity and ways in to television, rather than fears of selling out.[20] Haizlip felt that *Soul!* had tremendous potential to bring attention to artists whom he believed merited a larger audience. Novella Nelson, one of these artists, remembers that Haizlip had "an internal compass about what was beautiful [and] what was not beautiful that was unwavering and exquisitely sensitive, which is why, as a producer, he proved so prescient, giving many artists their first television exposure."[21] As Haizlip would proudly note, *Soul!* hosted the national television debuts of Melba Moore; Nelson; Roberta Flack (figure I.4); Bill Withers; Donny Hathaway; Herbie Hancock; Earth, Wind and Fire; The Spinners; Al Green; and Billy Paul.[22] It offered a national platform to black female political leaders—from New York's Democratic congresswoman Shirley Chisholm, who would go on to mount a historic run for the presidency; to Queen Mother Moore, the pan-Africanist, Garveyite, and long-time advocate for reparations for slavery—who were marginalized by mainstream black leadership. Politically and culturally, it bridged generational and political factions, welcoming icons of the "classical" phase of civil rights, like Belafonte and the musician Odetta (figure I.5), alongside poets, activists, and performers more identified with black arts and Black Power. It planted seeds in viewers as well, offering them a broad-minded exploration of black politics and culture that was a weekly source of delight, instruction, and inspiration on matters ranging from Third World critiques of capitalism to tips on natural skin

I.4. Roberta Flack at the piano (and a drummer in the background) on *Soul!*, circa 1970.

care. Frequent images of in-studio audience members—care of the directors Ivan Curry and, later, Stan Lathan—conveyed an ambience of black community that sent forth powerful messages of black political solidarity and cultural pride. But they were also helpful to young viewers in far-flung towns and small cities across the United States, who wanted to know about the latest fashions and hairstyles. As a national program, *Soul!* transmitted a New York–centric sense of emergent black identities to a geographically dispersed audience, exploring the simultaneous diversity, disunity, solidarity, and shared interest of a black audience shaped by multiple diasporas, displacements, and migrations.

I.5. Odetta on *Soul!*, April 1971.

Soul! was groundbreaking in form, as well as adventurous politically and aesthetically. Its combination of talk and performance, initially modeled after *The Tonight Show* with Johnny Carson, enabled it to venture beyond the limitations of the era's commercial fare (shows like *The Mod Squad*, *The Outsiders*, and *Room 222*) and noncommercial national public-affairs programming (including *Black Perspectives on the News* and *Black Journal*), notwithstanding the adventurous turns that both formats might occasionally take.[23] Unencumbered by realist demands for accuracy and verisimilitude, or by the weighty expectations placed on programs purporting to offer black viewpoints, *Soul!* could instead pursue questions of identity and community through multiple or even competing modes of address. Indeed, *Soul!* sought out politically and aesthetically challenging material of the sort that Carson pointedly eschewed. In the late 1960s, the popular late-night host took the *Tonight* franchise to new levels of profitability by offering the program to viewers as a diverting nightcap, an electronic elixir to ward off bad dreams incited by the disturbing images of the evening news.[24] If Carson's show also supported the careers of such pioneer-

I.6. A teenage Hall performs as Arsenio the Magician, *Soul!*, April 1971.

ing black comedians as Flip Wilson, Bill Cosby, and Redd Foxx—all of whom would go on to be important black TV stars and producers in the 1970s and 1980s—it was in part because they worked in a performance register that softened critique with laughter.

Soul! did occasionally feature comic performers. Irving Watson, a Carson favorite, and Foxx both appeared on early *Soul!* programs, and an episode from April 1971 featured a young magician by the name of Arsenio (figure I.6), later familiar to millions of late-night TV viewers as the host of the *Arsenio Hall Show*. But in general Haizlip shared the wariness of the poet Carolyn Rodgers and the novelist John Killens, both *Soul!* guests, about a legacy of TV representation—epitomized by *Amos 'n' Andy*—that cast blackness itself as an object of hilarity. In his personal papers, Haizlip kept a copy of Rodgers's poem *A Long Rap: Commonly Known as a Poetic Essay*, a searing black feminist critique of the *Flip Wilson Show* that was published in 1971, at the height of the comedian's popularity.[25] And he would have known *The Cotillion*, Killens's satire of the same year, with its simultaneously hilarious and nightmarish depiction of *The Tonight Show* as a stage for the symbolic lynching of the novel's black radical (anti)hero. If there was any confusion about where Haizlip, as producer, stood on the question, on the eve of *Soul!*'s first episode he curtly informed a *New York Times* reporter that the program welcomed white viewers, as long as they did not tune in "to watch a lot of darkies strumming and singing."[26]

Overlapping for three seasons with both Wilson's and Carson's shows, *Soul!* offered itself as a program that would use the variety format to address a diverse black audience, but would reject the format's racially saturated history of comedic performance and its evasion of politics.[27] Instead, *Soul!* would give the spotlight to a variety of organic intellectuals, based on the assumption (shared by members of the black arts movement) that a black television show had a responsibility to communicate with its audience rather than speak (down) to it. Whereas conventional television wisdom of the period held escapist (commercial) programming apart from educational (noncommercial) fare, *Soul!* proposed that pleasure and knowledge were two sides of the same coin, and that most television programming that purported to enlighten black audiences only reinforced existing class and gender hierarchies. In Haizlip's alternative formulation of "educational television" (a term that preceded today's more familiar "public television"), a concert by Mayfield and the Impressions might be "more meaningful than a three-hour lecture." Conversely, and consistent with the outlook of black arts practitioners, *Soul!* did more than any TV program of the era to promote poetry, conceived not as a rarefied art form but as accessible oratory rooted in longstanding African American aesthetic traditions.

In its emphasis on music, *Soul!* bears an obvious resemblance to *Soul Train*, the popular music-and-dance show that debuted in 1970, as Haizlip's program entered its second season. In fact, during the years that they overlapped as national productions (roughly 1971–73), the two TV shows—one commercial, the other noncommercial—booked many of the same acts. Both celebrated and incubated black musical creativity, and Haizlip respected the work of his friend and counterpart, Don Cornelius, but *Soul!* and *Soul Train* worked toward divergent visions. *Soul Train* began as a local Chicago youth and dance show sponsored by Sears, Roebuck and Company. Tweaking the formula popularized by *American Bandstand*—and explicitly refuting that show's racist legacy of resisting the integration of its dance floor—*Soul Train* tapped into the growing commercial market for black pop in the 1970s, epitomized by the success of Motown Records, which touted itself as "The Sound of Young America."[28] On *Soul Train*, the roving eye of the camera subordinated the relatively static image of musicians to the more dynamic spectacle of dancers as they responded to and creatively interpreted the music; on *Soul!*, the spectacle of musical production garnered more attention, with camera operators working to convey a sense of the emotional immediacy and intensity of live performance even when episodes were taped. Moreover, and unlike *Soul!*, *Soul Train* was a self-consciously entrepreneurial enterprise, in line with Berry Gordy's Motown. The program indeed anticipated the geographical trajectory of the Detroit-based record label when, in 1971—after Johnson Products Company, the maker of Afro Sheen, signed on as a major sponsor—it moved its base of operations to Los Angeles. The show's westward migration confirmed *Soul Train*'s power as a cultural arbiter, but it also conflated black success with the abandonment of local black communities, which were then confronting the forces of deindustrialization that would lead to the concentration of poverty in the inner city.

Soul! projected an image of soul culture that ventured beyond the youth and black pop demographic and retained a connection to New York's black arts and political scenes—and, perhaps, a slight whiff of black New Yorkers' sense of superiority to the residents of Detroit, Chicago, and Los Angeles. Shaped by the idealism of educational television, the urgency of the black freedom movement, and the eclecticism of Haizlip's tastes—cultivated during his student years at Howard University in the 1950s and his early career in theater—*Soul!* had the air of a TV program in pursuit of lofty goals, certainly something much higher than ratings or sponsorship. Whereas *Soul Train* embraced Black Power in an economic sense, manifesting its politics primarily at the level of style and image, *Soul!*, imbued with greater earnestness, self-consciously pursued black performance as a site for progressive black mobilization. It paid tribute to black popular culture yet devoted equal time to less popular arts (for example, concert dance) and to musicians whose genius was largely ignored by the commercial mainstream: from Nelson, the singer and actor who figures centrally in this book, to "New

Thing" jazz virtuosos like Max Roach, admired by the black intelligentsia yet lacking mass appeal, and Puente, who enjoyed international popularity but in television appearances was often expected to play music accessible to the Anglo majority.

The chapters of this book chart *Soul!*'s innovative, even visionary, explorations of black culture and politics, while bearing in mind the material conditions and structural challenges that simultaneously shaped the program's history and, at times, its expression. *Soul!* was a vehicle of black radical critique on public broadcasting, a medium embedded within the state and reliant, in this period, on the patronage of the Ford Foundation, the liberal philanthropy that had underwritten U.S. public broadcasting since the 1950s. The program's emergence coincided with a brief period when government officials and broadcasting executives, in response to the long-standing petitioning of black activists, looked to public television as a vehicle for redressing widespread sociopolitical discontent, and its demise occurred at a moment, soon afterward, when the state and, in its wake, broadcasting institutions abruptly reversed course, withdrawing support both for public television generally and for liberal programming in particular.

Others have narrated the decline of public television in these years.[29] *It's Been Beautiful* supplements existing scholarship by attending closely to how the state mobilized in response to civil rights successes, appropriating integrationist discourse to pursue its own interests, and how the *Soul!* community—an imagined public consisting of both its producers and its viewers—navigated repeated instances of existential threat. The first of these moments came in 1969, near the end of *Soul!*'s first season, when the Ford Foundation declined to renew a crucial programming grant that covered operating expenses; the last came in 1973, when officials at the quasi-governmental CPB announced that they were directing public monies away from *Soul!* and toward programming that would emphasize the image of integration—of black and white bodies within a single visual frame—thereby superficially projecting an ideal of racial harmony and of black citizens as the equals of whites within the formal political sphere. The story of *Soul!* is from this perspective a story of ongoing effort—in the form of public diplomacy, behind-the-scenes maneuvering, and organized protest—to secure the very conditions of possibility for the program's existence. The history of *Soul!* is particularly instructive in displaying how the noncommercial sphere of broadcasting, which had offered itself as a site of cultural possibility and formal experimentation not available in the commercial realm, ultimately proved to be vulnerable to countermobilizations of the "racial state" in the immediate post–civil rights era.[30]

Closely related to the issue of *Soul!*'s conditions of possibility is a set of concerns in *It's Been Beautiful* about the relation of *Soul!* to a broader political and social history of the period between 1968 and 1973. The black arts and Black Power movements, which came of age in these years, registered the shift from a post–World War II era of protest politics, which had produced a "face of public unity" to combat state-sanctioned racism, to an era of proliferating imaginations of black interests in light of novel expressions of state power.[31] In its five seasons on the air, *Soul!* harnessed energies and strategies associated both with civil rights and Black Power, reflecting the liminality of the period. A proudly black show on a television outlet better known for programs like *Great Performances* and the British import *Civilisation*, it combined the civil rights movement's critique of the uneven distribution of state resources and citizens' rights with the black arts and Black Power movements' rejection of the state as an ultimate arbiter of black freedom and embrace of alternative paradigms of value, belonging, and authority, as signified in the very word "soul" itself. If *Soul!* had a political patron saint, it was Malcolm X (figure I.7), whose 1965 murder the program commemorated in special episodes featuring the late leader's widow, Betty Shabazz, a friend of Haizlip. Yet the show's spirit of bold defiance was influenced by a distinct spirit of somber introspection that was inseparable from the lingering grief over the assassination of Martin Luther King Jr. and questions about the direction of the movement he had spearheaded. (It was in fact the anguished and angry public response to King's 1968 slaying that forced the U.S. government to make available the public resources that forged a path for *Soul!*) As this study illustrates, the *Soul!* archive is saturated by affective intensities that alternately gave voice to black hope and despair, celebration and mourn-

I.7. Anna Horsford in front of an image of Malcolm X, on the *Soul!* set

ing, Afro-optimism and Afro-pessimism.[32] It is an archive that refutes the notion—ably critiqued more recently by Jacquelyn Dowd Hall and others—that the immediate post–civil rights era was one of declension, decline, and the dispersal of black political energies and efforts.[33]

I find the protean energies of this period reflected and refracted in *Soul!*'s programming choices, its aesthetic of juxtaposition, and its ongoing experimentation with format. For example, in the repeated presence on the show of the poet and activist Felipe Luciano, I find an affirmation of the centrality of Latinos—especially Puerto Ricans, who had protected their property in Newark during the 1967 riots by writing "soul brother" on shop windows and doors—within post-1968 black cultural and political formations. In the two-episode conversation between Giovanni and Baldwin, I discover the simultaneous display and deconstruction of familiar categories of identity and political ideology, as well as powerful enactments of gendered tensions and romantic love within the Black Power movement. The dynamism of the era is evident as well in the memorable 1972 episode devoted entirely to the jazz virtuoso Rahsaan Roland Kirk, who evoked New World rebellions going back to the revolution of Haitian slaves and on to Selma and Newark by dramatically demolishing a chair after a performance of the gospel number "Old Rugged Cross."

As these examples suggest, *Soul!* affords us a vision of black culture and politics in the late 1960s and early 1970s that was more fluid, less predictable, and more open to difference than many scholars who work within a more traditional sense of the political have recognized. Whereas the evening news and public-affairs shows represented Black Power through the figure of the angry or militant male revolutionary, on *Soul!* a viewer was as likely to see radical consciousness and creativity embodied in Labelle, the female trio who appeared on a 1972 episode doing an inspired cover of the Who's "Won't Get Fooled Again." The proud and beautiful faces of women—first Nelson and later the actor and associate producer Anna Horsford, both wearing "natural" hairstyles—flashed on the screen during *Soul!*'s jazzy opening sequence, anticipating the opening sequence of *Saturday Night Live*, another edgy, New York–centric variety show that would debut not long after *Soul!* went off the air. And there was Haizlip, the avatar of soul style and sensibility, a gay man who engaged in warm and mutually admiring conversations on the program with Baraka and Farrakhan, whose sexual politics would seem to have positioned them as his adversaries. The *Soul!* archive casts light on such obscured networks of black arts and Black Power conviviality, in which figures seemingly set apart by difference of creed, sensibility, and ideology were represented as mutually familiar and respectful of one another, and in which invisible alliances and proximities (such as those between African Americans and Puerto Ricans in Harlem and between gay and straight black men within the movements) found an avenue of cultural representation.

The problem of understanding the political formation of *Soul!* in relation to received notions of Black Power is partly, I find, one of presentist historical inclination. Given my own intellectual formation in the late 1980s and early 1990s, engaging with the *Soul!* archive has meant shedding prevalent assumptions about 1960s and 1970s nationalist political culture as a homophobic and patriarchal monolith. If the Black Power movement has gotten a reputation for absolutism and intolerance because of some of its most visible and notorious expressions, then *Soul!* indeed offers us a different perspective, in which a common sense of purpose offered black people of divergent sensibilities, backgrounds, and political commitments pathways for representing and negotiating difference. Especially in chapter 4, *It's Been Beautiful* works to recuperate the finely woven social textures of the black arts and Black Power movements—not to idealize the period or to deny the pettiness and narrow-mindedness that coexisted with tolerance in this formation, but to subject it to new understanding.[34] For example, *Soul!* showed black women as occupying roles that diverge from and complicate those critiqued in Michele Wallace's 1979 manifesto, *Black Macho and the Myth of the Superwoman*, which took to task Giovanni, *Soul!*'s most recognized female intellectual, and set the tone for a certain feminist analysis of 1960s and 1970s black radicalism.[35] At the same time, Haizlip is revealed to be an important and overlooked protagonist of the black arts and Black Power movements: a cultural impresario and anthologist of soul culture, on a par with "New Negro" anthologist Alain Locke and the cultural rainmaker Carl Van Vechten, who left a lasting impression on the scores of artists and intellectuals he mentored or otherwise supported, but who is overlooked in academic black queer projects of historical recuperation. On *Soul!*, the idealized family of the black modern nationalist imagination is subjected to respectful critique—not to disparage varieties of nationalist politics and desire in this era, but to force its most visible spokesmen to address the dissenting expressions within this formation.

Two recurring keywords assist me in these investigations, threading their way through my narrative. The first is *affective compact*, a term I use to explore *Soul!*'s pursuit of intimacy and connection with viewers, despite the distancing, cold mediation of television. In practice, the affective compact, explored in detail in chapter 2, encompassed everything from *Soul!*'s mode of address (for example, Haizlip's use of words like *we* and *our* when speaking to the camera) and the knowledge it assumed viewers had (about racism, for example, or black public figures) to its tacit understanding of audience participation as a necessary element of live performance. The notion of an affective compact particularly assists me in understanding the activism of the heterogeneous and geographically dispersed community of *Soul!* viewers, who passionately supported Haizlip and the program in moments of crisis. It also helps me tease out *Soul!*'s resistance to widely embraced notions of television as a medium that, by its very nature, encouraged political passivity, social conformity, and social isolation.

At the center of the affective compact is a heuristic concept of black experience that binds viewers of *Soul!* to its representations and, through the synchronous experience of watching television, to each other. Haizlip alluded to this concept in a 1968 interview with *R 'n' B World*, telling a reporter: "Our main point is to attract the black TV audience. . . . We'd like to give the audience a common experience through its blackness. The thing is to pull all those brothers together on Thursday nights and let them have the common experience of enjoying Soul!"[36] As producer, Haizlip was tasked with giving material expression to the idea of black experience from segment to segment, week to week, and season to season. Not unlike the black arts movement's celebrated poets and dramatists, he incubated a vision of black cultural self-definition that refused to accept white aesthetic standards and, in so doing, contributed to the emotional and spiritual well-being of the collective. "We're trying to create programs of black love, of black encouragement," Haizlip explained, looking into the camera, at the conclusion of the occasionally fractious 1972 episode featuring Farrakhan. "We hope that you agree with what's going down."[37]

Where the affective compact is concerned, I am less interested in critiquing the idealism of particular moments or constructs of *Soul!* than in understanding the basis of their appeal, in both senses of that word: that is, in their solicitation and mobilization of a sense of solidaristic affiliation and their power to stimulate viewers' emotions and interest. Like the literary critic Stephen Henderson—who, in the influential introduction to his 1973 anthology, *Understanding the New Black Poetry*, proposed "saturation" as a keyword for understanding "the philosophical meaning of phrases like 'Black is beautiful'"—Haizlip posited a notion of soul that resisted the integrationist logic of American cultural pluralism.[38] For him, as for other black intellectuals engaging with concepts of cultural nationalism, black experience and black culture were empowering constructions that countered the historical erasures of white supremacy. Houston Baker Jr., looking back on Henderson's essay about saturation, declared them to be an expression of the era's "metaphysical rebelliousness," in which radical intellectuals sought to liberate themselves from critical traditions that marginalized black expressive culture.[39] Such metaphysical rebelliousness is likewise at the heart of the *Soul!* enterprise and a hallmark of its own spirit of restless and repeated self-creation.

My second keyword is *vibrations*, a term I derive from Haizlip himself, who used it to describe the affective atmosphere conjured by notable *Soul!* conversations or presentations. Haizlip elaborated on the concept of vibrations in a brief producer's note that he wrote for programs for Soul at the Center, a black performing arts festival largely inspired by the television show, which he co-organized at Lincoln Center in the summer of 1972. In the note, Haizlip—a native of Washington, D.C.— recalled the "warmth" he had felt seeing concerts, plays, and poetry recitals in the black performance spaces (including makeshift venues like churches) of the segregated capital city, and he wrote affectingly of the transformative power of black performance, both on the individual and the collective.[40] As an example of how performance could change people's sense of space itself, he cited his memory of Marian Anderson's historic 1939 recital at the foot of the Lincoln Memorial on the National Mall, after the opera singer had been peremptorily denied the use of Constitution Hall, the venerable Washington venue controlled by the Daughters of the American Revolution. Recalling the ways the amplified pulsations of Anderson's powerful voice filled and warmed that cold space (although it was Easter, the weather was distinctly wintry), he ascribed the efficacy of her performance to its "vibrations" and, in a bold historical leap, imagined a version of these vibrations pulsating through Alice Tully and Philharmonic Halls, venues designed with European high-arts traditions in mind.

In his original proposal for Soul at the Center, Haizlip elaborated on the significance of black people's "occupation" of "white" spaces. "The Black Experience Revival," he wrote, using his initial title for the Lincoln Center festival, "would take place at Alice Tully Hall," a space specifically designed for chamber music performance. "I am aware that it would be best to hold the fete in a relatively culture-free, nonestablishment location so that the ego-presence of the American Black people would be the unifying force, rather than the architecture of the buildings or the solemnity of the locale, yet one purpose of this event (which I hold firmly in my mind) is the urgency of making Lincoln Center a more relevant and responsive institution within the total community."[41] In the producer's vision, the "vibrations" of the collective were linked to the material transformation of white spaces and resources. "The Black Experience Revival" might have been staged at symbolically black spaces such as the (white-owned) Apollo Theater in Harlem, for which black New Yorkers felt a sense of cultural ownership and collective belonging, but then it would not have changed the dynamics of culture in New York, or the sense of the newly constructed Lincoln Center campus—a premier venue for New York performing arts—as a venue for symbolically white performance.

Through his concept of vibrations, Haizlip centered the production and negotiation of affect in performance settings that explicitly blurred the boundary between producers and consumers. Indeed, his idea about vibrations anticipates, even while it complicates, contemporary affect theory through its grounding in the African American performance aesthetic of call and response. As illustrated in the example of remembered concerts or recitals at Howard's Rankin Memorial Chapel, for Haizlip black performance was always a site of dynamic exchange between performers and audiences. The vibrations he associated with black performance were inherently social, resonating within the body of the collective and constituting the collective as a resonant social body. These vibrations also had a transtemporal dimension, insofar as they called on embodied memories of past performances while anticipating new feelings and states of being.

Haizlip was not alone in thinking about vibrations, a term from acoustics, as a metaphor for the efficacy of black performance, the condition of possibility for which is its own disappearance. A range of creative intellectuals including Kirk, John Cage, Sun Ra, Dorothy Ashby, Albert Ayler, and even Beach Boys band member Brian Wilson pursued similar ideas in their work—especially Ra, whose musings on music as sonic transport heavily influenced Baraka's writing and laid the foundation for later Afrofuturist and queer utopian theorizing.[42] Like Ra, Haizlip conceptualized the concert space as a quasi-sacred arena, where performers and audiences engaged in the mutual exchange of energy, and he recognized the bodily sensation of musical vibrations as a source of knowledge and power, not only (erotic) pleasure.[43] Yet where Ra's thinking pushed up against the limits of rationality and science, advancing unconventional beliefs in reincarnation and interplanetary travel, Haizlip grounded his utopian concept of vibrations in more terrestrial black cultural traditions, most notably those of the black church.

In an era when it was fashionable on the Left to denounce religion as a haven for passivity and false consciousness or to embrace systems of belief (such as the Islam of Elijah Muhammad) as alternatives to Christianity (conceived as a European or "white man's" religion), Haizlip's explicit embrace of black Christian cultural and social practices distinguished him from many of his contemporaries. Haizlip grew up in a Holiness congregation, and he regarded the African American church as a living archive of historical black consciousness.[44] Under segregation, churches had afforded black communities a weekly opportunity to experience shared vibrations in spaces largely outside of white surveillance. Moreover—and notwithstanding the inevitable fac-

I.8. The TV set as church: the New York Community Choir performs on *Soul!*, February 1971.

tionalism, hierarchy, and petty infighting—the church offered a flawed but useful prototype of the sort of warm black counterpublic space that Haizlip wished to create on television (figure I.8). Perhaps equally important to Haizlip—who, as a TV host and producer, did not conceal his homosexuality—the church had long accepted the presence of "sissies," "bulldaggers," and other queer bodies in the collective, as long as they were not too visible or disruptive.[45] Alice Hille, *Soul!*'s associate producer between 1968 and 1971, gave voice to this congruence when she touted *Soul!* as "one-hour of relief once a week."[46] Her phrase referred to concrete TV time bands, but it hints at an equivalence between television and daily life, in which a weekly hour at the church or mosque (or their secular equivalent, the nightclub) offered an analogous reprieve from the stresses of daily life. A May 1969 *New York Times* display advertisement appealing for corporate underwriters for the program at a time of crisis touted *Soul!* as a show that "turned the black community on," a phrase that usefully draws together affect, or the production of "intensities" associated with the erotic and manifested in spirit possession and related practices of the Sanctified Church, with the operation of consumer electronics such as television sets.[47]

Haizlip's interest in the vibrations of black counterpublic spaces links his concept, finally, to my notion of the affective compact. The 1960s and 1970s saw the increased use of the word *soul* as a signifier for blackness, the term resisting white appropriation insofar as it refused to be pinned to a specific quality or possession of black people. In this sense, the familiar phrase "if you don't know what it [soul] is, you don't have it," while humorous, succinctly locates the source of soul's signifying power in its very elusiveness as a concept. Haizlip referred to this power when asked about the title of his TV program or about whether it was also for white people. "Soul" is "a shared experience that only a suppressed, oppressed minority can express and understand," he told one white journalist, insisting that while whites might watch *Soul!*, it ultimately cared little whether they watched.[48] Haizlip's assertion of black cultural power through indifference to white viewers and white opinion was expressed as well in the exclamation point in the program's title, a mark of emphasis that resembled an upside-down Black Power salute.

I discuss Haizlip's concept of vibrations in more detail in chapter 5, which focuses on *Soul!*'s final season and on the producer's refusal to concede finality in the face of the withdrawal of CPB support, advancing a notion of the program's disappearance as distinct from its demise. Yet Haizlip's 1972 producer's note, the eloquence and originality of which moved me to write a book about *Soul!* in the first place, permeates this project in more comprehensive and also less explicit ways.[49] It influences my method, which draws idiosyncratically—but, I hope, coherently—on cultural history, cultural analysis, and literary studies, and which is informed throughout by oral history, even when I am not directly quoting from interviews.[50] Haizlip's concept of vibrations also informs the specific examples I home in on from among the dozens of hours of tapes of *Soul!* that are available. Although I cannot possibly hope to represent *Soul!* in its entirety in these pages—indeed, one of the challenges of writing this book is making five seasons of an ever-changing TV show both engaging and coherent—I have endeavored to narrate moments that strike me as exemplary in their materialization of the program's affective atmosphere or "vibe," as well as moments primarily interesting for their unusual, provocative, or extraordinary content.

With few exceptions, I draw these examples from *Soul!*'s second through fifth seasons, or from January 1970 through March 1973. My omission of most of the show's episodes from the 1968–69 debut season is driven by necessity. Of the thirty-five episodes of *Soul!* that aired live on Thursday nights at 9 o'clock on Newark-based WNDT during this period, only one exists in its entirety; as far as I and others have been able to tell, the tapes from this period were either lost, discarded, or repurposed for other recordings. Exacerbating this gap in the early *Soul!* archive is the fact that *Soul!* does not circulate widely, either commercially or via social media. As of this writing, the program has no significant presence on YouTube and is not available for purchase in analog or digital format; the only publicly accessible collection of *Soul!* episodes is at the Library of Congress.[51]

I read the incompleteness of the *Soul!* archive as a performance of the erasures that characterize the relation of black performance to the archive of American performance.[52] Similar absences or erasures characterize the archives of many programs of the period, including the first decade of *The Tonight Show* with Johnny Carson. Yet in the case of *Soul!*, such archival absences—in this case, perhaps literally erasures, since technicians reused the expensive two-inch tapes on which it was recorded when possible—contribute to the absence of subordinated groups from the historical record, exacerbating social experiences of invisibility. Archives, moreover, are not just collections of stuff; they exist by virtue of intensive investments of labor and money, as a *New York Times* journalist writing recently about the digitization of the *Tonight Show* archive could not fail to observe. Although little "from the first 10 years of Carson's 'Tonight Show' . . . has survived," the journalist noted that copies of shows from 1973 on "were kept in storage . . . in salt mines in Kansas." We learn, too, from the *Times* article that the effort of preserving, digitizing, and transcribing the *Tonight Show* tapes demanded the combined labor of "more than 2,000 people."[53] Hence the absence of *Soul!*'s first season may be arbitrary, but it is not entirely accidental.

Scant resources must also figure into the narratives we construct about how certain stories—including the story of *Soul!*—are overlooked in our cultural histories.

In *It's Been Beautiful*, the lacunae in the *Soul!* library compel me to seek out alternative sources of documentation and methods of storytelling more suitable to a text that was a palette for ongoing creative discovery by its production staff, directors, camera operators, lighting technicians, sound designers, and stagehands. Each of the five seasons of *Soul!* saw different attempts—sometimes several within a single season—to showcase an ever-changing roster of guests in ever-changing representational formats. In later seasons, this included the novel arrangement of the studio environment to resemble a nightclub, Club Soul, complete with atmospheric candlelight and the clustering of members of the studio audience around small tables. *Soul!*'s aesthetic of multiplicity, juxtaposition, and improvisatory experimentation further demands that individual performances be read in the context of the narrative arc of particular episodes or even seasons. To understand the gospel singer Marion Williams's authoritative and restrained interpretation of Billie Holiday's signature ballad "God Bless the Child," from a Peabody Award–nominated October 1968 episode, for example, requires thinking of it as the performance that directly followed "Die Nigga!!!," the Last Poets' confrontational spoken-word piece. Indeed, it is the fact that such disparate expressions could coexist in a single episode that merits exploration.

Furthermore, although Haizlip was the show's most unifying and visible presence and is in many ways the protagonist of the *Soul!* story, it is noteworthy that he regularly ceded the host role to others, in a deliberate effort to give performers—including Mayfield, Joe Tex, Luciano, and Giovanni—opportunities to display untapped aspects of their talent and to refute, yet again, the pernicious stereotype of the one-dimensional black entertainer. (The list of *Soul!* hosts includes the psychologist Alvin Poussaint; Haizlip's cousin, the educator Harold Haizlip; the announcer and producer Gerry Bledsoe; and the radio personality Hal Jackson.) Unlike *Soul Train*, helmed by the honey-voiced Cornelius, or—closer to home—public broadcasting's *Black Journal*, later renamed *Tony Brown's Black Journal*, *Soul!* did not produce its affective energy only through a singular charismatic male personality.[54] Haizlip's commitments, tastes, and connections drove the show, but the show itself did not rise or fall on his celebrity.

Soul!'s complexities, both as a historical project and a performance text, do not prevent me from writing about the program chronologically—especially in chapters 1, 2, and 5—from its prehistory in discourses of educational television, civil rights, and the integration of mass media to the early 1970s disputes about racial representation that led eventually to its cancellation. Diverse institutions play an important role in this story: from major funders like the Ford Foundation, the CPB, and WNET in New York to more obscure organizations such as the Station Broadcasting Cooperative, the group of PBS affiliates tasked with voting on programs for national distribution. So does the liberal state—by which, as I have already begun to suggest, I mean the discourses, institutions, and political arrangements that constituted governmental power and authority in the United States during this period. It was the liberal state under President Lyndon Johnson that embraced the integration of television as part of an ongoing project of managing—not merely suppressing—black grievances after King's assassination, just as it was the liberal state, under President Richard Nixon, that hastily fought to reassert federal authority over television in the face of the resistant and transformative energies that the counterculture—and integration—had unleashed.

Overall, I conceive of the state as a controlling and often repressive force in the lives of the people it deems threatening, which—as vast government initiatives like the Federal Bureau of Investigation's Counter Intelligence Program (COINTELPRO) show us—black Americans in this period were per se understood to be.[55] Even as black access to public broadcasting was materially enabled in this period, black expression was unceasingly policed, contained, and suppressed. Yet I also believe the state to be neither omnipotent nor monolithic, and not particularly consistent or deft in its exercise of power. And although I find much compelling in scholarly work that rejects the liberal state, in particular, as a site of liberation or freedom or that sees public television as "politically subservient to the holders of state power," the case of *Soul!* suggests to me the need for a less hermetic conceptualization of the state's relationship to liberal or progressive interests.[56]

Implicit in my conceptualization of the state here is a claim about the agency of black cultural workers who depend on its largesse, even as they compel it through their activism, vigilance, and leadership to be more responsive to their needs (or even while rejecting its authority altogether). The many interviews I conducted with key contributors to *Soul!*—including most of its production staff—as part of my preparation for this book suggest that for most of these committed and talented people, especially for those who identify themselves as black, public broadcasting was a viable and valuable, if imperfect, alternative to network television. As Killens noted in *TV Guide*, the emergence of commercial sitcoms or dramas featuring prominent black characters did not translate, in the early 1970s, into heightened employment opportunities for black people in television.[57] Indeed, the superficial integration of television beginning in the late 1960s arguably helped to consolidate a premature national narrative of political accomplishment, when in fact black grievances, with the mass media and more generally, went much deeper than the vast majority of TV programming would allow. As disenchanted as Haizlip ultimately was with the politics of public broadcasting, and as aggravated as he and his staff were by the need to constantly justify *Soul!*'s existence, they saw little to cheer about in the representations or opportunities produced in the commercial realm. For *Soul!*'s guests, the show created openings—for greater TV exposure, different modes of creative self-representation, or more overt political expression—that network TV, with its bigger audiences, greater prestige, and higher pay scale, did not. The title of Gil Scott-Heron's iconic song "The Revolution Will Not Be Televised" is a convenient starting point for discussions of television's limitations when it comes to radical expression—one reason why the phrase has been the source of many a punning title for studies of television—but it has never been the last word on the matter, not even for Scott-Heron himself.[58]

What concerns me, then, is not the impurity of the *Soul!* enterprise—indeed, I take for granted the impossibility and undesirability of purity in any political or cultural formation—but the discursive shifts that are illuminated by its struggles to stay on the air beyond the early 1970s. By the time the CPB pulled the plug on *Soul!*, the liberal consensus created by earlier civil disorders and the rise of Black Power had been displaced by the new neoliberal political compact formed around resistance to race consciousness and an investment in an emerging discourse of color blindness. As chapter 5 argues, the declining fortunes of *Soul!* correspond to the rising fortunes of post-race discourse. In the end, *Soul!* fell prey to the manipulation of the notion—familiar in our own era—that any form of race consciousness is an impediment to race-blind justice.

My title, *It's Been Beautiful*, gives voice to the dialectical tensions— between optimism and pessimism, utopia and dystopia, permanence and evanescence, and transcendence and boundedness—that frame this study and gives shape to my own affective investments in the subject matter.[59] Like *soul*, *beautiful* is a keyword of modern black cultural and political expression, its meaning bound up with the challenges and pleasures of refusing the definitions of the dominant culture, whose notions of beauty, inherited from the European Enlightenment, have deemed black people and their cultural productions ugly, deformed, and deviant. Indeed, because beauty has never been a neutral concept, it is difficult to think of a significant black American deployment of the word *beautiful* that is not implicitly an engagement with the history of race and racism. But the counterdiscourse of the beautiful acquired particular significance in the era of Black Power, when to utter the phrase "black is beautiful" was not merely to associate oneself with an idea, but also to affiliate oneself, quite pointedly, with a larger struggle.

The spirit of solidarity, especially in the face of the fracturing of old political alliances, is the overarching theme of the episode from which I derive the phrase "it's been beautiful." The episode, from April 1973, features Haizlip in conversation with Stokely Carmichael, and it is uncharacteristic of other last-season episodes in that it lacks the enlivening presence of a studio audience. Titled "Wherever We May Be"—a richly ambiguous phrase that connotes both imminent loss (dispersal) and enduring connection (diaspora)—it was recorded at a time when Haizlip and his staff knew that *Soul!*'s days were numbered because of the withdrawal of crucial CPB funding. Established by the Public

Broadcasting Act of 1967, the CPB was designed to be a neutral administrator of government funding for public broadcasting. Although its budget was controlled by lawmakers, and thus ultimately embedded in the political process, in theory the CPB was supposed to be insulated from political pressures and free to disburse funds to entities or projects it deemed deserving. But from the outset, the CPB was vulnerable to political weather, particularly in an era of increasing rancor over the allegedly liberal bias of public broadcasting and powerful executive-branch pressures to curtail the scope and reach of public television. Accordingly, the organization had denied WNET (formerly WNDT) crucial funding to produce a sixth season of *Soul!*, investing its money instead in a new series, *Interface*, which was to include white guests and focus on crossracial dialogue. A letter-writing campaign in defense of *Soul!* had yielded thousands of affirmations of its importance to viewers but had done little to change the minds of the people who controlled budgets.

The spring of 1973 was also a sober time for Carmichael. In early 1972, the man credited with popularizing the phrase *Black Power* while a young activist with the Student Nonviolent Coordinating Committee (SNCC) had been referenced on *Soul!* by his wife, Miriam Makeba, in a manner that could not help but romanticize the pairing of two such attractive and important figures of global black freedom struggles. But by the time of "Wherever We May Be," Makeba and Carmichael had separated, and Carmichael, living in Guinea, was increasingly becoming estranged from groups with whom he had been allied, especially the Black Panthers.

In the course of the hour-long episode, Haizlip and Carmichael review the highlights of Carmichael's career and discuss his current take on a variety of issues, from King's enduring importance to Sékou Touré, the president of Guinea, and politically motivated witch hunts of Black Power activists. Although the two men were not friends outside of the studio, the relationship of their bodies throughout the conversation conveys intimacy and conviviality. Indeed, the air of comfort and mutuality on the *Soul!* set is a noteworthy departure from the antagonism characteristic of Carmichael's network TV appearances between 1966 and 1970, when white journalists prodded him to defend his rejection of nonviolence and the provocative and empowering slogan "by any means necessary." Through confrontational tactics of questioning Carmichael, journalists in those years were able to cast an unflattering light on Black Power advocates as the explosively emotional counterparts to such stoically rational heroes of the civil rights movement as King.[60]

This is not to say, however, that *Soul!* links Carmichael and Haizlip under the romanticized sign of racial brotherhood. The men's sympathy is evident from the outset, but their differences are also on display, as when Haizlip welcomes Carmichael "home" and is politely corrected by his guest, who notes: "Home is in Africa. You may welcome me back to America."[61] But the dominant "thermodynamic modality" of their staged encounter—to use Jason King's useful vocabulary of performance effects and affects—is not fire but warmth.[62]

The phrase "it's been beautiful" enters the conversation near the end of the hour, when Haizlip, perhaps on a signal from the director, abruptly brings the show to a close:

> *Ellis Haizlip*: Stokely, um, time's up [laugh], and uh . . .
>
> *Stokely Carmichael*: So soon?
>
> *EH*: Time's probably up for *Soul!* anyway. We probably won't be here much longer, but it's been beautiful, the people out there responded well. I am privileged and honored . . .
>
> *SC*: [in reference to Haizlip's allusion to the show's cancellation] Why is that?
>
> *EH*: You know why it is, but uh . . . let's not deal with that. There isn't time [smiles].
>
> *SC*: Well, see, if our community was organized that would not be.
>
> *EH*: I don't know. Maybe it is our evolutionary process that's necessary. But I'm very proud to have had this conversation with you. It's done a lot. And tonight I hope that whoever's listening has learned something. And it's been beautiful. We will find a way to communicate and get our message through. [They punctuate the exchange with a "soul" handshake.][63]

Haizlip utters the phrase "it's been beautiful" twice here, and both times the phrase serves as a heartfelt affirmation of *Soul!*'s achievements in the face of its imminent demise. At the same time, *it* in "it's been beautiful" has a productive quality of indefiniteness. The pronoun simultaneously refers to this particular episode, to the show's five-year history, and to the movement itself, insofar as the fact of Carmichael's self-exile and his display of both disillusionment and hope express a foreboding sense of future political wandering. The present perfect tense of "it's been beautiful" contributes to this expansive reading of the phrase's meaning. Grammatically speaking, the present perfect in English expresses a past that has continuing effects in the present. We say "it's been lovely to meet you" to signify that a social contact has been a pleasure and to indicate an implicit anticipation of further encounters; we say "it's been raining" to indicate that yesterday's rain is continuing today. The temporality of the present perfect is that threshold where past meets present and where present gestures toward an indeterminate future (since our pleasure and the rain have no predetermined end in sight). Like the future perfect theorized by José Muñoz, the present perfect holds past and future in productive tension.[64]

In the context of the "Wherever We May Be" episode of *Soul!*, with its swan-song atmosphere and theme, "it's been beautiful" might therefore be read as a counterpoint to Haizlip's repeated observations about the end of time. When Carmichael asks why *Soul!* is ending, Haizlip's response—punctuated by the phrase "there isn't time"—conveys a need to move on: there literally isn't time left in their allotted hour to talk about it, and besides, he seems to suggest, this particular fight for the TV show's survival is over. In this sense, "time's up" is an acknowledgment of finality—the finality imposed by the conventions of the medium or, more existentially speaking, by the refusal of funding. Following Laurent Berlant, we might also read phrases like "time's up" and "there isn't time" as indicating a sense of crisis or intensified temporality, as in the expression, "It's nation time" (also the title of a poem and 1970 poetry collection by Baraka).[65] "Time's up," as observation and directive, renders this crisis tangible for both Carmichael and the show's audience.[66]

In contrast to the phrase "time's up," "it's been beautiful" resists closure and emphasizes pleasure and hope in the face of crisis. It does not ring of triumphalism—in fact, it communicates a profound humility in the face of history—but neither does it express resignation. It is, in fact, how Haizlip manages to end a show about crisis on a future-facing and affirmative but not Pollyanna-ish note, with a direct address to the audience ("whoever's listening"—a phrase uttered for the camera, in anticipation of future viewers) and an assurance of resilience in the face of constraint ("we will find a way to communicate and get our message through"). The men's handshake seals the deal, offering visual confirmation of their solidarity in the pursuit of a "beautiful" future, however different their strategies are. "Wherever We May Be" assures viewers that this has been the first act; there will be others.

The phrase "it's been beautiful" invites us to circle back to Haizlip's concept of vibrations as a means of negotiating the dynamic of affective imprint and material evanescence that defines our relation to performance. Vibrations are physical matter, but the human body does not always register their presence in the form of hearing or other embodied sensation. Vibrations are in this sense an apt metaphor for the expression of utopian possibilities in performance, which affords both performers and audiences a means of momentarily tapping into the undetected, extrasensorial universe of energy. It was the producer's hope that the vibrations of black performance would awaken their creators to new possibilities, and that, like the vibrations studied by physicists, they would have an enduring and theoretically infinite afterlife in popular consciousness and memory.[67]

I do not wish to overstate the impact of *Soul!* or idealize its interventions. The program was seen by far fewer people than *The Mod Squad*, cannot boast the legacy of *Soul Train* or the longevity of black public-affairs shows (either national programs such as *Black Journal* or local ones such as *Like It Is*, which aired in New York on WABC), and did not give rise to obvious imitations or successor programs—although *Soul!* indirectly blazed a path for later cable programs such as *Russell Simmons Presents Def Poetry*, the well-regarded HBO series that brought "spoken word" into the twenty-first-century cultural mainstream, and for Arsenio Hall's emergence as a significant TV personality. It did not radically alter the racial power dynamics of television, although it was part of a shifting TV landscape in which, increasingly, black people would be visibly present and in which, after efforts that began in the early 1970s, they would own cable networks such as Black Entertainment Television. Haizlip looked back on his experience with *Soul!* with enormous pride but also with some frustration, declaring public broadcasting to be "limited and limiting" in a letter to a lover.[68] Yet *Soul!* did and does have an afterlife, particularly in the communities of shared interest and affect that coalesced around its representations of black politics and performance, and in the scores of artistic and other careers that were facilitated through Haizlip's mentorship and support. On these counts alone, the show merits a prominent place in our canons of late twentieth-century American culture.

That said, I do not want to discount my own experience of the power of this affective archive in producing nostalgic effects and affects. Nostalgia is typically understood as the longing for a never-experienced past; by definition, it constitutes the object of its desire. Nostalgia can be retrogressive, papering over national trauma and rationalizing brutal projects of repression. Moreover, one has only to think of *Gone with the Wind* to appreciate the key role of visual media—from photographs to film and television—in producing and perpetuating such dangerously nostalgic narratives. But to the degree that nostalgia is about fantasy, it may well have a role in celebratory projects such as this one. If nostalgia is for a utopia that never existed, perhaps nostalgia, when it is created by cultural productions of the past, can also reveal the ongoing appeal of their utopian imaginings. If *Soul!* taps into a nostalgic vein of African American scholarship on performance, in other words, maybe that is because many of its fundamental hopes and desires have yet to be realized, even in our post-soul age.

1 *Soul!* and the 1960s

Ellis [Haizlip] said the civil rights movement made his show
possible. Black people made the show possible. Not the Kerner
Commission or the Ford Foundation or executives at WNDT.
—Novella Nelson, interview

Soul! emerged from the shattering events of the 1960s. In a sense, it bears a dialectical relationship to the riots, protests, assassinations, and violence that punctuated the decade, especially in its later years. In other words, *Soul!* was not simply a child of the 1960s or a cultural mirror for the historical and social changes associated with the era. Neither was *Soul!*'s emergence or the particular form it took inevitable. Rather, the creation of a space for black programming on public television, and the idea of a prime-time, hour-long show presenting an innovative— and, for the times, unusual—mix of culture and politics, performance and talk, materialized through ongoing cultural labors that paralleled, even as they were shaped and enabled by, struggles in the proverbial streets.

As Ellis Haizlip, the producer of *Soul!*, avowed—in words recalled by his friend and colleague, the singer Novella Nelson (figure 1.1)—the civil rights movement was the show's condition of possibility. It was the movement that framed television—or more precisely, the near-total exclusion of black people from employment or nonstereotypical representation in TV—as a significant social and cultural problem in American life. It was the movement that protested the exclusively white ownership and oversight of broadcast institutions, and the movement that

1.1. Novella Nelson performing on *Soul!*

compelled a variety of state and nonstate actors—including government agencies, media and telecommunications policy makers, philanthropic organizations, and public TV managers and executives—to take substantive action to address these problems. And it was black cultural workers who came of age with civil rights, Haizlip among them, who seized on openings in public broadcasting in the late 1960s to appropriate television as a tool of social change: not merely as a visible manifestation of integration, but more audaciously as a means of articulating, critiquing, and disseminating new modes of black consciousness.

In *A Dying Colonialism*, published in a mass-market English translation in 1967, Frantz Fanon—the theorist of colonialism whose work deeply influenced U.S. Black Power activists—had written hopefully of Radio Algiers, which transformed a medium previously associated with repressive state power into a revolutionary instrument of public information. Seeing their national struggle as part and parcel of a larger global movement against colonialism, apartheid, and imperialism, Haizlip and other black television pioneers dared to imagine using a medium that had largely failed to include black people in its visual representations or imagined audience as a way to raise consciousness and build community. Mindful of the example of the Black Panther Party, which used arresting iconography and visual symbolism to communicate with the black masses, and cognizant of television's particular capacity for expressing and enabling public feeling, Haizlip and his cohort sought to capitalize on the resonant and felt dimensions of the era's preeminent visual medium to enact, or at least envision, a more beautiful society.

As I tell it here, the story of *Soul!* and the 1960s is thus slightly different from the one usually associated with the articulation of television and civil rights—that is, the story of television as a medium that abetted, even as it altered and was altered by, movement politics. As numerous scholars have shown, the fact that television, as a form of domestic entertainment, and civil rights, as a defining postwar social movement, coincided in time means that television and civil rights are deeply implicated in each other's histories.[1] Among other things, civil rights activists developed sophisticated media strategies, recognizing television as an important tool for disseminating images of local efforts to repress African American citizenship on a national stage. "We are here to say to the white men that we no longer will let them use clubs on us in the dark corners," Martin Luther King Jr. had declared in 1967, the day after a sheriff's posse beat peaceful protestors in Montgomery, Alabama. "We're going to make them do it in the glaring light of television."[2] In its broadcasts on the evening news programs that Americans collectively watched of images showing state-sponsored violence against civil rights activists, television was indispensable to mainline civil rights organizations' ability to portray local fights as national crises in need of swift and decisive federal response and to arouse national sympathy for civil rights protestors.

Wittingly or not, the producers of TV news aided civil rights organizers by recognizing that the spectacle of such violent confrontations were both compelling political drama and compelling television. Like the movement against U.S. intervention in Vietnam, then, the civil rights movement was both culturally framed and experienced by viewers as something that was happening on television. For those at a distance from the front lines of these struggles, in other words, watching civil rights protests, marches, and speeches, as well as scenes of violence and the abuse of state power, became a powerful and distinct mode of cultural consumption and affective engagement with the movement itself.

Soul! was not unrelated to these efforts to use television to make civil rights protests and their repression visible, or to the practice of watching television as a mode of both knowing and feeling about the civil rights movement. Yet it was distinct from both of these in the sense that it grew out of African Americans' new access to television production. Although the visibility of black people on television had increased throughout the decade, it was not until 1968 that shows like *Soul!*—that is, shows primarily imagined and made by women and members of racial and ethnic minority groups—found a foothold in television. Originating in both public broadcasting and network outlets, often as local productions, these programs typically focused on news and public affairs. Better-known examples included Boston's *Say Brother*, New York City productions *Inside Bedford-Stuyvesant* (on public television), and *Like It Is* (on the local ABC affiliate), and—after a protest that led to the ousting of its original white producer—*Black Journal*, a nationally televised newsmagazine. As the label *newsmagazine* indicates, although they did not directly compete with the network news broadcasts, such shows worked within, even as they experimented with, the established format of public-affairs programming, through which the civil rights movement itself had come to visibility as a series of spectacular TV events. Here, too, *Soul!* was an exception among exceptions: a show that put creative expression, rather than reporting or documentary, at the forefront of its representation; that was topical, albeit unconcerned with the news cycle; and that articulated politics and culture rather than subordinating the latter to the former.

This chapter narrates how *Soul!* came to be: how it grew out of a fragile alliance of liberal and radical interests, both public and private, that sought to integrate television in the late 1960s, and how it came to take shape as a platform for the sort of entertainment content typically shunned by educational television. In the chapter, I trace the development of a certain discourse of public television in service to a black audience, and although this discourse did not originate in the National Advisory Commission on Civil Disorders, convened by President Lyndon Johnson in 1967 while Detroit was still burning, nevertheless it was given important public expression in its widely influential *Report* (popularly known as the Kerner Report after the commission's chair, Illinois governor Otto Kerner Jr.).[3] Yet I open with the epigraph from Nelson because her recollection of Haizlip's privileged perspective on the origins of *Soul!* illuminates a methodology for narrating the show's prehistory while remaining attentive to the limitations of official or policy-oriented discourses and archives. First, in starting with the observation that the civil rights movement made *Soul!* possible, and then restating and refining this claim (to "black people made the show possible"), the quote from Nelson instructively points toward a theory of historical agency, conceptualizing civil rights as a social practice rather than an abstract thing in which people participated. Moreover, in insisting that not the Ford Foundation, WNDT executives, or the U.S. government bore primary responsibility for *Soul!*, the quote serves as a useful reminder that it was the civil rights movement that emboldened, or in some cases compelled, institutions and people to pursue social justice in, as well as via, the mass media. Indeed, attributing *Soul!* to the Ford Foundation, WNDT, or the Kerner Commission sets in motion a narrative in which Haizlip and his creative team availed themselves of opportunities provided by beneficent individuals or institutions, but in the quote from Nelson, such openings are suggestively reframed as a response to movement strategies and demands.

One can hardly deny the importance of institutions in the emergence of *Soul!*—indeed, the following pages discuss precisely those named by Haizlip in his comments to Nelson. But the inroads they created in television for new modes and uses of the medium were paved at every step by black people who were motivated by their collective and individual experiences of exclusion, as well as by their many and diverse allies. In this sense, Nelson's quote contains a useful warning about the limitations of a narrowly top-down approach not merely to the history of *Soul!*, but also more generally to the history of television's incorporations of difference. For example, if we allow the state to prevail in the story we tell of how TV news operations came to feature black reporters, we might start and end with President Johnson's 1965 executive order requiring that the recipients of federal monies—including commercial TV networks—"take affirmative action" in hiring.[4] Although the president's mandate was consequential, it tells us little about how the civil rights movement itself made the hiring of black reporters essential to TV news operations. Even before Johnson's order could be implemented, the 1967 uprisings in Detroit and Newark brought the need for black reporters to the forefront. When violence erupted in these cities, white TV programmers, who may already have sympathized with the movement, realized that they could no longer delay in hiring black reporters and camera operators. The integration of TV newsrooms was thus at least as much about survival and self-interest as it was about political solidarity or dutiful compliance with a governmental dictate.[5]

Such recognition of the varied agencies of change, whether reformist or radical, helps to clarify this book's argument about the authenticity of cultural productions embedded in networks of capital or the state. The fact that *Soul!* was a production of public broadcasting, and thus tethered in important ways to U.S. government and private philanthropy, did not render it inauthentic as an expression of black sensibility and affect in the late 1960s and 1970s. Haizlip's characterization of *Soul!* as a show made possible in the first instance by the civil rights movement and black people anticipates this claim, usefully complicating the conventional opposition of black art and white money that inheres in many accounts of twentieth-century black creativity. Unlike the poetry broadsides, writers' workshops, and community theater or arts spaces typically and justifiably celebrated in histories of the black arts movement, *Soul!* was costly to produce (episodes cost $15,000–$20,000 each) and, in its four seasons as a national program, relied on an unwieldy and politically contested system of PBS connections.[6] Inasmuch as financial independence and independent distribution were never even remote possibilities, *Soul!* is a case study in the complex negotiations that underlie the making of progressive black cultural productions amid white ownership of the cultural apparatus.

Fragile alliance, my own term, is meant to call attention to this complexity, acknowledging *Soul!*'s efforts to give expression to utopian desires in the less-than-utopian context of office politics and bureaucratic protocols, including the corporate reports and grant proposals necessary to keep the money flowing. This chapter offers a broad picture of the discursive and material conditions in which *Soul!* took root. It also emphasizes the sometimes conflicting, sometimes mutually reinforcing nature of distinct discourses of black audiences, educational television, and minority programming, so that *Soul!*'s political, ideological, and aesthetic negotiations of such discourses may be better understood.[7]

Before I move on from this chapter's epigraph, I would like to use it to make a final introductory point, which has to do with the function of the black audience in this story. As I have begun to argue, *Soul!* marked a turning point in the concept of delivering targeted television content to black viewers, conceptualized—sometimes in conjunction with racializing socioeconomic markers, such as the phrase *ghetto residents*—as a distinct demographic group. As one of the first TV shows to target black viewers explicitly and to differentiate their interests and needs from those of mainstream (usually understood as white) audiences, *Soul!* participated in the imagination of a black audience constituted in and through a common TV-watching experience.[8] This claim, too, is anticipated in the epigraph. Although it may not strike us at first reading, the phrase "black people made the show possible" conveys an implicit concept of black audience, particularly if we read "black people" as those who watched *Soul!*, not only those whose labors created the conditions for the show's emergence.

In this sense, the epigraph likens the vision of *Soul!* to that of the era's black arts movement practitioners. Like the movement's poets and artists, the program blurred boundaries between "platform and pit," high and low art, aesthetic universalism and beautiful black difference.[9] *Soul!* reinterpreted the role and function of audiences for television, envisioning what I am calling an affective compact between black viewers and black producers and performers. Indeed, through the notion of an affective compact, as I began to outline it in this book's introduction,

Soul! in many ways sought to transcend the limitations of television as a medium that offered few, if any, avenues of dynamic engagement between its representations and those positioned as viewers.

Just as a notion of black audiences and their affective investments in black programming was necessary to the making of *Soul!*, so the black audience was a vital fiction for those institutions and discourses that abetted the show's emergence. The authors of the Kerner Report needed the notion of a black audience to support their finding that it was underserved by the preponderance of white faces and viewpoints on television. Likewise, the Ford Foundation, the most significant private funder of public television from the 1950s to the early 1970s, required the notion of socially and culturally distinct audiences with distinct representational needs to support the establishment of grants for minority TV programming. Haizlip employed a concept of the black audience every time he used the word *we* on camera, or when in 1973 he told Stokely Carmichael, a guest on the show, "it's been beautiful"—referring to *Soul!*'s five seasons on the air. Assumptions about this audience undergirded the very notion, important to Haizlip, of *Soul!* as a television show for "the community."

Who did the black audience consist of, what did that audience want, what was good or bad for it, and how might television in particular serve it—these questions constitute the discursive field of negotiation and conflict over black programming in the late 1960s and early 1970s in general and *Soul!* in particular. They imbued the 1968 Kerner Report, which provided rhetoric supportive of the notion of minority broadcasting, as well as the deliberations of the Corporation for Public Broadcasting (CPB) that led to the cancellation of *Soul!* in 1973. Often discourses of the black audience were overdetermined: for example, in the case of a Ford Foundation grant program for minority television that attracted applicants who justified their projects through appeals to minority interests and minority viewing populations. From this viewpoint, it is not surprising to find battles over *Soul!*'s funding conducted on the symbolic terrain of black people's interests, or (as I discuss in later chapters) to discover Haizlip and his team rebutting existential threats to *Soul!* by calling on surveys demonstrating that "blacks watch educational television more than do whites" and "make a point to tune in programing [*sic*] more oriented toward them."[10] Nor should we be surprised to learn that the era that saw the emergence of *Soul!* also saw the constitution of black consumers as an exploitable market for TV advertising, as well as the creation of demographic tools that produced "black families" as an object of statistical knowledge and analysis.[11] In all of these cases, the black audience was an instrument for particular discourses and outcomes. The story of *Soul!* is thus also a story of which version of this construct would prevail at any given moment.

The Kerner Commission delivered its sobering report to the nation in late February 1968, a little less than eight months before *Soul!*'s debut as a local program. Barring "a commitment to national action—compassionate, massive and sustained, backed by the resources of the most powerful and the richest nation on this earth," the commission's members found, the United States would continue on its trajectory of producing two unequal societies, one black and one white.[12] The rioting in the black ghettos of Los Angeles, Chicago, Newark, and Detroit was a sign that reformist policies, such as the Voting Rights Act of 1965, had failed to address black Americans' fundamental grievances, including pervasive and persistent under- or unemployment, inferior housing, and police intimidation and brutality. Most provocatively, the commission held white America accountable for the conditions that led to the "disorders," asserting that racist practices had created the ghettos that were now the sites of popular unrest. "White racism," it averred in perhaps its most radical conclusion, "is essentially responsible for the explosive mixture which has been accumulating in our cities since the end of World War II."[13]

King, who would be assassinated five weeks to the day after the Kerner Report was released, embraced it as "a physician's warning of approaching death, with a prescription for life," portraying the nation as a mortally or morally ill patient in need of the strong medicine the commission prescribed.[14] (He was perhaps echoing Johnson's comparison of violence in American cities to a "massive disease" in the body politic.[15]) Others noted that the report's recommendations were tempered by a strong condemnation of "a climate that tends toward approval and encouragement of violence" and the firm assertion that "The community cannot—it will not—tolerate coercion and mob rule."[16] As the *New York Times* observed, the Kerner Report "also warned that a policy of separatism now advocated by many black militants 'can only relegate Negroes to a permanently inferior economic state.'"[17] Even given the commissioners' efforts to echo Johnson's pledge to the nation that violence would not be "tolerated," their report proved too radical for the president, who—rejecting many of its premises—disregarded most of its policy recommendations.[18] Despite or perhaps because of Johnson's repudiation, the report touched a national nerve, selling two million copies when it was released in paperback.

It was in fact at Johnson's behest that the Kerner Commission came to devote an entire section of its report to the media. In remarks he delivered on signing the order establishing the commission in July 1967, the president posed a series of questions, one of which was: "What effect do the mass media have on the riots?"[19] This question reflected a growing unease with television as a shaper of narratives about urban uprisings, not just a neutral narrator of them. In viewing the media and the riots through the concept of effects, moreover, Johnson's question to the Kerner Commission was enabled by the notion that television might itself be a cause of civil disturbance. Advocates of this idea accused TV news programs of complicity with publicity-seeking black troublemakers. "The manner in which television uses its vast influence can determine which men become heroes, and which villains," declared one such advocate, in testimony before the Senate in October 1967. "It has the power to convert a virtually unknown extremist with a handful of followers into a national figure. Each time a network decides to feature a Stokely Carmichael or a Rap Brown on its news and commentary programs, it is assisting such irresponsible agitators to achieve recognition."[20] A September 1967 *TV Guide* article, titled "Do TV Cameras Add Fuel to the Riot Flames?," lent support to the "recognition" thesis, distinguishing between a television audience of the majority of blacks and a dissident fringe drawn to the cameras. "During spring and summer," the author noted, doing little to hide his scorn, "almost daily interviews with 'Negro leaders' predicting a holocaust were visible on television.

Many of these men were spokesmen without a following, ambitious activists eager for exposure. But their words created an air of tension and expectancy, convincing the ghetto dwellers that violence was indeed imminent. Nobody was surprised when it came."[21] Such critiques were explicitly framed as claims about representation: about how and whether the very presence of TV cameras produced the news that television purported to cover, whether by altering "the shape of events it touches" or by being "manipulated by the show business appeal of special pleaders."[22] Yet their implicit message was one of social control: A "law-abiding" black citizen watched the TV news; he did not make it.[23]

At the same time, such critiques rested on a powerful, if less explicit, distinction in the modes of black spectatorship of TV representations of riots and special pleaders. In particular, the critiques assumed the affective susceptibility of black audiences, whose members might be incited to riot merely by watching the spectacle of rioting on television. Building on 1960s-era social-scientific knowledge that the Kerner Commission would go on to cite—that black Americans were more likely than whites to get their news from television and that television had penetrated American ghettos almost as thoroughly as it had penetrated American suburbs—such assumptions cast black political radicalism as a social virus and black TV viewers as its unprotected victims. In their vulnerability, black viewers were imagined as being like the children who, it was widely feared in the 1950s and 1960s, might naively act out the violence they saw represented on television. The notion of television as a channel of racialized irrationality also coincided with the era's prevailing wisdom about political protest, which held that protestors were highly susceptible to the emotional power of the crowd.[24] As the political theorist Deborah Gould has explained, such a viewpoint was premised on a belief that, "in contrast to legitimate actors in the polity," protestors were compelled to act out of "natural impulses that interfered with reason." As a form of "acting out," such protest was in fact not political at all.[25]

Affect was also at the forefront of the Kerner Report's discourse on black audiences, albeit in quite different terms—the Kerner Commission saw black TV viewers as the victims of emotionally hurtful representations. Johnson saw media coverage of the 1967 riots as itself inflammatory and laid the groundwork, in his charge to the commission, for a finding that would hold TV news programming partially responsible for blacks' discontent. However, the commission produced a set of policy recommendations based on the notion that television was insufficiently attuned to the needs of black citizen-viewers.[26] The main problem with television, the commission argued, was not that it had been reckless in its coverage of the uprisings (although the report chided TV news operations, along with newspapers and radio, for resorting to sensationalizing tactics of reporting), but that it had not offered sufficient alternative representations of black people as productive and law-abiding citizens. Moreover, television, especially entertainment programming, drew unhelpful attention to racialized economic disparities. As the report asserted in its summary, elevating Johnson's lone question about the mass media to place of prominence, television had "flaunted" images of white wealth that was altogether beyond the reach of "the Negro poor and the jobless ghetto youth." Later, in the report proper, the commission repeated and even amplified the point, saying such images were "endlessly flaunted" and dubbing television "the universal appliance in the ghetto."[27]

Here the commission implicitly refuted the terms according to which Johnson had authorized its inquiry, turning its attention away from news media to focus instead on mid- and late 1960s popular TV dramas and sitcoms, in which the American family was generally white and affluent, gender roles were clearly and traditionally defined, and African Americans were absent—or, if they were present, were limited to supporting or comic roles. Although confined to the evening news, images of African American discontent were a jarring counterpoint to, and a refutation of, this televised America; moreover, by the commission's reasoning, the televised America of the sitcoms and dramas exacerbated black Americans' sense of dispossession. In later portions of its report, the Kerner Commission would elaborate on television's denial of the televisual presence of black people as members of the American polity (and thus, in TV terms, the American family). In the commissioners' view, if television had a role to play in the disorders, that role was less as a medium of instigation or mimesis than as a medium of insult, irritation, and neglect.

It is important to note here that in locating the problem of television in the kind and quality of its representations, the commission could be sanguine about the medium's potential for change. "Constructive steps are easy and obvious," the report asserted. "For example, Negro reporters and performers should appear more frequently—and at prime time—in news broadcasts, on weather shows, in documentaries, and in advertisements. . . . In addition to news-related programming, we think that Negroes should appear more frequently in dramatic and comedy series. Moreover, networks and local stations should present plays and other programs whose subjects are rooted in the ghetto and its problems." Here we can see that the commission envisioned television producing in black viewers a more robust sense of national belonging while encouraging in white viewers a habituated ease with the (visually normalized) presence of African Americans in the nation. Furthermore, the commission understood such "incorporation" of the black televisual image as the incorporation of black citizen-viewers into capitalist market relations. On the notion of the black citizen as a citizen of the marketplace, the commission was quite plain. "Any initial surprise at seeing a Negro selling a sponsor's product," it wrote, "will eventually fade into routine acceptance, an attitude that white society must ultimately develop toward all Negroes."[28]

The Kerner Commission thus came to very different conclusions than the president when he charged it with investigating the media's "effects." Nevertheless, in taking up the notion of television's social agency, even from a liberal viewpoint, the commission echoed Johnson's discourse of causality. Indeed, the report's liberalism abetted the notion of television as containment. As its recommendations made clear, the commission saw the question as not whether television could play a role in abating blacks' grievances, but how such an end might be expeditiously achieved. Moreover, although the commissioners rejected the more patronizing and depoliticizing implications of the thesis that TV coverage of the riots had inflamed black emotions, they did recognize the affective dimensions of television as a medium and see in TV representation opportunities for exacerbating or improving the national "mood." Just as television had stoked unrest by portraying the disturbances as "race riots," so its representations could be a balm for black viewers' affective wounds of racialized noncitizenship and a means of quelling the anxieties and fears of white viewers.[29] Finally, whereas the commission was in some sense spurred into being by the spectacle of black people on television, embedded in its recommendations was a notion—which others would act on—that race conditioned television viewership. The racial divide was reinforced and perhaps even produced at the level of watching television as a cultural practice.

Although the Kerner Report was aimed at the three major commercial broadcasters that dominated American television in 1968, it resonated powerfully among public broadcasters, whose self-definition was intimately bound up with the idea of a television as a public good, and who interpreted the commission's recommendations as a mandate for their own ongoing projects. They were encouraged in this interpretation by various U.S. government officials, who publicly asserted in the spring and summer of 1968 that the nation's noncommercial TV stations had a special role to play in addressing the racial divide that figured so ominously in the Kerner Report. As Laurie Ouellette writes, following the report's finding that "the average ghetto rioter was an unemployed high-school dropout," such officials called on public television "to address the 'poverty of hopelessness and despair.'" U.S. Commissioner of Education Harold Howe called public television "the only hope for providing the continuing education that can prevent our marketplaces from becoming riot places." Vice President Hubert Humphrey chimed in, calling on public television "to provide education and guidance to the disenfranchised urban poor."[30]

Such goals, consistent with the historical mission of educational television—known after the 1967 Public Broadcasting Act as public television, the modifier expressing a more populist branding and outlook—were deeply embedded in a discourse of patronage that saw black ghetto residents as not merely economically and racially oppressed, but also culturally and morally disadvantaged. As Ouellette and several others have shown, from its origins in the 1950s, educational television (ETV) had been imagined as an instrument of uplift, a conduit of cultural literacy in European traditions of ballet, classical music, and theater that were believed to constitute a foundation of ideal U.S. citizenship.[31] From the start, then, ETV's self-definition as noncommercial—and therefore presumably removed from market pressures to cater to the desires of the masses—was conflated with the goal of disseminating minority cultures and tastes, understood in the Arnoldian sense as "the best which has been thought and said in the world."[32] Although Ouellette associates educational television with the Leavisite view of culture as the exclusive possession of a culturally and educationally superior citizenry, in fact, the ETV model simultaneously assumed that such culture might be broadly disseminated and that the cultural uplift of the masses was in the broad interest of the state. In ETV's admittedly somewhat self-aggrandizing vision, television could be an important educator of the people and, in this role, a partner of the state.

As the 1950s gave way to the 1960s, the ETV paradigm shifted somewhat. For one thing, by the late 1960s, broadcasters could no longer speak of minority audiences and mean the educated few; the civil rights movement had changed the term's preferred meaning, so that *minority* now referred to those discriminated against on the basis of race, ethnicity, or color, in conjunction with demographic understandings of this group as a statistical minority within the overall population.[33] Yet even as public television absorbed the findings of the Kerner Report, its investment in the cultivation of a more enlightened citizenry through television prevailed. In an August 1968 essay titled "ETV and the Ghetto," which echoed the Kerner Report's optimism about television as a balm to social discontent, Richard Meyer wrote of "the new sense of pride, the grasp of basic facts and the discovery of American ideals which the poor may acquire from this electronic medium."[34] Here public television's role in empowering "the poor" is entangled with its function as a (compassionate) dispenser of knowledge, negating the possibility that "the poor" themselves possess insight into the "basic facts" of American life and "American ideals"—or, more radically yet, that "the poor" might teach the nation to realize these ideals.

The National Association of Educational Broadcasters, a lobbying organization and professional group for public television and radio professionals, would come to a similar—if by that point somewhat belated—conclusion in *Broadcasting and Social Action*, a November

1969 publication that urged broadcasters around the country to develop "minority" programming as a "service" to underrepresented groups, especially black Americans. "For the first time," the handbook's opening essay averred, "virtually all broadcast licensees are united in responding to American problems. Commercial and noncommercial stations alike are developing special services designed to help erase the ugliness of bigotry and the shame of inequality."[35] (An appendix in the handbook cited *Soul!* as an exemplary program.) Throughout, the handbook underscored the National Association of Educational Broadcasters' political and ideological affinities with the Kerner Commission.

African Americans hired by public television outlets in the wake of the Kerner Report rescripted the Great Society rhetoric of public broadcasting institutions for their own, sometimes quite different, ends. In addition to seizing employment opportunities, black people employed at WNDT and other public television outlets in the late 1960s worked to turn the notion of television as a source of cultural uplift—endorsed by policy makers and public TV executives alike—into a practical and serviceable tool for black self-empowerment and self-definition. They would do so through a rejection of Europe as a privileged site of culture and a strategic repurposing of what the Kerner Commission had identified as television's emotional appeal. Whereas Johnson saw TV news coverage of riots and other spectacular displays of discontent as a potential threat to public order, playing on the emotions of black viewers and leading them to self-destructive and socially disruptive ends, and whereas the Kerner Commission and public broadcasting officials saw television as a potential tool for improving the mood of the alienated and enraged black collective, Ellis Haizlip and the *Soul!* staff seized on the affective dimensions of television to spark interest and emotional investment in contemporary questions of black politics and identity.

The producers of non-news TV programming in the 1960s largely conceived of their role in terms of responding to audience desires— even if this meant that television lagged behind other mass media in reflecting contemporary social and cultural realities. In contrast, the makers of *Soul!* imagined themselves to be communicating with viewers in a dialectical fashion that presumed the cocreation of television's affects and effects. Culture was central to this project because the display of black creative genius spoke to powerful emotional and spiritual needs that facilitated and fed a sense of collective pride. Haizlip "loved black culture so much and he knew it so well," recalls the actor Anna Horsford (figure 1.2), who served on *Soul!*'s production team. The program "was a celebration. Look what we've produced *in spite of.*"[36] The notion of experimenting with specific modes of address to black TV audiences was also a key component of *Soul!*'s reworking of the late 1960s discourse of television's mediation of public feeling. Or, as Haizlip put it, cleverly turning the educational mission of ETV on its head, "we cannot again sacrifice the black audience to educate white people—they will have to find their education elsewhere."[37]

Interest in the sorts of projects lauded in *Broadcasting and Social Action* was particularly pronounced among public broadcasters in influential urban production centers such as Boston, New York, and San Francisco. Yet, as with many enterprises involving public television, enthusiasm outstripped resources. The Kerner Commission had put television at the center of its report about the national crisis, and official interpreters of the commissioners' mandates had located public broadcasters at the center of the national discussion about television, yet neither Congress nor the executive branch was particularly interested in funding public TV projects, especially those associated with minority interests. Neither, it should be said, did cash-starved public broadcasting executives, themselves facing a series of disruptive industry shifts and reorganizations that coincided with domestic and international unrest in the late 1960s, muster the political or economic will to shift funding priorities in the wake of the Kerner Report. Instead, when it came to realizing TV's ability to address social inequalities, they looked to the private sector to provide what the government would not—both dollars and practical incentives.

In effect, this meant turning to the Ford Foundation, the liberal philanthropy established from the estates of Henry and Edsel Ford. Since the early 1950s, the foundation had been public television's major source of private funding, investing hundreds of millions of dollars in TV infrastructure, the establishment of noncommercial channels, and educational initiatives. In New York, Ford had funded the development of NET, the nation's most significant noncommercial TV distribution

1.2. Anna Horsford on *Soul!*

and programming agency, and it had helped launch WNDT (Channel 13), the metropolitan area's main public TV station. With the creation of the CPB in 1967—and, with it, congressional assurances of a certain level of government support for public broadcasting—Ford's role shifted slightly. From then on, the foundation would operate an Office of Public Broadcasting and work with the CPB, supporting progressive public TV enterprises where congressional will to do so fell short.

The Project for New Television Programming, launched in the same season that saw the publication of the Kerner Report, was one such post-1967 Ford program: a two-year, $5 million grant-making effort aimed in part at supporting public TV shows for audiences neglected by commercial television.[38] The goals of the project included stimulating "pluralism and diversity in programming" and enhancing "understanding of urban and minority problems," and it was a turning point in the prehistory of *Soul!* on at least three accounts.[39] First, it acknowledged the fact that public broadcasters could not look to the state as a ready or reliable source of support for television aimed at black audiences. An information paper submitted to Ford trustees in March 1968 noted that the newly created CPB was unlikely to come up with "money for programming, especially controversial programming, in the cultural and public affairs areas . . . both because the funds at its disposal will be extremely limited and because of a concern not to risk offending influential members of Congress."[40] Second, by encouraging public TV executives to submit proposals for precisely the type of minority and urban programs endorsed by a variety of those executives in cities like Boston and New York, where public television stations were relatively strong, the Ford project created a tangible pathway through which intentions regarding television and minority audiences—the term is understood here as primarily including African Americans and Latinos—could be realized. And finally, the project's mission included funding the national distribution of successful locally produced series that it provided seed money for. Thus, the project imagined a future in which geographically dispersed minority audiences might be constituted as a viewing public, or televisually mediated minority public sphere.

Given Ford's role in enabling the creation of late 1960s public TV shows such as *Soul!* and *Black Journal*, launched in spring 1968 with a separate grant to NET, it is worth pausing here to consider these goals, which convey a complicated and even contradictory message about audience. The Ford project looked to support programs that appealed to racial and ethnic minorities, but it also positioned these new programs in relation to white middle-class viewers, understood as the largest demographic group in public TV's audience and thus its largest base of potential subscribers. The assumption of a dual audience for minority shows is especially evident in Ford's hope that funded programs would increase "understanding of urban and minority problems," the phrase implicitly projecting a set of primary viewers set apart, geographically and socially, from those affected by "urban and minority problems" and subsequently understanding the relation of these viewers to public television's images of minorities through the lens of liberal values of tolerance and acceptance.

Although such tensions were constitutive of Ford's vision for the Project for New Television Programming, they were not unique to Ford, and I do not raise them here to cast aspersions on the foundation's intentions. Rather, they reveal the representational tightrope that the first generation of black TV producers and supportive white TV executives in the late 1960s were compelled to walk to secure initial and ongoing funding for shows like *Soul!* As these producers and executives well knew, black and Latino viewers would not be the only, or even the primary, arbiters of the success of shows aimed at black and Latino audiences, notwithstanding the commissioning of expensive studies to determine such audiences' tastes and TV-watching habits. Once it became broadcast nationally, *Soul!* would also have to satisfy the needs of local station managers and programming directors, working under the watchful eyes of public TV boards, wealthy patrons, and politicians and keenly attuned to the judgment of influential TV critics. (In this sense, local programming was somewhat more protected from the scrutiny of groups hostile to minority representations.) In the end, service to black viewers was imagined within the scope of the tolerance of these almost uniformly white actors, who lurk as viewers of black intimacies rendered as public TV spectacle.

Although these shows were aimed at specific groups, in other words, many constituencies would be watching. (Some, however—such as the

Alabamans served by public TV stations owned by the white supremacist Alabama Educational Television Commission, which refused to carry *Soul!* and *Black Journal*—would not be watching.) And given the tremendous symbolic weight under which such programs would labor in the late 1960s and early 1970s—they were, after all, supposed to be not merely good television shows but also good social instruments— many viewers would feel entitled to voice their opinions. Journalists and critics candidly argued about the quality, authenticity, and social value of commercial programs like *Julia* and *Room 222* in the late 1960s, debating the realism of their depictions of black characters, but such shows were never asked to bear the representational burden of speaking for the enterprise of commercial television itself. Such was not the case with those late-1960s public TV programs that were perceived as experiments in connecting with black urban communities. For example, after watching *Talking Black*, a three-part series on local black culture and cultural activism that aired just before the Ford project got off the ground, a *Variety* reviewer deemed it "a most persuasive argument for the development of a new public television."[41] "Commercial TV couldn't have done the job and wouldn't have let these young militants try," the reviewer continued, in ambiguous phrasing that makes it unclear whether the "young militants" in question were the black cultural workers in the shows (which featured, among other subjects, the Schomburg Collection of the New York Public Library's Harlem branch) or those behind the programs. The *New York Times* reviewer George Gent, whose columns were closely followed by the managers of WNDT (Channel 13), weighed in with a similar opinion. As "an exploration of the new consciousness of blackness as a positive concept among Negroes," *Talking Black*, he wrote, began slowly but "built into a fascinating look at aspects of Negro life and thought not ordinarily covered in the usual programs about race relations in America." Gent also observed that "it was the first program in this reviewer's experience to capture the sense that viewers were really hearing the voice of the Negro when he wasn't shouting angrily during riots or explaining his just demands for a decent place in American society."[42]

A great deal was at stake, then, in the packaging of TV expressions of black needs and interests. Those that appeared as news, or that erupted onto television in a seemingly unscripted fashion, were seen as strident; yet angry shouts could just as easily issue from cultural programming that gave a platform to demands expressed in the form of a love poem, a popular song, or a saxophone's music. The reception of *Talking Black* suggested that cultural representations might, in a sense, fly under the radar where the policing of black political expression was concerned. This did not shield a show like *Soul!* from constant scrutiny about its content. Like *Talking Black*, *Soul!* would be both positively reviewed and carefully watched for evidence of militancy that exceeded liberal tolerance. Moreover, like *Talking Black*, it would have to calibrate its representational strategies to satisfy audiences of presumably different minds about what constituted militancy or fascinating "aspects of Negro life and thought." But *Soul!* would also significantly develop the promise of *Talking Black*, a series whose last images are of Sarah-Ann Shaw, then an advisor to the federally funded Model Cities Program in Boston, wondering aloud (in Gent's description) whether "someday Negroes might be given a program that was designed by Negroes rather than whites. Her eyes sparkled at the fadeout."[43]

At WNDT in New York, the announcement of the Ford grant competition spurred Christopher "Kit" Lukas, the station's young white director of cultural programming and the son of a prominent civil rights lawyer, to make good on an idea he had been mulling over for a "Black Tonight Show." "We had all seen too much television about poverty and 'riots,'" Lukas recalled recently, echoing the *New York Times* reporter's positive appraisal of *Talking Black*. "I wanted our audiences to know that the Black communities were rich in other qualities."[44] Lukas's idea—an outgrowth of his four-year friendship with Haizlip, who introduced him to the New York black arts scenes—and his implicit distinction between economic and cultural poverty, was innovative by 1968 standards. Unlike TV news representations that associated blackness with the irrationality and emotionalism of protests and riots, the show he proposed would offer up images of black people engaged in intellectual and creative work. Moreover, unlike shows that aimed to be relevant—a term that implied traditional public-affairs content—the program he proposed would draw on public TV's historical strength in showcasing the performing arts, emphasizing the "timeless" over the "topical."[45] By appearing on the same station that brought New York viewers concerts and theatrical productions (often British imports), such a show would implicitly convey the idea that African Americans had produced a significant corpus of music, dance, and theater. In that sense, it would speak to the Kerner Commission's recommendation that television be used to produce positive affects such as hopefulness and pride, rather than discontent and alienation, in the nation's black communities. Finally, it would help realize the aspirations of young WNDT executives to raise the profile of the station, regarded by many as out of touch with the local communities it supposedly served.[46]

In March 1968 WNDT submitted a proposal to Ford for "Where It's At . . . ," a biweekly show addressed to "black communities in the metropolitan area," which it subsequently revised in April, following King's assassination, proposing an augmented series of "thirty-nine programs, in color, directed at, and utilizing the services of, the black communities in the metropolitan area." "Entertaining in spirit, it contains elements of music, comedy, drama, and chatter," the application projected, "but it also has African history segments, youth debates, local community instructional and informational inserts, news, memorials to American Negro heroes, and documentary segments. Its aim is to enlighten our audience both black and white and also to continue Channel 13's efforts to create understanding between the races in the New York City area."[47] Citing brief passages from the Kerner Report's chapter on "The News Media and the Disorders," the proposal offered a list of the program's goals: "To give a voice to a segment of the population still not heard enough; still not hearing enough; To enlarge Channel 13's audience to include more black men and women; To provide an arena for continual exposure and debate in what is obviously America's most urgent domestic matter; To educate Channel 13's white audience about the nature of that portion of black American nearest to them; To entertain and enlighten."[48]

Lukas's last formulation is crucial, not merely in addressing public broadcasting's self-definition as a pedagogical apparatus, but also in making the case for performance as a means of attracting urban African American viewers—the "ghetto" audience of Meyer's "ETV and the Ghetto." Boosters of public TV had long argued that edifying programming need not be tedious or pedantic; a certain strain of wisdom even held that entertainment was a necessary sweetener to help the educational message of public TV programming go down.[49] In the case of "Where It's At . . . ," the familiar conjunction of entertainment and enlightenment would serve the additional goal of attracting viewers who (it was thought) might otherwise eschew public broadcasting for commercial fare. The show, the grant proposal promised, will distinguish itself from the "pompous, anxiety-ridden programs unwatched by the very audience we seek. . . . The *average* black viewer must be our concern."[50] Although the proposal does not specify who an average viewer might be—presumably Lukas and others were thinking in economic terms—it notes that public television had seldom, if ever, concerned itself with black audiences, and proposes that addressing this neglect would also require a fundamental rethinking of public TV's approach to programming. In particular, ETV would have to overcome its aversion to entertainment as either ancillary to its mission or a code word for culture thought to appeal primarily to the masses (so that baseball and popular music were entertainment, while opera and ballet were something else). Furthermore, public broadcasting would need to realize the limited appeal of its own "pompous, anxiety-ridden" approach to public service. "Because it's good for you" was a familiar enough phrase of parents at the dinner table, but it was an infantilizing and ultimately doomed approach to broadcasting. As Haizlip put it in carefully chosen words, he would take Lukas's premise: he boasted to a reporter that "there was nothing pedantic or intellectual about" the new show he had produced.[51] He did not mean that *Soul!* would not be thought provoking, but that it would not assume a position of intellectual superiority to its audience.

Consistent with Ford's guidelines, Lukas's proposal for "Where It's At . . ." voiced a commitment to hiring black people to work on the show. As he and his colleagues had realized, problems of racial representation on television in the late 1960s could be addressed only through changed employment practices. As he put it, the time of "whites doing programs about blacks"—often without even consulting black people—was over.

The furor then unfolding at NET over the appointment of an all-white production staff for *Black Journal* was instructive, and neither Lukas nor his bosses at Channel 13 wanted to repeat the mistakes of their colleagues. Recognizing that the lack of opportunities for African Americans in television meant that there were very few black people with experience in the medium, Lukas's proposal held out the possibility of hiring white producers to support black production staff members, at least until the new show got off the ground.

Lukas's rejection of the old ETV paradigm "whites doing programs about blacks" constituted a sharp critique of the sense of noblesse oblige on the part of liberals who offered sympathetic TV portrayals of African Americans but resisted a shift in power relations behind the camera; this was change at the level of surface (representation) rather than depth (production).[52] The novelist John Killens, in a 1970 article for *TV Guide*, would make a related claim, arguing that commercial shows like *Julia* and *Mod Squad*—heralded as a notable shift in African American TV representation—merely papered over a lack of fundamental change in employment in the industry.[53] Countering the self-congratulatory rhetoric of the networks, Killens asserted that as long as black people were denied opportunities as TV producers, directors, and especially writers, the black characters on the screen would be "white men in black skin." Careful to clarify that his beef was not with black actors, Killens channeled the late Lorraine Hansberry—who had written a never-aired teleplay about slavery, commissioned by NBC—in wishing for shows in which black people exercised creative agency.

Of course, the exercise of black authority over television representations of black people was no guarantee of their content, and neither Lukas nor Killens was making such an assertion. Rather, both recognized that the problem of black representation on television in the late 1960s was profoundly rooted in the denial of black access to the means of production.[54] However, access was not synonymous with control or creative freedom; black TV professionals would still be operating in a context of creative constraint and heightened surveillance. This was especially true at the networks, monopolistic enterprises that depended on sizable corporate sponsorship: one had only to think of *The Nat "King" Cole Show*, which was canceled despite its namesake's otherwise bankable charm.[55] The fundamentally commercial nature of network television—in which airtime was bought and sold, and programming content served as entertaining filler designed to keep viewers tuned to the advertisements—posed additional challenges to its use as a tool of black self-expression, let alone black liberation. As Robert Allen observed in his trenchant 1969 book *Black Awakening in Capitalist America*, time and again, capitalism had demonstrated its aptitude for reducing the black nationalist requisite of "ownership and administration of the cultural apparatus" to "an extension of democracy into the cultural field."[56] Allen's insight could be applied as well to public television, which was not driven by profit but was nevertheless embedded within a patronage system exemplified by Ford's support of *Soul!* In some ways, public TV shows were subject to greater levels of scrutiny and restraint, because so many different interests might be positioned as stakeholders in the public.

Indeed, although Ford envisioned the Project for New Television Programming as providing seed money for a new generation of public TV professionals as well as public TV shows, the philanthropy's financial authority over minority shows created its own set of structural pressures, embedded within (and exacerbated by) racialized power relations. Ever since 1966, when Ford Foundation President McGeorge Bundy declared the struggle for Negro equality "the most urgent domestic concern of this country," Ford had been on the front lines of philanthropic support for reformist projects of racial integration.[57] Yet as demands for civil rights gave way to demands for black power and self-determination, many African Americans questioned whether white money tainted or undermined black civic and cultural projects. Perhaps nowhere is this better illustrated than in African American fiction of late 1960s, which saw the emergence of a dubious new figure: the Ford Foundation–funded black character who was the tool of whites, and who put financial and professional self-interest over collective advancement. In Sam Greenlee's 1969 satire, *The Spook Who Sat by the Door*, the craven leader of a fictitious Chicago social services organization, the South Side Youth Foundation, confides to the protagonist that if his group's work in infiltrating black youth gangs succeeds, "we should be a cinch for the Ford grant. And you know that means substantial raises in pay and allowances for both of us."[58] In a similar vein, the black working-class protagonist of Nathan Heard's *A Cold Fire Burning*, after attending a black theatrical production with his white middle-class girlfriend, wonders at the contradiction of a black playwright "who scream[s] rage and pain and curse words at the audience with a subtle underlying plea to white people for a piece of the capitalist action." "The playwright," he concludes, "was sort of a Ford Foundation–approved revolutionary."[59] (Heard would appear as a featured *Soul!* guest in early 1969.) And in his political autobiography, *Die, Nigger, Die!*, H. Rap Brown portrays investments in black capitalism by the Ford Foundation and the U.S. government as furtive threats to black revolution: "We must study how revolutions are aborted, how independence movements are stifled, how people are cheated of the fruits of their efforts, how the foot soldier or the Mau Mau gets betrayed by the bourgeois nationalist—these are things that all revolutionaries must understand."[60]

Haizlip would confront the anxieties associated with white patronage of *Soul!* by being upfront about Ford's underwriting of the show. In the fifth episode—which I discuss at greater length in chapter 2— he notes on camera, and seemingly not for the first time, that *Soul!* was made possible by the Ford Foundation. This was at least as much an educational gesture (a way of informing the show's viewers about philanthropic support for various projects of black culture in the late 1960s) as a political one (a way of noting that corporations, despite their expressions of goodwill in matters of civil rights, were reluctant to invest in black cultural expressions they could not control). Significantly, Haizlip was resolute in his insistence that *Soul!* not contain the usual appeals for viewer donations tacked on at the end of programs; the implication was that black people had long and repeatedly paid for such programming in the form of their invisible or unacknowledged labors for the nation.

Extending this line of argument in an interview with a TV critic from *Newsday*—and anticipating his later comments to Nelson about the origins of *Soul!*—Haizlip characterized the money as reparative rather than charitable. "It's about time Ford returned to the community some of the money it's been taking out all these years," he quipped. "Look at all the Fords up in Harlem."[61] Haizlip's remark suggests that capitalism owed a debt to black consumers and rejects the role of poor supplicant to wealthy philanthropic interests. In addition, it purposefully conflated the Ford Foundation and the Ford Motor Company, which operated as separate entities despite having a common namesake. That a foundation cofounded by Henry Ford, a notorious and avowed racist and anti-Semite, could go become associated with liberal projects of multicultural reform—including, after 1968, the establishment of black studies programs on college and university campuses—may well have struck Haizlip not merely as richly ironic but as a kind of warranted historical payback.[62]

Channel 13 put considerable energy into promoting Lukas's proposal—particularly after King's assassination, which occurred just two weeks after its original submission. In the modified program proposal dated April 25, 1968, WNDT flagged "Where It's At . . ." as a priority for the station. By that point, NET had signaled its intention to rush *Black Journal* into production, and both CBS and ABC had announced they would air specials on African American history in the summer months.[63] In its revised application, Channel 13 distinguished "Where It's At . . ." from these offerings, arguing that the show would transcend the daily hullabaloo. The show "does not have a summer crisis atmosphere about it," the new proposal asserted. "It has continuity for the summer which does not abandon the field come the fall and winter."[64] WNDT/Channel 13 president John W. Kiermaier differentiated "Where It's At . . ." from *Black Journal* in personal correspondence to the Ford Foundation's Fred Friendly. "Although the NET 'Black Magazine' will be of value," Kiermaier wrote, "given its national approach and its once-a-month nature, it cannot possibly make the sophisticated local contribution to the racial problems of the New York area which is needed. This series we propose can."[65]

In June the Ford Foundation—at the recommendation of a panel of judges that included Ralph Ellison, who had expressed some trepidation about the proposal—granted WNDT the $631,000 it had requested to produce "Where It's At . . . ," described as a "social, cultural and artistic panorama of the Negro community in the New York metropolitan area, in magazine format."[66] At Lukas's urging, Haizlip was hired to produce the show, sharing the credit initially with white public TV veteran Michael Landwehr and then with Andrew Stern, and taking full control of production several episodes into the season. Haizlip's assets as a producer included an extraordinarily broad network of connections to black artists and performers. "Ellis always carried a thick appointment book and wrote in it with a real pen, using real ink," Lukas recalled. "Into that book went not only his calendar, but addresses and phone numbers and ideas for gifts and projects. He had a million of them."[67]

The contents of Haizlip's appointment book transformed the show that WNDT/Channel 13 had proposed into one that bore the imprint of his aesthetic and political vision.[68] This vision was pithily encapsulated in "SOUL!," the striking and evocative title (which appeared in uppercase letters on program stationery) that Haizlip proposed to use instead of "Where It's At . . ." A keyword of twentieth-century black political and expressive culture, *soul* evoked the pleasures of black community as well as the enduring spirit of black humanity, despite pervasive violence and material deprivation. In African American literature, the word reached back to W. E. B. Du Bois's turn-of-the-century masterpiece *The Souls of Black Folk* and extended forward to Eldridge Cleaver's contemporary best seller *Soul on Ice. Soul* was a word that bridged generations and class identities, appealing both to those who remembered Du Bois as an NAACP pioneer and those who thrilled to Cleaver's rejection of the cultural politics of the black bourgeoisie. In addition, *soul* bridged the sacred-secular divide. In both Christian and Muslim religious traditions, it referred to an inviolable essence that linked individuals to the Almighty, whereas in a worldly context it named a commercially and critically ascendant black cultural style of the 1960s. In music, the reach of *soul* extended from Ray Charles, Otis Redding, Aretha Franklin, and "Little" Stevie Wonder to gospel music (in 1968 a Grammy was awarded for soul gospel), the "Negro folksong" that Du Bois dubbed "the sole American music," and the new thing in hard bop, sometimes called soul jazz.[69] "All blacks have soul," Haizlip noted matter-of-factly. "No matter what their economic or educational or social level. Soul is something that all black people have experienced at one time or another. It unites them. It's a shared experience that only a suppressed, oppressed minority can express and understand."[70]

As this definition suggests, Haizlip's name for the show signaled above all its orientation toward and address to the black community—a construct he preferred to the black audience, with its distancing, sociological overtones and capitalist construction of black television viewers as an untapped market. As the word *soul* implied, the show was primarily concerned with black viewers. Dispensing with the cautious bureaucratese of grant applications, he declared frankly to a *Newsday* reporter that *Soul!* would be produced without regard for "the white structure and Mr. Charley's idea of what black people want."[71] Whereas Lukas's proposal for "Where It's At . . ." had envisioned a multiracial audience, appealing both to liberal ideals of understanding between the races and to Ford's interest in funding programming that was new and yet not too radical, Haizlip made no bones about who *Soul!* was for, who was behind it, or what its intentions were:

> We don't give a damn if white people do or don't tune in. . . . Although if they do watch, it might be educational for them, fit into Ch[annel] 13's educational television pattern. No, we're interested in aiming at the black community. We have a black host, a black orchestra leader, and for the first time, black entertainers who aren't necessarily stars accepted by the white establishment, but are performers who are important to and in the black community. They'll perform things that are meaningful to them as blacks and are therefore meaningful to their black audiences.[72]

In this one karate chop of a remark, Haizlip splintered two decades of educational television discourse, including some of its more fanciful notions of the needs of "ghetto audiences" and national crises of mis-education. At the same time, he redefined the public of public television, suggesting that black people—not public broadcasting executives, patrons, or politicians—would measure the new program's success. By referring twice in this statement to "the black community," Haizlip signaled a discursive shift from market value to affective value, according to which the success of *Soul!* as a television show would be judged not by the metrics of market shares, celebrity appearances logged, or patron dollars generated, but by whether it was "meaningful"—a concept that I discuss further in chapters 2 and 3.

In light of the history I have traced here, Haizlip's insistence on the notion of "the black community" as the source, object, and arbiter of *Soul!* represents a noteworthy break from the black audience as a social abstraction wielded by a variety of different social actors in the culture wars brewing over television in the late 1960s. Whether it was used by the liberal authors of the Kerner Report, by conservative politicians who feared the emotiveness of the black crowd, or by Ford and Channel 13 as a means of differentiating "Where It's At . . ." from other public television fare, the black audience was a racial abstraction founded in notions of blackness as difference. Despite the terms' grammatical similarity—syntactically, *the black community* is no different from *the black audience*—Haizlip's preferred term strives for a de-abstracted notion of black people as a heterogeneous collective with a common history and experience of racialization. His intention to use *Soul!* as a platform for black performers whom this community deemed important, rather than stars whose celebrity status was, in part, a function of the importance already ascribed to them by the white majority, articulates this distinction most clearly, calling attention to the material effects of segregation on cultural access and reception while insisting on a freedom to pursue programming choices regardless of white cultural validation.

Other formal and aesthetic changes flowed from the show's new name, all of them bound up with the artistic world recorded and contained in Haizlip's legendarily thick appointment book. Lukas's original wish list of guests, highlighting established stars familiar to TV audiences, was reformulated by Haizlip to feature black performers with little or no previous access to television, either because of mainstream oversight or aversion (they were considered too black) or because their work did not support conventional conceptions of black art (they were seen as not black enough). "Our primary responsibility is to present black artists to a black audience that is almost ignored on television," Haizlip explained, connecting the dots between spectacle and spectators, neglected black artists and neglected black audiences.[73]

To be sure, Haizlip's intention to use *Soul!* to give TV exposure to emerging or ignored artists was an overt rebuke to the white entertainment establishment. But it also implied a reproach of black media institutions. According to the *Soul!* writer Alonzo Brown Jr., whose musical tastes gravitated toward avant-garde jazz and whose political explorations ranged to Buckminster Fuller, there was a conscious effort on the part of the show's core staff to reject an "*Ebony*-style" approach to entertainment, in which the focus was on spectacle, celebrity, and the display of wealth and a narrow conception of black female beauty and gender distinction was rigorously enforced, in both advertisements and editorial content.[74] Harold Haizlip, Ellis's cousin and contemporary who briefly hosted the show in its first local season before Ellis established himself as a regular in the role, echoed Brown's observation, recalling that *Soul!* went "beyond the pictures in *Jet* magazine and *Ebony* and whatever print media, the African American newspapers, and so on. . . . Here was something that seemed to be harnessing people, up-and-coming and established African Americans, whom we had heard about but hadn't seen much of."[75]

Both of these comments reflect a sense that black media—exemplified by the immensely popular magazines produced by Johnson Publications—had shortchanged black audiences, not by ignoring them but by incorporating them into capitalist logics and enforcing the myopic tastes of the commercial market. This was not a wholesale rejection of the magazines, which played a powerful cultural role in allowing black readers to picture themselves in the context of familiar American ideals of achievement and belonging. Yet, consistent with public TV principles, it was a repudiation of surface in favor of depth, a principled refusal of the equation of commercial popularity with aesthetic value. Few of the artistic heroes of the black intellectual class of the 1960s—the jazz experimentalists and the writers who ventured beyond realist conventions—were likely to be celebrated by integrationist publications like *Ebony*, which often focused on black success in white contexts. Perhaps more important, the stance of Haizlip, Brown, and others suggested *Soul!*'s implicit and explicit affiliations with the various expressions of capitalist critique within Black Power discourses—whether socialist, Marxist, or cultural nationalist. In an era when domestic African American struggles were being effectively articulated to the struggles of Third World peoples (either still or formerly colonized), when anti-imperial and anticolonial movements were experimenting with forms of socialism, and when many young activists of many stripes were advancing King's critique of the interpenetration of capitalism with forms of oppression, the *Ebony* model of celebrating black inclusion in American capitalist fantasy was hopelessly out of touch. What New York black viewers wanted, Haizlip was betting, was a show that revealed the cultural work that thrived despite the lack of capitalist investment in black communities and arts institutions.

Haizlip's commitment to *Soul!* as a platform for black artists who were not also celebrities was also driven by a conviction that viewers would respond generously to images and sounds that challenged them to question their assumptions—including their assumptions about culture and blackness. If the phrase *role models* was not a part of Haizlip's discourse, it was not because he scoffed at the influence of such figures, but because the phrase assumed that black ghetto residents had no such models in their own communities or that ordinary communities could not also nurture an artistic avant-garde. The Kerner Report referred to black audiences as "the Negro poor," an objectifying formulation that could only reinforce a collective experience of invisibility. In contrast, *Soul!*'s assemblage of performances hailed the community as a source of cultural and social wealth, echoing Lukas's notion of black cultural "riches." Whereas others would presume the cultural impoverishment of such invisible and excluded urban black populations, *Soul!* drew directly from the range of cultural expressions produced within ghetto spaces.

Chief among these was music, which Haizlip regarded as an accessible entry point into the new black consciousness. Although chapter 3 will explore Haizlip's claims about music in greater detail, it bears remarking here that his understanding of music as a significant means of communicating with black audiences further refined Lukas's challenge to the traditional public TV distinction between entertainment and culture. And although WNDT executives allowed Haizlip a great deal of latitude, there is evidence that his emphasis on music gave rise to worries—not so much of offending viewers more used to European entertainments, but of displeasing Ford officials by straying too far from the balance between entertainment and education mentioned in

Lukas's original vision for "Where It's At . . ." "When we first proposed 'Soul' we envisioned a series which would have an ever larger share of public affairs content although starting with an essentially entertainment base," WNDT's Kiermaier wrote to David Davis, television program coordinator at the Ford Foundation, in January 1969, after *Soul!* had been on the air for four months. "Indeed there has been substance on 'Soul' but not perhaps of the hard core local public service type we once thought advisable. . . . Possibly a more consistently cerebral programming approach is preferred by some. We think our present mix of entertainment and general substance is the most effective format to reach a black audience."[76]

Guided by his concept of the black community, Haizlip rejected and reworked such rhetorical and ideological divisions. If *Soul!* was to educate black viewers, it would do so in the etymological sense of leading them, not directing them from above. If it was to attract them as an audience, it would do so by presenting local and national examples of black cultural expression, not through patronizing discourses of cultural deprivation. Consistent with the religious connotations of *soul*, the show promised the "warmth" Haizlip associated with black churches, both as sites of worship and as intimate counterpublic spaces.[77] Just as churches were places where worshippers gathered each week to get in touch with their souls, so *Soul!* would aim to be a television space to which the black community might tune in each week. This was television imagined as a tool of black "encouragement," as Haizlip would put it, rather than as a tool of liberal social engineering, emotional and political containment, or cultural edification according to a European standard.[78] It was television imagined as for the very people who had made it possible.

2 The Black Community and the Affective Compact

There are no ratings taken north of 96th Street, but if
"Soul!" goes well, the audience is there. And if we can stand
there in our blackness and be beautiful, others may follow.
—Ellis Haizlip

If New York was a house, Ellis's *Soul!* was the kitchen.
—Nona Hendryx, interview

Soul!'s first season was a bold experiment in television produced under
the sign of the black community. Over the course of thirty-five episodes
aired between September 12, 1968 and June 5, 1969, the New York–based
show, aired in color (and, after October 24, 1968, live) on Thursday
nights on Channel 13 (WNDT), welcomed remarkable talents from the
worlds of music, dance, the visual arts, and literature, as well as accomplished creative intellectuals, politicians, and cultural celebrities. The
production of these episodes was—unsurprisingly in the first season of
a program that had gone from conception to broadcast within a matter
of four months—a seat-of-the-pants affair, with scouting and booking
during the week, followed by rehearsals at eleven on Thursday morn-
ings and broadcasts the same evening at nine. (Viewers who missed
the live airing could catch a broadcast of the taped show on Sunday.) In
its first season, the new program also experienced predictable growing
pains in the form of changes in key personnel, both behind and in front
of the camera, and unevenness in production, as it sought to establish a
signature format and feel. But *Soul!* also charted remarkable successes,

drawing an unprecedented number of black viewers to Channel 13 and earning the loyalty of its audience through provocative and engaging programming.

As African Americans in the New York metropolitan region in the late 1960s were inventing themselves as black, and as Puerto Ricans and other Latino populations in and around the city were exploring alternatives to whiteness, *Soul!* imagined television for "the black community." The program's producer, Ellis Haizlip, preferred that phrase, with its linguistic affiliation to the idea of the commons and its racially and ethnically expansive possibilities, to terms like *black market*, understood as constructing black people as exploitable resources, or even *black audience*, a term that retained the whiff of social-scientific categorization. This chapter examines how *Soul!* sought to forge what I call an affective compact with viewers, reaching out to them through representations that appealed to and facilitated feelings of pride, racial distinction, and racial unity. Neither Haizlip nor *Soul!* assumed that a community of such viewers existed on account of race; rather, the show's producers understood that this audience, inured to commercial television's distorting images, and, in the case of educational television, its legacy of racial superiority, would need convincing that the new program was worth the investment of an hour's time. And although critics often assumed that earning black viewers' trust amounted to pandering to popular taste and thereby, it was thought, being no different than network shows, *Soul!* just as often crafted its appeal to viewers by venturing into the territory of the avant-garde and the culturally unfamiliar. This is brilliantly realized in the program's fifth episode, regarded by Haizlip as one of its best.

Although little footage from the first season exists, we can piece together an idea of how *Soul!* achieved such a compact with black viewers through the existing video, supplemented by journalistic accounts, oral histories, archival documents, and other cultural texts from the period. It is also through the notion of an affective compact that we can understand the extraordinary outpouring of viewer support for *Soul!* that followed the spring 1969 announcement of its possible cancellation, after Ford rejected its bid for a second year of grant funding. Chapter 1 pursued the implications of Haizlip's notion that black people made

Soul! possible. This chapter explores the ways that *Soul!* constituted the black community or audience that in turn worked to save *Soul!*, ensuring its survival for a second season and its national distribution through PBS. The outpouring of support for *Soul!* was indeed powerful evidence in defense of Haizlip's view that television could be a means of "turning the community on."

My notion of an affective compact draws liberally on affect theory to situate the "transmission of affect" in the context of the late twentieth-century African American transmission of televisual sounds and images.[1] Just as the preacher's message does not register without the "amen" of the congregation, so the concept of an affective compact emphasizes a dynamic negotiation between parties, in this case between *Soul!* and its viewers. Although the terms of this negotiation are always shifting and not always smooth, the affective compact indicates a degree of mutual understanding and sympathy between parties on either side of the television transaction, secured from moment to moment and episode to episode. Indeed, it complicates the clear division between production and consumption, deconstructed decades ago by Stuart Hall in his groundbreaking essay "Encoding/Decoding," which characterized the relationship of cultural producers and audiences in terms of tensions, unevenness, and struggles for authority.[2] Mindful of Hall, this chapter draws on an intellectual tradition going back at least to Frederick Douglass that emphasizes the coconstruction of the meaning of black performance, thereby bringing black intellectual and cultural practices into productive conversation with scholarly concerns about the role of public feeling in the making and shaping of resistant collective identities.

The notion of an affective compact also affects my methodological choices and investments here. Although professional pollsters gathered data about the audience of *Soul!* in its 1968–69 season, I seek to understand *Soul!*'s work as a television show for the black community through moments in which the show hailed viewers as a racialized group linked by shared knowledge, experience, and affective investment. Relying on close readings of the few preserved moments from the first season and situating these in the history of late 1960s television, I portray *Soul!* as a show that was not only acutely mindful of its imagined audience but also acutely attuned to inviting viewers into its affective field. Finally, continuing work begun in chapter 1, this chapter narrates the ongoing struggles of *Soul!* in the context of capricious financial support, the policing or suppression of black political expression, ongoing debates over the respectability of entertainment on public broadcasting, and continued contestation of the meaning and significance of educational television. The spring 1969 campaign to save *Soul!* demonstrates that the enterprise of programming for the black community required constant strategic refinement, interrogation, and protection.

Soul! premiered in the wake of an unprecedented $15,000 marketing and outreach campaign targeting black viewers in the New York City area. Never before had WNDT, a station whose signal extended across the vast multicultural metropolis, courted black people so explicitly or so broadly, and never had it invested so pointedly in bringing minority viewers into the fold of public television. Notices of the new show were placed in the *Amsterdam News*, the city's preeminent African American newspaper, and *Muhammad Speaks*, a weekly magazine of the Nation of Islam, and thousands of promotional posters were plastered on walls in Harlem; Bedford-Stuyvesant; the East Bronx; and Newark, New Jersey. Mindful of the large Puerto Rican population in El Barrio, the upper Manhattan neighborhood sometimes known as Spanish Harlem, WNDT—at the urging of Haizlip—placed advertisements for the new show in Spanish-language papers. The station also mailed notices of *Soul!* to a hundred black community organizations, and it placed orders for "SOUL!" shopping bags, buttons, and other souvenirs emblazoned with the program's logo so that in-studio guests could carry word of *Soul!* to the places where they lived, worked, or went to school. In support of the September launch, Sylvia Spence, Channel 13's director of public information, even hired a young black woman whose charge, for three months, was to talk the show up in black neighborhoods.[3]

However, WNDT refrained from characterizing *Soul!* as a program "produced and controlled by the black community," as the Ford Foundation's David M. Davis noted in a memorandum recounting an August

1968 meeting with Channel 13 president John W. Kiermaier and director of cultural programming Christopher "Kit" Lukas. Although the
phrase accurately captured the spirit of black self-determination infus-
ing the new program, it obscured the presence on the early *Soul!* set of
a white producer, Michael Landwehr, who worked with Haizlip on the
first episodes, and later Andrew Stern, a white TV news veteran hired as
Landwehr's replacement. It also ignored the key role played by Lukas,
an ally of Haizlip's who had helped secure the initial Ford Foundation
funding for the show. As the memorandum noted, WNDT station executives had taken extra precautions with language to try to "avoid any
blow up such as happened with NET's 'Black Journal'"—referring to a
recent strike by black employees of the TV newsmagazine to protest the
lack of black senior production staff.[4]

Accordingly, the early publicity campaign for *Soul!* emphasized its
connections to black audiences, placing stress on the "for" part of the
"by and for black people" formulation. Public television had historically
promised its audiences cultural enlightenment, a formulation based in
freighted notions of the superiority of European culture and bourgeois
taste, but in contrast publicity for *Soul!* promised audiences cultural
relevance, implying a shift in power relations and an analogous recon-
ceptualization of cultural value away from whiteness and white people.
Print advertisements made explicit that *Soul!* would be "devoted entirely to and aimed at the metropolitan area's 2 million black population" [*sic*]—a phrase which, even while meant to dodge the question
of ultimate control over the program, nevertheless communicated its
novel valuation of an audience that had previously been written off by
public broadcasters.[5] In interviews, Haizlip likewise emphasized *Soul!*'s
relationship to black viewers as a defining concern, insisting on an understanding of black programming that put audiences—and implicitly,
the cultural practices and expressions these audiences most valued—at
the forefront of consideration. "Even though '*Soul!*' is not of or by the
black people," he told the *New York Times*, alluding to the contributions
of Landwehr and others, "we're trying to focus it, channel it, into a contribution that will be meaningful to the black community."[6]

Haizlip's notion of the "meaningful"—reiterated in later public comments, including a statement explaining *Soul!*'s emphasis on music—

conveys his pointed critique of the white or European aesthetic standards that dominated cultural representation on television in the 1960s. By insisting on a standard that rendered the needs and interests of black audiences paramount, Haizlip was implicitly resisting patronizing liberal discourses that infantilized working-class and poor people of color and signaling a rejection of the traditional black middle-class prerogatives of uplift, whereby the black professional classes might dictate cultural value to their impoverished brethren. Moreover, and in contrast to the Kerner Report's liberal discourse of minority representation, the standard of the meaningful allowed for the possibility of black television programming that communicated in modes other than realism—that is, in registers that did not function through tropes of accuracy or true-to-lifeness. A representation that was "meaningful to the black community" might not claim to represent black experience, nor might it necessarily even be liked by a majority of black viewers. A spectator watching *Soul!* might find significance in the voicing of an opinion with which she did not particularly agree or a performance that she found boring. A Marxist critique might be "meaningful" to a non-Marxist who nevertheless valued black intellectual diversity, especially when it made powerful white people nervous, just as a ballet might be "meaningful" to a viewer who did not care for ballet but who was gratified nevertheless to learn about black artists working in that European dance medium. The "meaningful" thus brokered a path between discourses of authenticity rooted in monolithic conceptions of black community and discourses of social uplift, through which middle-class values would prevail in deciding what was good for the whole. In short, meaning was to be found in a wide variety of representations and performances, including those that stretched the limits of black audiences' familiarity, knowledge, and taste.

Haizlip's insistence that *Soul!* answer, first and foremost, to community standards of meaning permits us to locate the program, despite its technological mediation and mass nature, on a continuum of black counterpublic social and cultural projects, where performers—whether preachers, musicians, or poets—were understood to take on the privilege and responsibility of communicating with and for black audiences.[7] In this sense *Soul!* was not unlike Spirit House, the influential

Newark-based black arts center chartered by Amiri Baraka, or Harlem's East Wind performance loft, an incubator space for innovative black performance that I discuss below in this chapter. But neither was it unlike the Apollo Theater, the storied, white-owned uptown performance venue, where black audiences were known to vocalize their aesthetic judgments to the delight or mortification of those confident enough to assume a position under the spotlights. Indeed, in the same *Times* article in which Haizlip elaborated on meaningfulness as an aesthetic standard, Lukas noted that *Soul!*, originally modeled on the *Tonight Show*, had been revised at Haizlip's and Landwehr's urging into something "much jazzier . . . that would appeal to people who go to the Apollo."[8]

Lukas's reference to "the people who go to the Apollo" signaled *Soul!*'s particular investment in working-class black viewers, who had long played a key role in shifting the center of popular music culture toward black practices and sound ideals (from the Jazz Age to the era of rock-and-roll), but who had rarely, if ever, been imagined as a TV audience, let alone one worthy of respectful address.[9] In the *Times*, Haizlip elaborated on the implications of putting "the people who go to the Apollo" at the top of his agenda as a producer, suggesting that even cultural narratives that attempted to weave black people into the story of American culture tended to do so in response to the needs of the culturally and socially dominant. "We cannot again sacrifice the black audience to educate white people," Haizlip told the *Times*. "They will have to find their education elsewhere. Making the black community aware of Eldridge Cleaver is much more relevant than debating the Revolutionary War role of Crispus Attucks."[10] (Later he would make a strikingly similar comment about the value of a performance by Curtis Mayfield and the Impressions compared to that of "a three-hour lecture."[11]) Strategically reinterpreting public television's mandate of public service, Haizlip held an awareness of black liberation struggles to be more "meaningful" to the black community than revisionist narratives of American history. Where Crispus Attucks represented the integration of American history, Eldridge Cleaver represented the interrogation of American history—including its most cherished narratives of heroic national struggle against British oppression—from the perspective of the "undercommons."[12]

Seeking to make good on these promises and commitments, the opening episode of *Soul!* brought together a wide range of guests, including local artists and those whose talents had not yet received widespread recognition. In a further link to the Apollo, Haizlip had succeeded in convincing the saxophonist Reuben Phillips, the theater's longtime musical director who had performed with the likes of Andy Kirk, Count Basie, and Louis Jordan, to bring his talents to *Soul!*'s midtown studio, promising viewers an in-house orchestra "made up of leading jazz and rock musicians."[13] As a marquee attraction, Haizlip and Landwehr had also booked Julian Bond, the young civil rights activist and Georgia state representative, who had only recently returned from a star turn at the August Democratic National Convention, where he had briefly been a nominee for vice president. As musical guests, Haizip had enlisted Patti LaBelle and the Bluebelles, the Philadelphia-based recording artists also known as the Sweethearts of the Apollo; as well as the singer Barbara Acklin; the vocal quintet the Vibrations; the gospel musician and educator Pearl Williams-Jones; and the singer and actor Novella Nelson (figure 2.1). The episode's host, Alvin Poussaint—a trailblazer in the field of psychiatry and a civil rights veteran—contributed gravitas to the proceedings. His assistant was a vivacious young woman named Loretta Long, who would soon afterward successfully audition for the role of Susan in a new production of the Children's Television Workshop called *Sesame Street.*

What is noteworthy about the reception of the *Soul!* opener—only snippets of which are available on tape or preserved in still photographs—is how the episode's musicians and its female guests most captured contemporary observers' imaginations. Advance press releases for the opener had highlighted Poussaint and Bond, men who commanded relatively high levels of name recognition among white public television audiences and who contributed most obviously to the ends of minority programming imagined from a public-affairs perspective. In published reviews, however, writers reserved their greatest appreciation for the women who, although less professionally recognized in their fields, seemed to them to better embody the creative vision of the fledgling program. In an appreciative and thoughtful column, for example, Barbara Delatiner, a white *Newsday* TV reporter, contrasted

2.1. Novella Nelson was a highlight of the *Soul!* debut in October 1968. Here, she performs in a later episode.

Poussaint's "awkward" turn as host of the opening *Soul!* episode with Long's poise and energy. Delatiner deemed Poussaint's interview with Bond unremarkable—implying that there was nothing about it that distinguished it from interviews Bond might give on mainstream public-affairs programs—but she praised the dynamism of Patti LaBelle and the Bluebelles, who performed "He's My Man" and their trademark "Over the Rainbow," turning the signature song of Dorothy Gale, a fictitious Kansas farm girl, into an expression of black female longing for a "land that I've heard of." Delatiner also singled out for special mention the revelatory, stirring performances delivered by Nelson and Williams-Jones. These female artists—not the male civil rights activists who might have been imagined as offering the episode's more substantive educational content—were for Delatiner harbingers of *Soul!*'s "bright future" on television.[14]

Although Nelson was not a headline attraction that evening, she played a particularly crucial role in establishing *Soul!* as a show addressed to the black community, broadly and inclusively imagined. For starters, Haizlip had decided to use his friend's image—not the image of a more recognizable black political or cultural hero—in the brightly colored montage, jauntily scored by Billy Taylor, that served as the program's title sequence for the 1968–69 season. The choice of Nelson as the first "face" of *Soul!* represented a conspicuous departure from the convention of representing black cultural and political aspirations through male figures, and it constituted a powerful visual statement of the program's inclusion of black women under the *soul* umbrella. Although Nelson's Afro was not remarkable among a certain cadre of young black women in New York, it was certainly a notable visual turn away from the black feminine norm on television and in the mainstream black press. At the time understudying for Pearl Bailey in the acclaimed black-cast Broadway production of *Hello, Dolly!*, Nelson also had the honor of both opening and closing the *Soul!* debut, setting it in motion with a dramatic rendition of "Johnny I Hardly Knew You," the nineteenth-century English ballad that had become a staple of the anti-war movement, and bringing it to an emotional climax with "I Wish I Knew How It Feels to Be Free," the Billy Taylor composition best known through Nina Simone's commanding 1967 interpretation.[15]

According to Nelson, she sang "Johnny I Hardly Knew You" at Haizlip's insistence.[16] Haizlip knew, and assured his friend, that the material and its arrangement played to her dramatic gifts as a singer. Yet both performer and producer understood the song as an aesthetically and politically audacious opening statement, defiant of what Haizlip had publicly disparaged as "Mr. Charley's idea of what black people want."[17] Nelson sang the song from the small stage at WNDT's Studio 55, with little to detract attention from her commanding visual presence and fine contralto. As folk tradition allowed and even encouraged, she inflected the lyrics to acknowledge the particular circumstances of her performance, singing "We'll never send our sons again," a line that, through its use of the phrase "our sons," drew attention to the sacrifices of black servicemen in Vietnam, although among politically aware viewers, it almost certainly would have evoked the anticolonial critiques of American power advanced by Martin Luther King Jr., Malcolm X, and many others.[18]

The spectacle and sound of Nelson performing a folk song narrated in its original version by an Irish woman powerfully asserted that neither Nelson, nor, by extension, *Soul!*'s audience, would be limited to outsiders' definitions of blackness or black art; it might even have been read as an expression of cross-racial solidarity with other working-class Americans whose "sons" had no alternative to fighting in Vietnam. Moreover, although the lyrics did not refer overtly to race, they fashioned a powerful appeal to black viewers as a collective aware of the sacrifices of soldiers and civil rights freedom fighters alike, who laid their bodies on the line in pursuit of cherished national ideals. Consistent with this notion of sacrifice in the service of black popular liberation, Nelson's closing selection of the show was a secular hymn to the "freedom dreams" of the collective.[19] It, too, lacked overt references to race, but—like the Paul Laurence Dunbar poem "Sympathy" that it self-consciously echoed—it voiced an unmistakable hope for the transcendence of racism:

> I wish I knew how it would feel to be free
> I wish I could break all the chains holding me
> I wish I could say all the things that I should say

say 'em loud, say 'em clear
for the whole round world to hear.

At the close of her performance, the studio audience rewarded Nelson with a standing ovation, applauding, we might imagine, both the singer's virtuosity and the song's expression of communal desire, conveyed in the language of the singer's private "wishes." Like Dunbar's poem, "I Wish I Knew How It Feels to Be Free" harnessed the individualized and privatized "I" (Dunbar's poem includes the line: "I know why the caged bird sings") to give voice to the collective. Through a complex metaphorical chain, Taylor's song linked wishing with knowing with feeling with saying, establishing connections between the wishful subject of the song and the singer's own performance of the defiant speech act. In Nelson's choice of song, the audience gathered in the *Soul!* studio and in various locations throughout the city might have felt the presence—or, to use Haizlip's favored word, the vibrations—of Nina Simone, a singer who, as Daphne Brooks has observed, "would shape the bulk of her career in response to an aesthetic conundrum: what should a black female artist sound like?"[20] In the longing for self-expression in Nelson's song, *Soul!* audiences—both in the studio and in front of their television sets—might have heard as well an articulation of the program's own aspirations simultaneously to defy aesthetic expectations attached to black performance and to say things that other TV programs would or could not say.

While unremembered in the annals of television, Nelson's performances on the *Soul!* opener are significant not only in and of themselves, giving us insight into how *Soul!* crafted its appeal to black people as a viewing community, but also in light of the history of leftist political performance in the period. Indeed, they bear a remarkable resemblance to two highly celebrated moments on the *Smothers Brothers Comedy Hour* that have come to exemplify both the power and the limitations of commercial broadcasting as a medium of political dissent in the late 1960s. Two weeks after the *Soul!* premiere, CBS executives in New York rejected a Harry Belafonte performance intended for the third-season opener of the Smothers Brothers' enormously popular variety program on the grounds that it violated network standards of propriety in political speech.[21] The banned performance consisted of a satirical medley built around the calypso song "Don't Stop the Carnival" and featured Belafonte performing against a backdrop of video footage of police battling antiwar protestors outside the site of the 1968 Democratic convention in Chicago. Like Nelson in her performance of "Johnny I Hardly Knew You," Belafonte tweaked the lyrics of his song to relate it to contemporary conditions in the United States. In the traditional lyrics, "don't stop the carnival" expresses the speaker's appeal to Trinidadian officialdom not to shut down the annual revelry, which gave celebrants the opportunity to thumb their noses at authority. Take away Christmas and New Year's, the speaker of the song implores, but give us the "Creole bacchanal." In Belafonte's satire on the *Smothers Brothers* show, "Creole bacchanal" became "American bacchanal," delivered with the singer's trademark suavity while violent images of clashes between police and protestors floated disconcertingly behind him. However, network executives spared Belafonte's version of "I Wish I Knew How It Feels to Be Free," performed with Tom and Dick Smothers as a statement of cross-racial political solidarity.[22]

The parallels between Nelson's performances on the *Soul!* opener and Belafonte's taped performances (both the banned medley and the Taylor song) for the September 28 season premiere of the *Smothers Brothers Comedy Hour* indicate that *Soul!* was from the get-go artistically and politically ambitious. In this instance, *Soul!*, a local television unknown—like Nelson—had a distinct advantage over the *Smothers Brothers* show, a popular and well-funded program renowned for its irreverence on topics ranging from civil rights to premarital sex. Indeed, as a Ford-funded experiment in minority programming, *Soul!* was expected to embrace a style and politics associated with the new black consciousness, and both WNDT and Ford executives were prepared to defend the show on the basis of not wanting to censor black expression. In effect, its special status as television for black viewers, together with its newness and ostensible educational function, afforded *Soul!* a freedom to experiment with what television could say and do that may have eluded more visible commercial programs. This is not to say that *Soul!* enjoyed any special protections from interference—quite the opposite, given the fragility of its funding and the burden it bore of being expected to bring black viewers to public television—but rather that the fledgling program took full advantage of the openings offered by its novelty and geographical restriction to viewers in the New York City area.

The performances on the *Soul!* opener established it as a television program whose significance, both for television generally speaking and for New York black viewers in particular, was reducible neither to the backstage presence of black producers nor the onstage presence of black performers. As the first episode promised, *Soul!* would also distinguish itself through programming choices that embraced a range of performance modes, repertoires, and aesthetic sensibilities and through representational strategies that emphasized the *Soul!* studio as a forward-looking (that is, visually modern) space of cultural exchange between performers and audience members.

Nowhere were these qualities of the young program better illustrated than the show's fifth episode. Broadcast live on October 24, 1968, this episode celebrated local, especially Harlem-based, talent, including actors, musicians, and journalists. Like the first episode, it gathered a notable—and notably eclectic—group of guests, including the gospel great Marion Williams; Barbara Ann Teer, founder of the National Black Theater; the actor and journalist Clayton Riley, a contributor to the influential leftist black magazine *Liberator*; and Duke & Leonard, a soul duo with a single out on the New York–based Stomp Town label. But the show would be remembered chiefly for hosting the television debut of the Last Poets, a new performance collective based (along with Teer's theater) in the East Wind loft on 125th Street.[23] Their three electrifying performances that evening would grab the attention of the white jazz producer Alan Douglas, who later told an interviewer: "I heard a snatch of material on television one night, and it stopped me short. It was on PBS, so I called the station, and I got an address and a telephone number."[24] (The fruits of Douglas's collaboration with the group include the 1970 album *The Last Poets*.) The group would also impress Channel 13 brass, who nominated the episode for a Peabody Award, the public broadcasting equivalent of an Emmy.[25]

The fifth episode of *Soul!* was also significant for featuring Haizlip's debut as the show's regular host. Five weeks into the premiere season, Loretta Long was still serving as assistant host, but Poussaint, temperamentally better suited to the show's talk segments than to the emceeing of musical acts, had made a graceful exit.[26] So, too, had Harold Haizlip, the respected educator and Ellis Haizlip's cousin, who filled in briefly for Poussaint. Ellis Haizlip was an unlikely candidate for *Soul!*'s most visible role. For one thing, although he had worked in the theater since his college days at Howard University, he had little onstage experience and had never performed in front of a television camera. Moreover, although he had an appealing quality of low-key composure, he lacked the professional—some might say commercial—polish of black male TV hosts like *Soul Train*'s Don Cornelius. And he was gay: the sort of black man who, in those days, was described as "flamboyant." When he ventured uptown with Phillips, the bandleader, his coproducer Andrew Stern remembers, Haizlip was occasionally addressed as "she."[27]

I return in chapter 4 to the question of the visibility and significance of Haizlip's non-normative sexuality, which was certainly recognized by gay and lesbian viewers even if the producer was never explicitly "out" on camera. But even putting aside the issue of his legibility as a gay man, anecdotal evidence and published reviews suggest that Haizlip's appeal derived from his "just another brother" vibe, distinct from the slick aloofness of a Johnny Carson or the soothing smoothness of a Cornelius, and that this air of approachability was not perceived by viewers as inconsistent with the producer's obvious college pedigree and off-stage familiarity with "practically every young, gifted, and black New Yorker."[28] Although intellectually commanding, Haizlip approached *Soul!* guests with a humility and respectful admiration that belied the supposed sense of superiority of the black bourgeoisie, secure in its knowledge and accomplishments.[29] At ease with artists and performers, in part because they made up a significant portion of his own social circle, he had empathy for the creative process and deeply sympathized with the special demands of black celebrity in an era of limited mass-media representation of black excellence or social authority. During performances, instead of sitting back and coolly observing from a host's perch on stage, he openly displayed his enjoyment, swaying or clap-

2.2. Ellis Haizlip and Georgia Jackson, mother of slain "Soledad brother" George Jackson, share a moment on the set, October 1971.

ping like any other audience member. Similarly, he conducted interviews on matters of great sensitivity—from the murder in prison of George Jackson with his mother, Georgia Jackson (figure 2.2), to the ethics of the representation of pimps and drug pushers in the era's new blaxploitation films—in disarmingly informal and relaxed tones.[30] The New York edition of *Variety* exulted that once Haizlip took the stage, "all of the academic uptightness that characterized the period of Alvin Poussaint's hosting, and was only somewhat reduced in the week with Harold Haizlip . . . was gone."[31]

The fifth episode of *Soul!*, devoted to the exploration of radical black theater of the late 1960s, includes several moments that display Haizlip's skill in encouraging and moderating conversation, and it is on three of these moments, which are also potent moments for *Soul!* viewers, that I focus before returning to a discussion of the work of the Last Poets. Before that, a brief overview of the hour-long episode is in order. Like the majority of *Soul!* episodes in the first several seasons, the fifth is fast-paced, juxtaposing talk with music or poetry, and it touches on a variety of emotional registers, allowing for moments of laughter and joy as well as sober reflection and fiery dedication to black liberation. Although the episode flows relatively smoothly from act to act, with no missed cues and minimal gaffes in sound, there are also moments that highlight *Soul!*'s newness. For example, after Haizlip is introduced by Long, he asks the viewing audience to "bear with us" because it is the program's first live broadcast, and he jokes about his "first goof on live television" after flubbing the title of a Last Poets performance. And although there is ample time for talk, music takes pride of place, with Williams providing the episode's opening and closing songs.

The first conversational moment of significance to my argument about the affective compact occurs about twelve minutes into the broadcast, after the Last Poets—David Nelson, Gylan Kain, Abiodun Oyewole, and the percussionist Nilija—have performed their first piece, "Lady Black," a love poem addressed to black women from black men. Following a shot of the audience applauding, the camera cuts to the side of the studio, where Haizlip, Long, and Teer, perched on stools in a tight circle, resume a discussion of the group's work with manager Russell Pitchford. Picking up on the ways the women in the studio audience, in particular, seemed to have been affected by "Lady Black," Haizlip asks Long and Teer to talk about what it made them feel. "I was thinking it's about time I hear something besides blondes have more fun," Long fires back, drawing a laugh from the studio audience. Teer, clearly moved, responds in a more introspective mode. "Listening to the Last Poets is a religious experience for me," she says. "You know, they make you feel like you can relax now, there's a new breed of black man." After she says this, the audience breaks into sustained applause.

The second noteworthy moment comes about forty minutes into the episode, when Haizlip is again talking with Teer and Long, this time joined by Clayton Riley, a journalist who had also appeared on stage and worked on the acclaimed 1964 film *Nothing but a Man*. Haizlip turns the conversation to the limitations of mainstream media representations of black people, prompting a negative comparison of the recent Hollywood film *For Love of Ivy*, starring Sidney Poitier and Abbey Lincoln, with the Last Poets' more aesthetically and politically cutting-edge performances. Then he switches registers, bringing *Soul!* itself into the conversation. *Soul!* was possible, Haizlip says, "because the Ford Foundation gave Channel 13 the grant to do it, but there are network television shows such as *Julia* [the new NBC sitcom starring Diahann Carroll] that have attracted network sponsors." As a somewhat puckish expression crosses his face, the producer asks his guests to speculate on the chance that the Last Poets will draw network sponsors, and then poses the question, "What do you really think about *Julia*?" He turns to Teer and asks her to answer first.

But before Teer can tactfully decline Haizlip's mischievous prompt, members of the group begin to smile, stopping just short of outright laughter. "I'll sort of go on the spot because I reviewed *Julia* for this month's *Liberator*," Riley volunteers (an introduction that does not bode well for *Julia*). "I will only say that I hope the Last Poets are never in a situation where they're on *that* kind of network television show." At this point, the studio audience again breaks in with approving applause, after which Teer weighs in with scorn for black actors who take on roles without regard for the well-being of "their people." *Julia*, she concludes, code switching momentarily, is a "fantasy world. It ain't about nuthin." More applause greets Teer's statement. Then, as if to settle the matter of whether the Last Poets are likely to be recruited by NBC, Haizlip introduces their provocatively titled poem "Die Nigga!!!" "The Last Poets are going to do a piece for us now, and I can only beg that everyone can accept it in the spirit in which it's delivered," he tells viewers.

The third conversational moment I want to highlight comes near the end of the broadcast, following Williams's stately delivery of "God Bless the Child" (the performance that directly follows "Die Nigga!!!"). Engaging his friend in casual banter between songs, Haizlip asks Williams about her plans, and she proudly mentions that her next album for Atlantic Records will draw from country and western and folk music. When Haizlip wonders about Williams's "switch" from gospel, the singer sweetly but firmly admonishes him, saying, "I don't think that's a switch. There's a relation." Her comment about what Baraka had called the "changing same" in black music wins Williams a "touché" smile from Haizlip and her own round of hearty applause from the audience, demonstrating that although she is a Christian woman wearing a conservative gown and a wig rather than a kente-cloth-inspired print and an Afro, her credibility is not to be trifled with.

In the end, Williams's confident self-assertion allows Haizlip to put a bow on the entire evening, the "bow" being his notion of the "beautiful." "I think one of the most beautiful things is that tonight on the show we have presented the Last Poets, we have presented Marion Williams and presented Duke & Leonard, and there's a unity among us all because we're all black," he says, turning to Williams. "Do you agree, Marion?" Not missing a beat, the singer smiles angelically and responds to Haizlip's preacherly "call" with the requisite response of an "Oh, yes." Then she launches into an authoritative performance of "How I Got Over," a song that allows the entire audience to enjoy a moment of church—we see Long clapping in double time at one point—before the credits roll.

Together, these disparate yet related moments reveal the ways in which *Soul!* negotiated its affective compact with viewers, as well as how the program incorporated into its representation both the atmosphere of the live set and, following this chapter's epigraph from Nona Hendryx, the air of a comfortable, counterpublic domestic space—an implicit rebuke to the idealized and sanitized domestic setting of commercial sitcoms, including *Julia*. In the first example, Haizlip invites Teer and Long to comment on what "Lady Black" made them feel, initiating a sequence of events that draws guests and viewers together as witnesses to the spectacle of four black men—their attire, dance movements, and drumming emphasizing the African and Afro-Caribbean roots of African American culture—performing a praise song for black women. Through the Last Poets' impassioned tribute to black heterosexual eroticism and love and Teer's and Long's modeling of different but equally appreciative responses to it, viewers, especially women who were the subjects of the performance but not its agents, are invited into a television space where it is possible for Long to drop her guard for a moment and engage in some signifying with her fellow guests and the audience. In the second moment, Haizlip uses *Julia*, another new program in the fall 1968 season, to represent *Soul!* as a philanthropy-funded alternative to commercial television. Asking his guests to imagine the Last Poets on network TV is a way of asking viewers to contemplate the significance of white ownership of television, and of the effects of ownership on programming. And in the third moment, in response to Haizlip's performance of puzzlement at her "switch" to country and western, Williams performs *Soul!*'s own investments in black aesthetic diversity and nonconformity, themselves embodied in the juxtaposition of the defiant, straight-talking Poets with the gracious gospel soprano. Her affirmation of Haizlip's parting message about black unity despite difference constitutes a cross-generational, cross-genre appeal to older viewers, including women, who may have appreciated the commentary of Long and Teer but not readily identified with their youthful style or with the Last Poets' boldly profane rhetoric.[32]

When *Soul!*'s affective compact with its audience is considered, the discussion of *Julia* carries particular weight. Once again, the viewing audience is positioned by the camera as though listening to the intimate conversation of a group of people gathered around an imaginary table, and once again the tone is relaxed and familiar, belying both the political and cultural stakes of the discussion and the implicit risks the speakers take in criticizing a black performer and a black TV show in public and on public television. The intimate vibe of the segment is also conveyed through the wealth of shared cultural knowledge implied in Haizlip's question to Teer and Riley: knowledge about Carroll as a black female entertainer who appeals to the white mainstream; about *Julia* as a heralded sign of progress in its nonstereotypical depiction of a black middle-class heroine; about a critical discourse of *Julia* as hopelessly irrelevant to contemporary black realities; and perhaps about the Ford Foundation as a liberal underwriter of black cultural enterprises, including Teer's theater company. The question itself is performative, in other words, because as everyone knows—or is presumed to know—the comparison of *Soul!* and *Julia* is preposterous, almost as absurd as the idea of *Julia*'s sponsors, Mattel and General Foods, underwriting a show starring the creators of "Die Nigga!!!"[33] The signs of this performativity, which is underwritten by shared knowledge as well as shared feeling, include the in-studio audience's applause when Riley and Teer deprecate the offerings of network television, precisely as Haizlip has teed them up to do. But it is also registered in the fact that Haizlip and his guests are able to make an example of *Julia* without finding it necessary, in a show otherwise quite self-conscious about dispensing information (for example, the address of the East Wind loft and details about an upcoming performance featuring the Last Poets and Sun Ra's Arkestra), to explain the premise of the sitcom, name its star, or elaborate on the various debates it has inspired—although, like *Soul!*, it had been on the air at that point for fewer than six weeks.[34]

Haizlip's questions and the answers they elicit construct *Soul!* as the anti-*Julia*, and in so doing, they imaginatively project a community of black viewers joined in their embrace of *Soul!* as an alternative to mainstream programming that represents black people. Whereas *Julia* is assimilationist, picturing a black woman almost exclusively in the context of her white neighbors and co-workers, *Soul!*, it is insinuated, will support the intimacy and pleasures of the black collective. Whereas *Julia* addresses white viewers, *Soul!* will be indifferent to them. Whereas *Julia* is answerable to executives at NBC, who are in turn answerable to corporate sponsors, *Soul!*—for example, in presenting the Last Poets' "Die Nigga!!!"—will be careless even of the liberal philanthropy bankrolling it. Whereas *Julia* is emasculated, representing Carroll's character as a widow, *Soul!* will depict black men as activists, intellectuals, artists, and lovers of black women; moreover, through Teer and Long—and even Williams, when she insists on her right to reject artistic barriers to her musical expression—it will picture black women as in the artistic and political vanguard. Whereas *Julia* is the (civil rights) past, *Soul!* will be the (Black Power) future.

These distinctions, as I have been arguing, are explicitly voiced in the interview segments of the show, but they are also, and perhaps even more powerfully, enacted in performance, especially in the work of the Last Poets. The collective's "Die Nigga!!!" is not only the episode's most enthusiastically received performance, but it is also its most definitive, and the one most aligned with Haizlip's aspirations. Featuring Nelson rapping, it is poetry as exorcism, a nearly three-minute piece that requires Nelson to say the word "nigga" dozens of times, in rapid-fire variations of the title phrase ("die nigga," "niggas dying," and "niggas die") that build in intensity until he arrives at the poem's cathartic last lines: "Die nigga! / So black folks can be born." As he raps, Nelson doesn't just speak the words to the poem; he spits them, as though to rid himself of the unclean taste of the racial epithet and the unwelcome images of the violated black body (assassinated, lynched, raped, and suicidal) that the poem conjures. The closeness of the camera as it watches Nelson underscores this effect; viewers can literally see the beads of sweat on his brow, the spray of spittle as he enunciates in the glare of the stage lights.

A poem about communal self-birth from the ashes of a dead identity, "Die Nigga!!!" is performed with *Soul!*'s spectators as well as auditors in mind. As Nelson declaims, the stage is a hum of activity; Kain and Oyewole rock and sway as they perform a background chant, and Nilija pounds out a beat on conga drums—sonic and visual signifiers of the Last Poets' multiethnic composition and New York Puerto Rican influences. In medium shots of the group, the viewer can make out the set designer Chris Thee's modernist metallic sculptures, suggesting scaffolding or perhaps ladders reaching toward the sky.

The tension on the stage builds palpably until the last line, which Nelson delivers with thunderous clarity. When the collective finishes, the audience does not just clap; it whoops its approval, and one camera offers us a view of Haizlip shaking his head back and forth in happy amazement. It is a performance worthy of Teer's earlier declaration that the Last Poets are a "religious experience," a phrase that links art and soul. The narrative trajectory of the show, in which "Die Nigga!!!" is followed directly by Williams's two closing pieces, indeed resembles the arc of the Christian religious service, in which the emotional and spiritual heat generated by the sermon is offset by music and other rituals that prepare the community to reenter the world outside the church. Williams's renditions of "God Bless the Child" and "How I Got Over" expertly perform this function, with the first introducing a slower tempo and a bluer mood and the second allowing the audience to go out on a buoyant note.

These performative elements of the episode supplement its more overt efforts to politicize its viewing audience through references to black cultural genius, discussions of aspects of the larger black freedom movement, and critiques of integrationist cultural productions (*Julia* being the chief example here). For the viewer unfamiliar with the East Wind loft, Teer's National Black Theater, Sun Ra (mentioned by both Teer and Pitchford), or the *Liberator*, the fifth episode of *Soul!* would have conveyed a sense of the tremendous creative and political effort being harnessed and expressed under the umbrella of black arts. Moreover, the work being cited as exemplary or even visionary on the program was also being produced locally, in the very neighborhoods from which viewers were watching the program. And finally, in its futuristic orientation toward the advancement of black liberation—whether expressed through Teer's heartfelt evocation of a "new breed of black man," Duke & Leonard's musical admonition to "Just Do the Best You Can," or Williams's vision of artistic freedom on and through her next album—we can discern elements of what Haizlip would hopefully call *Soul!*'s vibrations, the generative and sustaining energy it sent forth from the studio to viewers throughout the New York City region.

Haizlip and Channel 13 had every reason to believe that *Soul!* was doing well among black viewers—in other words, that the viewers were feeling these vibrations. A glowing *Variety* review of the October 24 episode with the Last Poets confirmed that critics appreciated *Soul!*'s experiment as "a new kind of television."[35] The small studio could not accommodate the number of fans who wrote to Channel 13 requesting tickets for live broadcasts. And Haizlip, as "Mr. Soul," was generating his own buzz.

  Soul! was not suffering any shortages of creative vitality, either. Thanks to Haizlip, Stern, and Alice Hille (figure 2.3), the young black associate producer who handled many of the musical guests, the show consistently spotlighted both established talents and weekly *Soul!* "discoveries," usually local performers. Between late October and late spring, *Soul!* welcomed dancers, writers (John Killens, LeRoi Jones [who would later go by the name Amiri Baraka], Ernest Gaines, Nikki Giovanni, Anne Moody, and Maya Angelou), cultural personalities (including the filmmaker Melvin Van Peebles [figure 2.4]), comedians, actors (Diana

2.3. Alice Hille, *Soul!*'s original associate producer. "I say just *having* blacks on television is 'educational,'" she once quipped.

2.4. Ellis Haizlip interviews Melvin Van Peebles, as the director Stan Lathan looks over the head of the camera operator, December 1971.

Sands, Vinette Carroll, and Raymond St. Jacques), and popular musicians (including Sam and Dave, Peaches and Herb, Ben E. King, B. B. King, Mary Wells, Roberta Flack, Melba Moore, Jerry Butler, the Five Stairsteps, Joe Tex Jr. Walker and the All Stars, the Impressions, the Vibrations, the Unifics, and the Delfonics).

Notwithstanding these abundant signs of life, *Soul!* was threatened with cancellation that spring when the Ford Foundation turned down its request for a renewal of grant support under the Project for New Television Programming. The previous winter, Ford had affirmed its commitment to a second year of the project, announcing funding of $5 million, an amount roughly equal to the entire congressional appropriation for the Corporation for Public Broadcasting (CPB) in its first year of existence. "The question of editorial freedom for controversial programming remains troublesome," the Ford Foundation noted in materials explaining the need for ongoing private investment in a public medium. "Insulated and adequate funds at the local level for public television's most sensitive and vital areas—programming—continue to constitute a critical need. This project is designed to demonstrate what public television stations are capable of doing when given both freedom and realistic budgets."[36]

Seeking a piece of the $5 million pie, Channel 13 submitted two grant applications to Ford in 1969: one for a second season of *Soul!* and the other—recycling an unfunded proposal from 1968—for a show to be called "New York Television Theater" that would feature hour-long productions of plays by "young writers concerned with the political and social dilemmas of our time."[37] The submission of two applications (no station could receive more than one grant at a time) indicated Channel 13's concern with ensuring continuous revenue in the face of uncertain government and local funding. But it also hinted at worries that *Soul!* might be poorly received by the independent panel charged with evaluating the show. In January WNDT/Channel 13 president John Kiermaier wrote to David Davis, Ford's television program coordinator, to assure him that *Soul!* still had an "increasingly strong appeal for the black community." But Kiermaier allowed that *Soul!*, in practice, deviated from the show envisioned in Channel 13's original grant application. "When we first proposed 'Soul,' we envisioned a series which would have an ever larger share of public affairs content although starting with an essentially entertainment base," he wrote. "Indeed there has been substance on 'Soul' but not perhaps of the hard core local public service type we once thought advisable."[38]

If his defense of *Soul!* read a bit like a concession, it was because Kiermaier understood substance and public service in traditional educational television terms. In the same letter, he built a case for *Soul!* based on a recent episode featuring Nathan Heard, whose debut novel *Howard Street* appeared in November 1968, a month before the author's release from the New Jersey State Prison, where he served eight years for armed robbery and parole violation. "The lesson of hope conveyed by an ex-convict reflecting on his success in publishing a novel proved a message of social significance and encouragement which goes beyond the more standard types of community aid we once thought 'Soul' would perform," Kiermaier wrote to Davis, extolling Heard as "an object lesson of hope for all people, black and white." (It is unclear whether he had read Heard's profane depictions of the black lumpen.) Kiermaier further justified *Soul!*'s "mix of entertainment and general substance" as a means of reaching black viewers. "While we cannot give conclusive proof, all of our fragmentary indications tell us that 'Soul' is getting through to the blacks, especially to those who are among the most deprived. . . . We hope that one experimental season will not be all that these people can expect."[39]

Because of the confidential nature of the Ford grant review process, it is impossible to say with any certainty why *Soul!*'s application for refunding was rejected. Yet we can deduce, from Kiermaier's almost apologetic letter to Davis and other documents, the context in which its worthiness and effectiveness as minority programming might be evaluated. In effect, the issues that defined *Soul!*'s prehistory—the question of what constituted community aid; the concept of culture as "uplift"; the notion of black performing arts as primarily diversionary rather than educational or cultural; the idea of entertainment as a carrot to attract black viewers, especially "the most deprived"— defined the terrain on which its value was to be judged. But these were precisely the sorts of criteria that Haizlip and his creative team had rejected as insensitive to black viewers' needs and ignorant of African American creative traditions. The history of black music making— from the work songs of slave laborers to the street-corner harmonizing of urban youths—attested to the close connections in black musical practice between sociality and sustenance. The black musical aesthetic (pace LeRoi Jones in *Blues People*) did not recognize a division between enjoyment (body) and substance (mind); rather, as the title of a memorable 1970 Funkadelic album put it, *Free Your Mind . . . and Your Ass Will Follow.*[40]

In other words, what was lost in the bureaucratic deliberations over whether *Soul!* had conformed to its original programming format was the richness of what *Soul!* had achieved, the myriad forms of "encouragement" it had given and "public service" it had performed, and its bold recalibration of the educational mission of public television, based on Haizlip's concept of addressing the black community as a counterpublic. Indeed, Haizlip's notions of educational television made with black viewers in mind had much in common with the concept of education advocated by college students organizing nationally for courses in black studies in the late 1960s. From California to New York, as Noliwe

Rooks has documented, multiracial coalitions of student activists campaigned for "relevant" courses, the hiring and retention of faculty members of color, and greater access to college for black and poor students.[41] A major underwriter of black studies through the 1970s, Ford spent millions to enable such efforts. Yet in 1969, the year it awarded its first grant for black studies, the foundation balked at supporting *Soul!* Of the seventeen programs eligible nationally for a second year of funding under the Project for New Television Programming, *Soul!* was among the three turned down in spring 1969. Instead, Ford announced it would support Channel 13's proposal for "New York Television Theater."

The news sent Channel 13 into crisis-management mode. Anticipating that the station would not be able to retain *Soul!*'s production staff through the summer, the number of shows was reduced from thirty-nine to thirty-five, with the remaining money banked for salaries. Kiermaier, Lukas, and others began working bureaucratic back channels, lobbying friends and allies at both Ford and the CPB. The corporation lent its support by commissioning an audience survey specifically to gauge *Soul!*'s reach among black viewers. Conducted by Louis Harris and Associates, the survey of black families in all five boroughs of New York City—including people in Harlem, Bedford-Stuyvesant, South Jamaica, and the South Bronx—found not only that black New Yorkers watched *Soul!* "in significant numbers" but also that the show garnered a Thursday-night audience that compared well with the audience for commercial TV, even though Channel 13 aired on the UHF bandwidth, which only newer TV sets could pick up.[42] According to Harris estimates, of the 400,000 black "households" (defined as consisting of four people) in New York deemed to be television viewers, between 170,000 and 250,000 tuned in to *Soul!* with some regularity. Even more significantly, 64 percent of the 912 survey respondents reported watching *Soul!* every week, and when asked directly, 75 percent said they wanted to see *Soul!* continue on Channel 13.

Kiermaier voiced his frustration with the fickleness of Ford support in a letter to Fred Friendly, who advised the foundation on its work in public TV, which was copied to both Davis and CPB President John Macy. "'Soul' represents a case history of everything that is right and wrong in public television," Kiermaier wrote. "First, we were given an opportunity by the Ford Foundation to experiment with a new black project. This is something that only public television could have done. Yet, after that experiment was proven successful by any objective test, it cannot be continued for lack of funds."[43]

Desperate, Channel 13 turned to corporations for support. The television program that had dared openly to discuss the politics of access to television of outspoken black performers was now in a position of seeking an underwriter. With the help of an advertising friend of Stern, the station placed a cleverly self-conscious display advertisement in the May 1 local edition of the *New York Times*. Under the words "For Sale: Soul" in large print, copy in smaller type read: "Only Channel 13 has it. And we are, frankly, looking for corporations to underwrite its continuation. SOUL! turned the black community on. It should not be turned off." Below this was an endorsement from the *Variety* review of the Last Poets episode—"Soul points the way to a new kind of television"—and a list of upcoming guests that read as its own argument for the show: Novella Nelson; LeRoi Jones; and the Pharoah Sanders Quintet, featuring Leon Thomas.[44]

Soul! press notices promoting upcoming episodes that spring included a statement from Lukas: "We are hopeful that a public-spirited corporation or foundation will recognize the contribution that SOUL! has made to the black community."[45] Notably, he phrased his appeal in terms of *Soul!*'s value to black people, rather than the value of black viewers as potential public TV patron members or the value of black consumers to advertisers. (The latter strategy would prove successful around this time for *Soul Train*'s Cornelius, who persuaded Chicago-based Sears, Roebuck and Company to buy airtime during the afternoon broadcast to market phonographs to young viewers, as well as for Tony Brown, who was able to secure commercial underwriting for *Black Journal* from PepsiCo.) The point that Haizlip had gone out of his way to make on the October 24 episode—that television shows like *Soul!* were rare because they refused to treat their audience primarily as an exploitable market and relied on potentially capricious philanthropic or government support—had been borne out in *Soul!*'s own brief history.[46]

"Mr. Soul" took the case for *Soul!* directly to viewers. In the previous months, Channel 13 had refrained from issuing on-air appeals for viewer contributions immediately before or after *Soul!* Yet in an episode in April 1969 (and possibly earlier), Haizlip went before the camera to announce that *Soul!* had lost its funding, and he urged everyone watching to express their support.[47] Letters and statements began pouring in, mostly from self-identified black viewers who characterized the show as a sustaining oasis in a television desert. The smattering of new commercial television shows with black actors and black public-affairs shows on public TV in 1968 had done little to alter these writers' perception of television as a white medium. Many spoke eloquently of *Soul!'s* educational function, joining their voices to Haizlip's in his critique of the narrow public broadcasting definition of that function.

More than 18,000 viewers petitioned WNDT during two weeks in May.[48] The *Amsterdam News* published a brief editorial asking readers to support the show, calling it "important" to the city's community, and by July 3 the number of viewers who contacted the station had grown to 51,000.[49] Ultimately Channel 13 submitted a petition with 8,000 individual signatures to Ford—most from viewers in the New York City region, but a few from Europe and Africa.

The variety of written appeals to Channel 13 was impressive. Some were typewritten; others were handwritten or, in the case of letters from children, illustrated. Some were from representatives of groups of workers or specific communities; others spoke for families or individuals. A letter from Port Jarvis, New York, began with the salutation "Dear Ellis." A black serviceman stationed at Fort Tilden, in Queens, composed his letter while he watched: "I am listening to LeRoi Jones and it sounds good. It is wonderful to hear my people expressing themselves in many ways (asides from rotting)." One viewer praised *Soul!* as "a particularly relevant vehicle for those of us in the white community," and specifically singled out the Last Poets' "Die, Nigga!!!", writing that "the power and majesty of that segment beggars description." The director of a juvenile detention facility in Orange County, New York, wrote to say that *Soul!* was important to his wards. Peter Long, Loretta Long's husband and public relations director at the Apollo Theater (yet another connection to the Harlem venue), weighed in with a heartfelt note about the ways exposure on *Soul!* had jump-started his wife's career, and pledged the Apollo's continued collaboration with the show.

Letters in defense of *Soul!* issued from high and low. Ralph Bunche sent a telegram; an inmate of Monmouth County Jail, in New Jersey, sent a letter that bore the warden's stamp of approval. A Brooklyn writer who identified herself as a "soul sister" wrote that *Soul!* was "the only show catering to the task of our generation (young)." Seven people from Jamaica, Queens, signed a letter that said: "Keep 'Soul' and educate, entertain, and maybe save a few false fire alarms, whitey's head, stores, and my sanity." "T.V. really was never *for me* before," wrote a grateful female viewer from Rego Park, New York. "In my opinion, 'Soul!' is too relevant to the social viewing needs of a group of minorities of the New York area as large in number as we are to be taken away." Another writer, identifying herself as "a widow woman" who had scrubbed hospital floors to educate her three grown children, concluded, "I think *Soul* is not only entertaining, but empowering, enlightening and hope-full [*sic*]." A Long Island City woman submitted an appeal in the form of a poem:

> My family has a five-hundred dollar
> colored television set
> that we turn on
> > once a week
> Thursday
> > 9 P.M.
> > Channel 13
> > SOUL!
> Because it's the only for real thing on T.V.
> Dig it?[50]

In referring to *Soul!*'s "realness," letters like this spoke implicitly about the possibility of political censorship conducted under the guise of bureaucratic procedure. In doing so, they linked the plight of *Soul!* to that of the *Smothers Brothers Comedy Hour*, permanently retired by CBS that spring on the basis of the producers' refusal to allow the network to review tapes before shows aired, so that material deemed objectionable could be censored. There is evidence that *Soul!* did indeed alienate some white viewers. After watching the fifth episode, one man wrote directly to Ford to question its sponsorship of the show. "While purporting to promote Negro culture, the extra aura was that of hate for white people," he wrote. "This was not particularly offensive until the last number, the title of which was 'Die, Nigger, Die.'" Another writer from Chatham, New Jersey, complained to Ford: "Instead of a medium for showcasing Black talents, it frequently turns into a smug laugh session full of innuendoes downgrading 'Whitey.' It frequently exhibits the bigotry we are all trying to eliminate."[51] And in its annual report for July–December 1968, Channel 13 acknowledged that some perceived *Soul!* as having "strong leftist leanings."[52]

It is unclear whether claims of *Soul!*'s "bigotry" held any sway with Ford officials, or whether the value of certain politically charged performers like the Last Poets was at issue in their deliberations. More likely, such predictable qualms with the show paled before the pressure brought to bear by Channel 13 officials, supported by an outpouring of support from viewers—"more than 51,000 requests from both the white and black communities," according to a statement from Kiermaier.[53] In any case, although Ford had denied WNDT funding under the Project for New Television Programming, pushback by viewers and Channel 13 eventually led to Davis's eleventh-hour authorization of $175,000 in direct Ford support for *Soul!* Together with a $40,000 appropriation from the CPB and WNDT studio production services budgeted at $143,000, this was enough to keep *Soul!* going for a second season—its first of national distribution—beginning in early 1970.

The experience with Ford illustrates the vulnerability of *Soul!* in 1969 despite its demonstrated success as measured in terms of critical reception, public viewership, cultural impact, audience loyalty, and artists' support (prominent performers were willing to appear on *Soul!* for little money). It also suggests that the promising political climate that had allowed for the planting of the seeds of television for the black community in New York in early 1968 had already changed by early 1969, when the novelty of such television had begun to wear off and the brief "fragile alliance" produced by grief over King's assassination had begun to dissolve. As far as my argument about the affective compact is concerned, the struggle for a second season of *Soul!* speaks to the strength of black viewers' identification with the show and their willingness to participate in the campaign to keep it on the air. We can attribute viewers' enthusiasm for cultural activism on behalf of *Soul!* to the show's own cultural strategies. Here I would recall one of the key moments of the program's fifth episode, when Teer—in response to Haizlip's specific questioning about the affective power of the Last Poets' performance—characterizes such power in terms of its ability to make the auditor or spectator (in this case, Teer herself) "relax . . . there's a new breed of black man." Leaving aside the question of gender and sexuality raised in Teer's comment, we can think about *relax* as a verb that conveys the release of tension and anxiety, the laying down of a burden, emotional or otherwise. To relax is to experience an affective state as a corporeal effect: when we relax, we let go of both other affects (fear, worry, and stress) and the embodied way we enact these affects (muscle tension and other corporeal symptoms). But Teer, I argue, is not referring only to a privatized feeling of relaxation; she is also naming a collective feeling produced by and though the Last Poets' performance. The relaxation she names is a collective disaccumulation of negative affects that has a powerful potential to produce what she and Riley, later in the episode, refer to as "new realities."

We can see Teer's comment on the Last Poets echoed in the letters composed by *Soul!* viewers in response to the program's threatened cancellation. Although the letters voice a range of very specific feelings about, and sets of arguments for, the continuation of *Soul!*, collectively they attest to a common experience of the program as a source of pleasure, relief, and recognition. Although the writers composed their letters about this experience individually or in small groups, in effect they constitute themselves as a community through the act of written expression. Through letters that attest to *Soul!* as an outlet for the release of negative feelings (the desire to pull a fire alarm or go upside "whitey's head") as well as a source for the accumulation of positive ones (pleasure and pride in the "wonderful" sounds of "my people expressing themselves"), viewers reflected their sense of being hailed as a community by responding in large numbers to Haizlip's call to save the program. In voicing their investments—political, emotional, and intellectual—in keeping the show on the air, they relayed some of this sense of connectedness back to *Soul!*, in a feedback loop of cultural agency and positive vibrations. Although Channel 13, the Ford Foundation, and the CPB bankrolled the program's production in 1970, once again it was black people—now constructed as members of the *Soul!* community—who made it possible.

3 "More Meaningful Than a Three-Hour Lecture"

MUSIC ON *SOUL!*

Our vibration is based on creative solidarity: trying to
influence the black community toward the same kind of dignity
and self-respect that we all know is necessary to live. We're
trying to put out survival kits on wax.
—Gil Scott-Heron

First of all, when people say "soul" they put you in one
category. . . . That's all they expect for you to sing and that's
all they want you to sing. But that's not true. Soul is being able
to . . . express yourself so much that people are able to relate
to what you're saying and what you're singing and to feel what
you're singing and to respond to what you're singing, and
that's one thing that we brought to this country.
—Stevie Wonder, the "Wonderlove" episode
of *Soul!*, December 1972

A man and a woman, each holding a microphone, take turns introducing themselves to the camera. "I'm Nick Ashford," says the man, his Afro extending beyond the frame of the close-up. "And I'm Valerie Simpson," says the woman, similarly coiffed. As a basso-voiced announcer welcomes the *Soul!* audience, the duo launches into "Keep It Comin'," a mid-tempo ballad about the sustaining power of romantic love. The singers are decked out in flamboyant style, their flowing garb and "liberated" hair conveying, in the words of the journalist Clayton Riley, "the

3.1. Nick Ashford and Valerie Simpson, from a May 1971 *Soul!* appearance.

urgency of a people's sense of themselves as a reborn, spiritually awakened 20th-century tribe."[1] Ashford wears a red-orange jumpsuit and a knee-length crocheted jacket accented by a metallic belt as large and imposing as a heavyweight champion's, while Simpson, a diminutive woman whose Afro adds several inches to her stature, wears a colorful striped halter dress that flutters around her ankles. (An earlier 1971 appearance, their first on *Soul!*, find them no less high-spirited, despite somewhat less exuberant attire; see figure 3.1.) "Keep it comin'. Keep it comin'." As she sings, Simpson raises her arm above her head, the dance gesture doubling as a revolutionary salute. Both she and Ashford are beaming, aglow with pleasure. As the camera pans back from the singers, it becomes apparent that the audience is, too. Heads keep time, feet tap gently; the room is softly alive and buzzing, the massed bodies a single unit, riding the song's gentle groove. "Keep it comin'. Keep it comin'." The repeated lyrics offer friendly but insistent encouragement. *Don't stop*, they say. *Don't give up. Let's do this thing together.*

Ashford and Simpson's radiant performance, from October 1972, sheds light on why Ellis Haizlip insisted that black music was the beating heart of the *Soul!* enterprise, not only in the show's groundbreaking first season, which culminated in the successful campaign of viewers in the New York City area to keep it on the air, but also during its nearly four-year run (1970–73) as the nation's most important television outlet for black performing arts. "*Soul!*'s emphasis is on music, because music is a significant way of communicating with all people," the producer noted in 1970, as the program was preparing for its national launch. "To begin to understand black music, is to begin to deal with and understand the attitude of blacks. . . . When Curtis Mayfield sings 'We're a Winner,' . . . that is more meaningful than a three-hour lecture on 'black is beautiful.'"[2] Haizlip made these remarks (which echoed earlier comments on "meaningful" television for black audiences) to a reporter for *Image*, the program guide mailed out to Channel 13's mostly white and well-heeled subscribers, in the summer before the show's national launch. But his statement goes beyond the defense of the culturally popular, the perennial argument for black music's artistic (as opposed to sociological) value, or the critique of narrow conceptualizations of the educational needs of black viewers. More audaciously, it suggests the agency of black musical performance in the very project of collective self-making denoted by the phrase "black is beautiful."

In affirming that political enlightenment can and must be pleasurable, and in positioning black music as both a sonic archive and a sonic vanguard, the producer's commentary on the value of a TV broadcast of a Mayfield performance expresses, for television, a notion that had deep roots in black American cultural critique. From Frederick Douglass's notion of song as an articulation of slaves' subjectivity as well as their suffering and Zora Neale Hurston's conceptualization of Negro folk expressions as oral annals of black Southerners to Sun Ra's far-out beliefs about discordant sounds as vehicles of transport to more harmonious spaces and places, the elevation of black music as a privileged expression of black consciousness spans the black intellectual tradition, drawing African, African American, and Afro-Caribbean cultures into productive conversation.[3] Such notions were avidly revived and reworked in the era of civil rights and Black Power by a range of intellectuals, most prominently by *Soul!* guest Amiri Baraka. In "The Changing Same," Baraka (then LeRoi Jones) put "socially oriented" R&B on the same plane of aesthetic achievement as the critically self-conscious work of post–World War II jazz musicians, whose sonic experiments found favor among the black arts intelligentsia, if not always with mass audiences of black people. Baraka's thesis—that "New Thing" jazz and commercially popular R&B were "the same family looking at different things. Or looking at things differently"—conceded the oppositional vitality of even popular, commodified music, a sticking point for Cold War–era leftist intellectuals concerned about the commercial incorporation of blues and jazz. "If you play James Brown (say, 'Money Won't Change You . . . but time will take you out') in a bank," Baraka wrote in a crucial passage, "the total environment is changed. Not only the sardonic comments of the lyrics, but the total emotional placement of the rhythm, instrumentation and sound. An energy is released in the bank, a summoning of images that take the bank, and everybody in it, on a trip. That is, they visit another place. A place where Black People live."[4]

The connections Baraka was drawing between music and environment, environment and energy, and energy and social transformation point to what Haizlip saw as the transformative potential of black music on television, as an intimate mass medium that joined image and sound. They also harmonized with Haizlip's notion of vibrations, which function like the "energy" that Baraka identifies with Brown's music and its effect on the social and material environment. If Brown could impose a disruptive black presence in the temple of capitalism through his syncopated vocalizations and funky rhythms so, perhaps, might musicians on *Soul!*—from Mayfield to the Staple Singers, singing of a transcendent place where "Ain't nobody cryin' / Ain't nobody worried / Ain't no smilin' faces / Lyin' to the races"—turn television into a place "where Black People live": not merely visually represented, but "present" in and through its energy or vibrations (figure 3.2).[5] Baraka's notion of music as a means of social transformation and movement joins up with and supports Haizlip's utopian vision for *Soul!* as a program that takes its audience to different spaces and places via its sounds and images.

The producer attempted to represent this energy, as I have noted, by inviting the community into the midtown Manhattan studio where, beginning in 1970, *Soul!* was primarily taped as live—that is, recorded in one take and broadcast unedited, creating the impression of live television.[6] Positioned close to the stage—sometimes on bleachers,

3.2. The Staple Singers, Pops on guitar, February 1971.

sometimes at small tables—studio audience members were invited to feel like part of the production and embraced spectatorship as a role. Occasionally they would allow themselves to be visibly transported by the music. The actor Anna Horsford, then part of the *Soul!* production staff, recalls that Debbie Allen—the actor, dancer, choreographer, and future producer of such seminal television shows as *Fame* and *A Different World*—jumped out of her seat during the taping of a 1972 Stevie Wonder episode. Similarly, in the episodes I discuss at length below, audience members are seen by the camera in states of absorption, concentration, rapture, amusement, and wonder. They are both visibly moved and visibly moving: in "Shades of Soul I," audience members get up to dance to the sounds of Willie Colón's band, and in "Shades of Soul II," a male audience member rises up from his seat to join the women of Labelle in their chorus of refusal: "We won't get fooled again." Such images of the faces and bodies of the *Soul!* studio audience served both to illustrate and to secure the notion of black music as a space of affective exchange and cultural cocreation. As producer, Haizlip sought to make this energy available to viewing audiences—to "catch the flavor of people *interreacting*," as he put it, notwithstanding technological mediation.[7]

Once again, this was a significant departure from the public broadcasting paradigm, which represented music—typically, the European classical repertoire—as an object of appreciation, to be enjoyed in a manner that supported the notion of the viewer's good taste, high standards, and cultural sophistication. The word *appreciate*, as a term for what public broadcasting audiences might do with televised musical performance, implied a hierarchy that positioned auditors and viewers as acolytes who received its message. Consistent with this concept of appreciation, most representations of classical music performance on public television kept audience members out of sight of the viewers and emphasized instead the grandeur of the concert setting, the virtuosity of the musicians, and the cultural importance of the musical enterprise.

Soul! upended the appreciation model, which imposed separation and distance between artist and audience, and which tended to represent music as a static event rather than a dynamic happening. As Haizlip put it, *Soul!* presented the image of an audience "in relationship to a performance that it is enjoying as opposed to a performance that is being presented *for* it."[8] Just as the appreciation model of traditional educational TV implied a specific aesthetic of representation, so *Soul!*'s interreacting model implied a distinct set of aesthetic choices: direction that encouraged musicians to play to and for the studio audience; camera work and microphone placement that included the studio audience in the visual and auditory frame of the transmitted sound and image, so that TV audiences could see and hear their on-screen proxies; interview segments that presented popular musicians as intellectuals; set design that encouraged horizontal interaction between performers and audiences, rather than placing performers in unapproachable settings above the audience; and the fostering, through props and lighting, of an on-set atmosphere of warmth modeled on the atmospheres of the church and the nightclub, two historically counterpublic spaces that provided the templates for *Soul!*'s approach.

The church, as I began to argue above, was a particularly important touchstone for *Soul!*, harboring robust traditions of cultural performance that Haizlip would creatively appropriate.[9] Indeed, his phrase "more meaningful than a three-hour lecture" hints at a relationship between overlong political speechifying and protracted church sermons.

But it also alludes to traditions of dissent within black churches, where music mediates productive tensions between male preachers, the officially vested seats of spiritual and moral authority, and various congregational voices—from the women seated in the mourners' benches to the nominally closeted gay men in the choir—who comment on this authority, sometimes shoring it up, at other times subtly challenging it. In a church service, a chord progression from the queer church organist might affirmatively punctuate a preacher's sermon, like a musical "amen," or it might interrupt him by triggering the congregation to break into song midway through his preaching. The shouts of female worshippers might incite the rest of the congregation to fall out in a manner that shifts the focal point of attention from the pulpit to the pews. Haizlip, a gay man who grew up in the church and respected its traditions, frequently talked about its cultural imprint on his aesthetic as a producer. "Ellis says his religion is the Gospel song rather than the Gospel . . . the Gospel According to Song," wrote the playwright Alice Childress in a 1971 *Essence* profile that is also one of the few published pieces to hint at the producer's non-normative sexuality, through an oblique reference to Haizlip as a widower.[10] It is all the more fitting, then, that in *Soul!* as Haizlip's church we find the musical undercommons— the voices of women, Latino musicians, gospel singers, and those who defied categorization—represented so generously.

Through diverse musical performances, moreover, *Soul!* created a space for the sonic exploration of pan-Africanism as a political orientation or ideology that cut across national, linguistic, and ethnic divisions. When the trumpeter Hugh Masekela appeared on a November 1971 *Soul!* episode with the band Union of South Africa, doing a set that included their chart-topping 1968 hit "Grazing in the Grass," audiences could listen in on a transnational conversation conducted by means of swinging brass and exuberant cowbell. Similarly, when the exiled South African songstress Miriam Makeba (figure 3.3) performed several songs in Xhosa on a January 1972 episode guest hosted by poet Nikki Giovanni, U.S. viewing audiences could perceive the linked struggles of black South Africans and African Americans in her rhythms and sonorities, even if they could not understand her lyrics. (The episode's other guest, boxer Muhammad Ali, furthered the theme of diasporic al-

3.3. Nikki Giovanni (left) interviews Miriam Makeba as audience members look on, January 1972.

liances through his well-known criticisms of the U.S. Armed Forces' recruitment of African Americans to "go ten thousand miles from home and drop bombs and bullets on brown people in Vietnam."[11]) Haizlip's diasporic orientation was particularly significant in facilitating the inclusion of U.S. Latino musicians in its representations of soul, flouting both U.S. public policy (which tended to categorize Latino populations as "white") and conventions of U.S. racial discourse.

In what follows, I briefly survey the representation of black musicians on television before moving on to examine three *Soul!* episodes, each of them exemplary from the viewpoint of this chapter's concern with the disruptive and transporting energies of black music. The first episode, from October 1972, features Rahsaan Roland Kirk, a virtuoso renowned not only for his mastery of wind and brass instruments but also for his outspokenness about the mass media's neglect of black music, especially jazz. The second and third episodes, from successive weeks in November 1972, are titled "Shades of Soul" and explore musical articulations of culture and identity that complicate and multiply notions of blackness. "Shades of Soul I," with the performer and activist Felipe Luciano as guest producer and host, focuses on New York Puerto Rican, or Nuyorican, artists, bringing together orchestras led by Tito Puente and Willie Colón, the latter featuring singing by a young Héctor Lavoe. Based on the previous summer's Soul at the Center festival at Lincoln Center, "Shades of Soul II" divides its attention between a band led by *conguero* (conga drum player) Mongo Santamaría and Labelle—the vocal trio composed of former members of the group Patti LaBelle and the Bluebelles, who had appeared on previous *Soul!* programs, including the 1968 series opener.

These episodes communicate with audiences in multiple ways and in different registers: through vocal and instrumental timbre and intonation; rhythm and cadence; repertoire and arrangement; and the performers' movement, bearing, dress, appearance, and attitude. The fact that they do so while centering on musicians at the margins—of generic categorization, commercial recognition, and/or recognition in dominant framings of American or black music—renders them additionally important in light of *Soul!*'s larger political and cultural project. Consistent with Haizlip's notion of the interreaction of musicians and spectators or auditors, I explore how members of the *Soul!* studio audience played an active role in the production of musical meaning and pursue more fully the producer's notion that black musical performance mediates practices of black collective self-definition and self-identification by representing the community, in sound and image, to itself.

As I began to argue in the introduction, *Soul!* was not unique in its strategies of representing music. *Soul Train*, which debuted as a local Chicago program around the same time as *Soul!* went national, is the obvious and most relevant example of a TV show that was similarly centered on the interaction of audiences and musicians; and other programs, from teen music-and-dance shows to variety shows like the *Smothers Brothers Comedy Hour*, experimented with in-the-round and other alternative stage formats.[12] Yet *Soul!* was exceptional in granting popular musicians artistic agency. Novella Nelson, for example, recalls that on *Soul!* there was no pressure to sing to the camera or to worry about making her work accessible to viewers for whom it might be unfamiliar. Thanks to a sensitive director and crew, she notes, "you could concentrate on the audience."[13] The early *Soul!* director Ivan Curry echoes this perspective, noting that he learned to let the artists perform on *Soul!* as they were accustomed to performing in nontelevised appearances—that is, with the stage setup, positioning, and choreography that they preferred—and let the TV cameras follow.[14] *Soul!* likewise opened doors for artists to pursue a broader repertoire than they could on shows that expected the plugging of a current single. Nona Hendryx, a member of Labelle and, before that, of Patti LaBelle and the Bluebelles, remembers that whereas on *American Bandstand* "you got up and lip-synched to your hit," on *Soul!* "you got to do your thing with a sympathetic in-studio audience."[15] Al Johnson, whose vocal harmony group the Unifics appeared on *Soul!* in 1969 and 1970, similarly recollects that they were able to bring all of their musicians and their stage manager to the TV set—setting the group at ease and helping them re-create "the concert atmosphere" for viewers.[16] And Luciano, who acquired his first TV experience through his work on "Shades of Soul I," notes that Haizlip gave him extraordinary latitude as a guest producer, allowing him to reimagine the *Soul!* studio as an intimate space where Nuyorican musicians and dancers fed off of each others' energies and rhythms.[17]

This is not to say that other TV programs' musical representations were inauthentic, either as music or as television. Among other things, the use of prerecorded audio tracks in lip-synched performances enabled TV producers, camera operators, and singers to focus on the creation of compelling visual images that also communicated powerfully with audiences, introducing new dimensions into the experiences of both performing and watching music. The Supremes' immaculate ensembles and hairdos and their finely honed dance moves, crafted to emphasize the small gestures and details that were visible on television (but not in the setting of a large concert venue), were at least as important to the Motown message of black self-empowerment and self-respect as the lyrics of their songs, the timbres of their voices, or the funkiness of their backing band.[18] Yet *Soul!*'s approach to music on television was distinct and, as we shall see, in many respects more affiliated with the naturalistic conventions of jazz and rock performance, which deemphasized the artifice of the TV apparatus. *Soul!* also took its cues from black radio, with its traditions of deejays as respected taste-makers and knowledgeable sonic architects of mood. Episodes thrived on the revelatory juxtaposition, mining the acoustic spaces between apparently unrelated musical guests (such as Labelle and Santamaría), and they placed a value on artists' abilities to display range as well as virtuosity.

The argument I pursue here has two separate but related dimensions: one concerning television as a means of visual and sonic representation, and the second concerning the pedagogical and inspiriting functions of black music in a period when racialized Americans were exploring new modes of identity and alliance. The first has to do with television as an affective medium, notable for its ability to represent liveness and to convey proximity and intimacy, notwithstanding its mass nature.[19] The second concerns the importance of television as the dominant form of domestic leisure during an enormously fertile period in black popular music culture. *Soul!*'s run as the nation's preeminent black performing arts showcase coincided with the peaking of Motown (the first Jackson 5 single topped the *Billboard* Soul and Hot 100 charts around the time of its second-season opener); the flowering of funk, salsa, and new jazz fusion styles; and the early years of what would later be called disco and hip-hop. The early 1970s saw black popular musicians, and popular musicians more generally, combining commercial popularity with political outspokenness on records that Gil Scott-Heron, one of the pioneers of rap, would liken to "survival kits on wax."[20] On *Soul!*, I am suggesting, these two registers merged, producing powerfully affective television spectacles in which musicians were troubadours of the new black consciousness, sonic ambassadors to what Stevie Wonder would dub "higher ground."[21]

Soul!'s associate producer Alice Hille, the woman responsible for getting many of the popular musicians who appeared on the show in its first nationally syndicated season, was unapologetic about its entertainment format. In the same *Image* article in which Haizlip made a case for the pedagogical significance of Curtis Mayfield, she was more blunt. "I say just *having* blacks on television is 'educational,'" she quipped.[22] To get a sense of *Soul!*'s significance where music is concerned, we have only to consider how highly restricted a milieu television was for black musicians prior to the late 1960s.[23] In most instances, television was accessible to only a few acknowledged superstars—figures on the order of Harry Belafonte, Sammy Davis Jr., and Lena Horne—or, after the rise of Motown and the widespread commercial success of just-different-enough black pop, to those who could perform black music as a desirable but not-too-threatening object of consumption for young white audiences.[24] Black musicians who were less easily incorporated into prevailing wisdom about the demands of the white youth market or who were seen as espousing values incompatible with those of southern TV network affiliates had far fewer opportunities to play for national TV audiences, and to do so in ways that allowed them to inhabit the roles of artists rather than entertainers.

Even the Supremes—who conquered the pop charts in part thanks to a concerted effort led by Maxine Powell, director of artist development Motown, and the choreographer Cholly Atkins to remove the signifiers of racial and sexual difference from their appearance, movements, and vocalizations—were not granted the freedom of their white male peers. In a bizarre sequence from a September 1968 *Red Skelton Show* that also featured the Jefferson Airplane, Skelton introduced the group prior to their performance and asked them, mock seriously, whether they were from "this country." When they affirmed, coyly and in rehearsed unison, "Sure, can't you tell by the way we talk?," Skelton laughed and said that their hairdos had fooled him, since they looked like the hairdos of "three boys from England." Skelton's joke made light of the mid-1960s commercial rivalry between the Supremes and British Invasion groups. But in its reference to the Supremes' trademark wigs it also unwittingly pointed to the ways television differentiated between white male groups like the Beatles, whose girlish hairstyles were the permissible—if sometimes mocked or excoriated—signs of youthful sexuality and rebellion, and black female groups like the Supremes, who were less free to display sexuality or sexual difference. The disparity in representation pointed to a larger contradiction, since British boy bands had fashioned their own sexually and culturally rebellious masculinities in conversation with the aesthetic practices of the Motown girl groups.

Whereas the Supremes were, in a sense, made for TV, other groups, especially those considered too political for advertisers or southern affiliates, were more reluctantly included on network programs. It took concerted negotiations with the producers of the *Joey Bishop Show*, for example, before Mayfield and the Impressions were allowed to sing "Choice of Colors" on a 1969 episode. In other instances, producers found ways to contain the threat of the group's outspoken lyrics by carefully controlling the visual representation of the musicians. To take but one example: when the group appeared on *Where the Action Is*, a mid-1960s *American Bandstand* spinoff, to perform their 1965 masterpiece "People Get Ready," they were pictured singing while sitting in a paddleboat in a lake in Los Angeles's MacArthur Park, the only black figures in a landscape populated by white boaters enjoying a day in the sun.[25] It is difficult to say whether this illustrated white producers' profound misunderstanding of the Impressions' music ("People Get Ready" had the status of a movement anthem), or whether it exemplified their resistance to representing black popular music as social and political critique. In either scenario, the "People Get Ready" segment illustrated how the oppositional power of black music was anxiously policed on television—whether by flanking black musicians with white go-go dancers offering awkward interpretations of their songs or, as in this instance, by inserting black musicians into racially integrated scenarios. The "People Get Ready" video also illustrated, none too subtly, television's policing of the threat of black male sexuality and sexual agency. Surrounded by male and female boaters who appear to be enjoying a carefree afternoon, the Impressions, awkwardly wedged into a paddleboat meant for two, provide the musical source of the scene's ambience of careless romance and innocent sexuality, even as they are excluded from it.

Opportunities on television for black musicians working outside of the orbit of commercial or youth music were even more limited. A sympathetic white journalist in Toronto enthusiastically plugged the 1970 season of *Soul!*—which some Canadian viewers could see on the public television station of Buffalo, New York—as a means of gaining exposure to "all the black singers and musicians most of us haven't heard of," a list that included Pharoah Sanders, B. B. King, Alex Bradford, and Marion

Williams.[26] We might venture to assume that the journalist writing these words had heard adaptations of jazz, blues, and gospel sounds in popular music of the era, and that the "most of us" he refers to simply failed to recognize black performers, or perhaps this set of performers, as musical progenitors in these genres.

In this sense, the journalist might have added to his list the various Latino musicians who in previous decades had fueled international dance crazes for mambo, boogaloo, and cha-cha-cha and who in the 1970s would produce salsa as a globally popular style. Even a figure like Puente—who in the late 1960s briefly hosted his own bilingual TV show, *El Mundo de Tito Puente*, on New York's Channel 47—was considered too ethnically and linguistically esoteric for national television and its presumably white and Anglophone viewing publics. As Puente noted in a 1981 interview, "you can't play a *guaguancó* [an Afro-Cuban style] on Johnny Carson because the people that he caters to don't know what *guaguancó* or a typical Latin tune is, so you have to go with a semicommercial thing. Maybe an 'Oye como va'"—the Puente composition made into a massive hit by Santana—"they might understand. . . . So it's a challenging thing." Moreover, Puente asserted, he could not rely on TV variety-show house bands, whose members, however accomplished, were not expert at playing the polyrhythms that formed the basis of much Latin music.[27]

Puente, finding few opportunities on television, focused on building his audience through an exceptionally prolific performing and recording career. In contrast, some jazz musicians briefly organized in the late 1960s to protest their exclusion from TV. The Jazz and People's Movement was a ragtag group that included Kirk, the trumpeter Lee Morgan, the drummer Elvin Jones, and the saxophonist Archie Shepp and that circulated a "Statement of Purpose" accusing the media of "obstructing the exposure of true black genius" so thoroughly that "many black people are not even remotely familiar with or interested in the creative giants within black society."[28] In the absence of invitations to appear as guests on variety shows, the group used guerrilla theater tactics to crash them, causing enough commotion to disrupt tapings. In August 1970 it disturbed a taping of *Merv Griffin*, blowing whistles and holding up signs that read "More Jazz Music on TV" and

"Honor American Jazz Music." *The Tonight Show* and the *Dick Cavett Show* were similarly targeted, as was the January 24, 1971, episode of *Ed Sullivan*, on which Kirk, ironically, was an invited guest. According to John Kruth, Kirk's biographer, Sullivan's producers had reached out to Kirk to preempt the group's threatened interruption of a live broadcast. The strategy backfired, however, when Kirk showed up with an all-star band (Archie Shepp, Charles Mingus, and Roy Haynes) to play Stevie Wonder's audience-friendly "My Cherie Amour," as previously agreed, but then surprised everyone on the live set by launching into a raucous version of "Haitian Fight Song," the Mingus composition named for the rebellion against slavery and colonial rule in the late eighteenth and early nineteenth centuries. It was a song about which Mingus had noted, "I can't play it right unless I'm thinking about prejudice and persecution, and how unfair it is."[29] "Once the sonic storm subsided," Kruth writes, Ed Sullivan "appeared looking pale and wooden, saying 'Wonderful, wonderful! Let's hear it for *Ramsam* [here the host flubbed his guest's name] Roland Kirk.'" (Years later, the popular TV host mortally offended Kirk by asking whether John Coltrane "had any albums out.") Some thought Sullivan's show a wasted opportunity to introduce jazz to middle America, but others, such as the critic Leonard Feather, came to Kirk's defense, calling it "a unique night in the history of jazz on the small screen."[30]

In the years when the Jazz and People's Movement was active, *Soul!* stood out as a national TV program that not only incorporated jazz into its representation of contemporary music, but also presented practitioners of jazz as venerated artists on a par with the greatest performers of Western classical music. In the course of approximately sixty episodes that aired between spring 1970 and spring 1973, the show hosted dozens of jazz performers, including Haynes; Thelonious Monk (figure 3.4); the Herbie Hancock Sextet; Betty Carter; Carmen McRae; Horace Silver; the McCoy Tyner Quartet; the vocalists Andy and Salome Bey; Hugh Masekela and the Union of South Africa; and King Curtis and the Kingpins, who replaced Reuben Phillips and his orchestra after the first season as *Soul!*'s house band. *Soul!*'s head writer, Alonzo Brown Jr., who had studied jazz under Martin Williams, brought an adventurous ear to the program, urging Haizlip to take risks on experimental groups such

3.4. Thelonious Monk at the piano, circa May 1971.

as M'Boom, an all-percussion ensemble led by Max Roach (figure 3.5). Others, like Cuban singer La Lupe, Miles Davis, and Ornette Coleman, were on Brown's wish list, although they never appeared on the *Soul!* stage.[31]

It would thus have been with considerably heightened expectations that Kirk accepted Haizlip's offer to appear on *Soul!* with his band, the Vibration Society (made up of the drummer Robert Shy, the bassist Pete Pearson, the pianist Ron Burton, and the percussionist Art Perry) in the fall of 1972. *Soul!* offered Kirk and his fellow instrumentalists a starkly different performance context than *Ed Sullivan*: a knowledgeable host (Haizlip had been enthusiastic about Kirk's performance at Soul at the Center the previous summer), a receptive audience, and leeway to perform the sort of overtly political material that Kirk had smuggled on to the *Sullivan* stage like so much musical contraband. Moreover, whereas Sullivan's producers expected Kirk's group to shoehorn its music into the variety-show format—play your song, chat briefly, and exit—*Soul!* made efforts to incorporate Kirk's anticorporate aesthetic into its format, staging, and technological design. Gone was the need to be on and off within five minutes (the relatively generous time allotted

3.5. Max Roach on the *Soul!* set, November 1971.

by the *Sullivan* producers); instead, Kirk and his band would have the better part of forty-five minutes to explore different aspects of their repertoire and develop a rapport with the audience. Gone, too, were the conventions of the proscenium stage, especially as a means of presenting music that made claims to being art; on the innovative Club Soul set that premiered that year, the studio resembled a cozy nightspot, with prop chandeliers and guests seated at small round tables.

Even with these accommodations, Kirk presented certain challenges for Haizlip and his colleagues. In addition to performing unusual feats of virtuosity, such as playing instruments with his nose or blowing multiple saxophones at a time (figure 3.6), Kirk was known in his live shows for his extemporaneous monologues and improvised stage antics that extended to the smashing of chairs. These qualities made him an exciting and unpredictable performer—posing challenges for directors and camera operators—and a figure susceptible to being reduced to the spectacle of his performance, which was only exacerbated by his blindness. Sensitive to these challenges, Haizlip began the episode with a brief montage of some of Kirk's more visually fantastic musical

3.6. Rahsaan Roland Kirk blowing several horns at once on the *Soul!* episode devoted to his music, October 1972.

feats, followed by a ten-minute interview to establish the basic outlines of Kirk's biography and his approach to playing. In this way, viewers learned of the musician's disability, the accommodations he was forced to make for sighted people who misunderstood his "not seeing too well" (the phrase Kirk preferred to "blind"), and his related interest in novel ways of producing sound, including ones that used unconventional body parts like the nose.[32]

At one point during their interview, Haizlip prompted Kirk to discuss the importance of the audience to musical performance, eliciting an answer that effectively validated the show's own investments in representing music as a collective practice that blurred the boundary between musicians and auditors. When Haizlip asked Kirk whether he thought it possible "for an audience to create anything that in turn forces you to create as you're performing," Kirk affirmed that the audience indeed played "a big part" in his work, and he went on to compare his best concerts to "beautiful revival meetings at churches," at which the people "get so wound up in the music they speak in other tongues." Defending a religious practice (glossolalia) often disparaged as merely for show—a bit like his own unconventional approach to playing, which some musicians accused of being gimmicky and self-promoting—Kirk challenged black audiences to allow themselves to be moved by music. "Black people have been so psyched out from our music that we don't want to let ourselves go anywhere," he told Haizlip.

The concert that followed the interview bore out Kirk's ideal, echoing and amplifying Baraka's notion of music as a transport to places outside the reach of racism and capitalism. This becomes evident about ten minutes into the concert, following the band's rollicking instrumental version of the popular gospel song "Old Rugged Cross." As the band segues into an extended vamp, Kirk—attired in maroon slacks and shirt, gold-rimmed sunglasses, and a black head wrap—suddenly stops playing and grabs a metal folding chair on which one of his horns has been resting. While blowing a whistle and occasionally banging a gong, he proceeds to pound the chair against the side of the tiny, carpeted stage, eliciting loud whoops, applause, and cheers of encouragement from the audience. When this pounding proves insufficient to destroy the chair, Kirk reaches for the satchel he wears to hold his instruments and opens a zippered front pocket to grab an object—perhaps a laminated badge—with which he attacks the red velvet seat cushion.

TV viewers see this spectacle unfolding from multiple points of view. One camera alternates between medium shots of Kirk with his band behind him and close-ups of the musician working feverishly to remove and destroy the cushion; another pans the audience from the back of the room to reveal Club Soul guests absorbed in the drama of the moment, including one young woman who seems to levitate, as if pulled by an invisible string, from her own folding chair. When Kirk finally manages to detach the cushion, there is an eruption of applause and cheers, and as he thrashes it against the stage and crushes it under his shoes, the audience rises to its feet. A jib-arm shot (from overhead) shows people leaning in to the stage, as Kirk—not yet finished with the chair and still whistling—disassembles the frame. When he has finished, he bangs the gong and then, turning to another pocket in his satchel, pulls out a conch shell, which he blows in triumph as the audience cheers again.

The power of Kirk's chair act is enriched by its allusions to spectacles of rioting and rebellion familiar from the evening news. Accompanied by shrill whistle sounds that evoke the police, Kirk's destruction of the folding chair is thus visually as well as sonically linked to contemporary black political protest and might indeed have registered with some viewers as a critique of civil rights strategies such as sit-ins.[33] So effective was the chair act on television that Frank London, the Klezmatics trumpeter, recalled being a "twelve-year-old white kid from the suburbs" watching Kirk on *Soul!* and feeling "totally freaked out! I thought the suburbs would be burnin' any day"—a description that nicely captures the ability of television to make its viewers forgetful of its mediation.[34] Telling, too, in this context is London's association of the destruction of the chair with burning and a specific fear that the white suburbs, not the black ghettos, are about to be set aflame. The faces of the studio audience members that the TV cameras briefly make visible on screen reveal a range of affective states, although fear is not apparent among them. Rather, there is amazement that Kirk is doing something so extreme, wonder that he is getting away with it (on national television!), intense absorption in the spectacle of the musician as he lets himself "go somewhere," pleasurable identification with the enactment of powerful emotion and the spectacle of physical aggression, apprehension at what is happening and whether Kirk will finally triumph over the chair, and (as echoed in the faces of some of the band members, who clearly have witnessed such behavior before and know the score) amusement at the musician's crazy behavior.

Putting aside the passage of time between the event and London's recollection, it is interesting that he links Kirk's destruction of the folding chair with the song "Blacknuss," which followed it. London's conflation of the two moments associates, quite correctly, I would argue, the destruction of the chair with the emergence of a new black identity— one that Kirk spells *blacknuss*. On the other hand, it forgets Kirk's blowing of the conch shell, a makeshift instrument associated with the history of black *marronage* memorialized in Mingus's "Haitian Fight Song" and in the famous 1968 bronze of the Haitian artist and architect Albert Mangonès, *Le Nègre Marron*, installed before the presidential palace in Port-au-Prince. In that sculpture, which survived the 2010 earthquake that struck the Haitian capital, a male figure can be seen breaking free of his shackles and, head tilted upward, blowing a conch shell.

In the context in which Kirk plays it, then, the conch is not merely another exotic instrument that the uncannily versatile performer can play, but a potent symbol and sounding of New World black rebellion and the musician's role as a leader of social rebirth.[35] The sound of the conch shell, announcing the completion of Kirk's destructive task, is the call to assembly that makes the declaration of blacknuss possible. Like the ram's horn blown on the Jewish Day of Atonement, it sonically symbolizes the people's resolve to act as a collective. In the *Soul!* episode, it precedes a rousing singing of the lyrics to "Blacknuss," in which the audience follows Kirk's lead in spelling out, again and again, the new word that also symbolizes the world to come.

It is worth noting here that compared with home audio systems, most television sets in the 1960s and 1970s had rather poor sound quality. "Squeezed through a midrange mono speaker the size of an ashtray" is how Scott-Heron describes sound on TV in his memoir, *The Last Holiday*.[36] The Kirk episode of *Soul!* addresses this problem through camerawork and direction that strive to create the feeling of being there, despite obvious sonic limitations. Indeed, the mediation of the television camera arguably renders the affective power of Kirk's performance more immediate and more suspenseful than it might have been in a nightclub setting. Through close-ups that reveal beads of sweat on the musician's forehead, the camera allows TV viewers to observe (or perhaps fetishize) the labor of Kirk's task, picturing his body as engaged in a frenzy of pulling and tearing. Kirk and his band contribute to the illusion of liveness by not returning the camera's gaze, and moments when the camera breaks away from the performer to look at the audience, or when its privileged sightline is blocked by a spectator rising from her chair, paradoxically reinforce this effect of realness. The suspense of the spectacle is amplified, moreover, by viewers' knowledge that Kirk cannot see the chair, and by cultural stereotypes that render the visually impaired person feeble and ineffectual rather than physically powerful and aggressive. Kirk's blindness also invites a reading of his extraordinary act as a bitter but perhaps triumphant commentary on the shameful rituals (such as those famously depicted in the "battle royal" scene early in Ralph Ellison's *Invisible Man*) that set blindfolded black male contestants against each other for the pleasure of white spectators.[37]

Simon Frith, a scholar of popular music, understands such strategies of visual representation, which are also hallmarks of documentary film, as particularly relevant to televised performances of rock—a genre characterized by its ideological and aesthetic investment in authenticity. A commercial medium that depends on absolute control over the image, often to the point of scripting liveness down to the quarter-minute, television would seem to pose challenges for rock that it does not pose for pop, with its unabashed celebration of surface. Rock "performers must seem authoritative, even as their impact is being created," Frith writes. On television programs that convey the feeling of live concerts, "we must believe that the performers are presenting themselves, even as their presence is determined by technology, by lighting, amplification, sound balance, editing, etc."[38]

The Kirk episode of *Soul!*—in both the musician's rock star antics and its visual strategies—productively complicate Frith's account, putting a different spin on his argument about TV's representation of popular music that, in terms of its own mythologies of realness, would seem to be opposed to TV's artifice. (Here, jazz as a genre seems ideologically closer to rock than to pop.) For Frith, the best rock performances on television are those that paradoxically stage rock's resistance to television. The chair act certainly qualifies as one such staging of resistance, yet there is an additional layer to Kirk's performance, linked to the artist's own activism around TV as an exclusionary tool of white European cultural hegemony. On *Soul!*, Kirk—denied access on account of race both to the mantle of rock and to the publicity of television—appropriates the cultural power of TV to render more broadly accessible the intimate spaces of black counterpublic performance, spaces where black genius, as well as black rage and black triumph, are abundantly on display. Whereas rock musicians in Frith's account must perform their indifference to being on television in order to retain their authenticity as rockers, Kirk and his musical kin are burdened by the need to perform a critique of television's indifference to their existence as musicians. As political theater, Kirk's smashing of the chair thus stages not only generalized contempt for an oppressive society, like Pete Townshend's destruction of his guitar on a famous 1967 *Smothers Brothers* episode that also saw Keith Moon's botched detonation of his drum kit, but also very specific contempt for the structures that render black musicians selectively visible as entertainers but invisible as artists.

Moreover, Kirk's chair act differs from Jimi Hendrix's famous burning of his guitar at Monterey in 1967 or the Who's theatrics in that it does not shore up normative masculinity—or, rather, it shores up masculinity, but in a manner that is related to blindness as a trope of feminized dependency. When male rock musicians torched, smashed, or otherwise attacked their guitars or drum kits in the 1960s and 1970s, they shattered norms of respectability while retaining, or even expanding, their claim to masculine authority as rock gods or guitar heroes. Through the destruction of an instrument, the male rock performer asserted his contempt for the laws governing property and value; in this sense, his act was also consistent with rock culture's rejection of commodity culture, with its worship of dollars. In contrast, in attacking the chair on which his instruments rest rather than the instruments themselves, Kirk channels a disruptive energy more linked to the everyday and to acts of civil disobedience, including those associated with urban riots. Furthermore, in wrestling with the chair over the course of four long television minutes—the time it would have taken him and his band to play "My Cherie Amour" on *Ed Sullivan*—Kirk enacts a protracted and suspenseful ritual of destruction. Will he vanquish the metal folding chair? Or will it resist his efforts? When Kirk ultimately dismantles the chair, the audience's standing ovation registers pleasure in the spectacle of his symbolic destruction of the old order, but also relief that his considerable mental and physical labors have paid off.[39]

Airing in mid-November 1972, six weeks after the Kirk episode, "Shades of Soul I" also culminates in a spectacle of collective exorcism, expressed not through an act of creative destruction but through an improvised TV dance party. As Willie Colón y Su Orquesta ease into "Timbalero," their third and last selection of the evening, members of the *Soul!* studio audience get up to join a pair of hired dancers on the stage. The song is an apt soundtrack for the display of Nuyorican soul, paying homage to the player of the timbales, the Cuban percussion instrument whose distinct sonorities and rhythms lay the groundwork for much Latin music.[40] But the song is more than a paean to the musical past or to the resourceful reworking of African rhythms in the Americas; it also gives voice to the musical imagination of the present-day Nuyorican barrio. To use Baraka's resonant metaphor from "The Changing Same," "Timbalero" sonically transports *Soul!*'s studio audience and its geographically disparate spectators to the "places"—the clubs, homes, and streets—where New York Puerto Ricans live.[41]

The lyrics of "Timbalero" invite the listener into this musically mediated Nuyorican counterpublic space. "Y oye la conga y el timbal," sings the lead vocalist Héctor Lavoe (then only seventeen years old), imploring dancers and musicians alike to "listen" to the drums, both conga and timbales, as they "talk" of sonic traditions brought to the Caribbean from Africa. "Y me voy pa' Cantanga," he intones, taking listeners on a musical trip to the Congolese "motherland" where the rhythms were born and nurtured.[42] As the band's instrumentalists take turns soloing, the camera lingers for several minutes on the dancers, alternating between medium close-ups of couples moving gracefully in time and panoramic shots of the dance floor as a swirling, pulsating mass of bodies. Thanks to inventive direction by Stan Lathan, overlaid images from different cameras create a montage of bodies and colors. Against these images, the credits begin to roll, announcing the end of the hour-long episode. But the spirit of the dance—or so TV viewers are encouraged to imagine—lives on, in other times and spaces.

Although *Soul!* had included Puerto Rican musicians and actors in its representations of black culture as early as 1968, "Shades of Soul I" was the only episode of the program devoted entirely to the vibrant expressive cultures of New York Puerto Ricans.[43] It did so amid a burgeoning Puerto Rican culture and political consciousness, particularly among young people. Inspired by national liberation struggles on Puerto Rico and by Black Power, young Nuyoricans in the late 1960s and early 1970s were questioning what they saw as the colonial mindset of their parents; their place in U.S. economic and racial hierarchies; and their culture's valorization of whiteness, which persisted despite myths of a raceless Puerto Rican society. Proudly pointing to their collective African and Taino ancestry, many young Puerto Ricans increasingly refused to identify themselves as white, regardless of their individual phenotype or ancestry.[44] In so doing, they rejected not only U.S. racial categorizations—which conditioned the social agency and cultural visibility of Latinos on an identification with whiteness—but also race itself, instead embracing new pan-national and pan-racial or -ethnic identities like Third World.[45]

When Haizlip handed over responsibility for "Shades of Soul I" to Felipe Luciano (figure 3.7), the artist and activist who had previously read his poetry on a *Soul!* episode featuring Herbie Hancock, the producer put his program in the hands of a charismatic personification of the new Afro-Boricuan consciousness.[46] As a member of the Original Last Poets (a subset of the collective that had appeared on the first *Soul!* episode), Luciano wrote and performed poetry that paid tribute to the cultural, spiritual, and social richness of the New York barrio, singling out its musicians—both immigrant and native-born—for special praise. And although it was never mentioned explicitly on "Shades of Soul I," he possessed political credibility for many young Latinos and Latinas as a founding member of the New York chapter of the Young Lords Organization, a pan-Latino cultural nationalist group inspired by the

3.7. Felipe Luciano performing his poetry, unidentified *Soul!* episode.

Black Panthers. Moreover, although Luciano had not previously hosted or produced a program for television, he was known in the Puerto Rican community as the host of the WRVR radio program *Latin Roots*, a weekly English-language showcase of Latino arts, politics, and current affairs very much in the spirit of Haizlip's TV show.[47] Finally, as a brown-skinned Puerto Rican who wore his hair in an Afro, Luciano embodied the Afro-Boricuan critique of race as a means of dividing populations linked by shared ancestry, culture, and political self-interest.

Luciano rewarded the trust Haizlip placed in him and, following the producer's example, hosted an episode that was groundbreaking on several fronts. Not only did "Shades of Soul I" break with U.S. sociological convention in representing New York Puerto Rican society as a multiracial and multihued "rainbow" (as Luciano put it in his opening poem, "Puerto Rican Rhythms"), but it also depicted this culture in English, thus directing its representations to Anglophone second- and third-generation Latino viewers as well as non-Latino audiences.[48] (In contrast, *Realidades*, the local Latino public affairs program that began airing on Channel 13 in 1972, was bilingual.) But "Shades of Soul I" was perhaps most notable for appropriating Haizlip's notion of the culturally meaningful to represent Nuyorican music without apology, translation, or sociological explication.

African American performers were gradually gaining a foothold on television in the 1970s, but Latino musicians in the era remained, for the most part, outside the cultural sights of the medium, although their sounds infiltrated and shaped American popular music. Sometimes this invisibility had its roots in musical genre. As a rock artist, the Mexican-born Carlos Santana achieved a degree of mainstream commercial popularity that neither Colón nor Lavoe would ever enjoy, although their hybrid sounds also appealed widely to young audiences. In other cases, the marginality of Latino musicians on TV was a result of the medium's solicitation of Anglo viewers. As Puente noted, Latin jazz musicians faced constraints on the material they could play in mainstream TV gigs. Moreover, like their African American jazz counterparts, to appear on television, Latino musicians typically had to accept conventions that preferred the three-minute pop song to the ten-minute improvised *descarga*, or jam session.[49] On his 1972 album

/

El Juicio (The judgment), Colón's "Timbalero" had occupied a full eight minutes and eighteen seconds—and even this represented an abbreviated version of what his group might play for a live club audience. Where on television could Latino musicians find a platform for musical performance that appeased their own desires for sonic expression, let alone the expressive needs of dancers?

Luciano responded to these representational challenges in "Shades of Soul I" by shining a spotlight on two exemplary Nuyorican bands, Puente's legendary orchestra and the up-and-coming Colón group, interlacing their musical performances with his own poetry, brief interview segments, and the screening of excerpts from the recent documentary *Our Latin Thing (Nuestra Cosa)*, which contained electrifying footage from an acclaimed 1971 Fania All-Stars performance at New York's Cheetah Club.[50] Empowered by Haizlip's example, Luciano specifically set out to avoid lowest-common-denominator representations of Latin music or musicians, producing the episode from a viewpoint that assumed audiences' familiarity with and respect for both.[51] His refusal to decipher Puerto Ricanness for viewers is exemplified in the episode's opening moments, which depict hands beating out a rhythm on bongo drums and which are closely followed by the image of other hands (later, we discover that they are Puente's) using timbale sticks to play a cowbell. No authority names these instruments, deciphers what the drumming means, or identifies their sounds with a particular national musical tradition, following the practices of ethnographic guidebooks or commercial TV shows that understood their task as one of translating Latin music for white audiences.[52] However, the camera does not linger on the players' hands with ethnographic curiosity, as though offering viewers an impromptu lesson in how to play congas. Rather, the images make the music present in a visually intimate fashion, while radically defamiliarizing the assumptions of racial or ethnic difference and exoticism that ground mainstream television representations of Latin musicians.

A critique of TV conventions governing the representation of Latin music also surfaces in the bands' respective repertoires. Although Puente was universally known to fans as el Rey del Timbal and was associated with mambo and other up-tempo genres of Latin music, for his second number—at Luciano's urging—he played "Tus Ojos" (Your eyes), a romantic ballad that allowed the *timbalero* to display his virtuosity on the vibraphone, an instrument associated with African American jazz musicians like Lionel Hampton. Likewise, a presumption of intimate knowledge of Nuyorican culture informs Luciano's interviews with Puente and Colón—which, while establishing basic biographical information about the musicians (where they were born, how they acquired their musical skills, and who they counted as influences) refuse to pander or condescend. For example, when Puente, in response to a question about the future of Latin music, mocks the tepid appropriation of Latin rhythms in popular American hits such as "Cherry Pink and Apple Blossom White" and "Can't Take My Eyes Off of You," drawing knowing laughter and applause from the audience, Luciano allows the joke and his own appreciative reception of it to go unexplained, in a way that echoes the reception of in-jokes about the TV show *Julia* in the fifth episode of *Soul!* (discussed in chapter 2). Similarly, when Puente praises younger musicians for returning to their sonic roots in earlier genres and Afro-Cuban rhythms, earning another round of audience approval, Luciano does not spend time clarifying this statement. In a telling conversational moment before Colón's band takes the stage, the "Shades of Soul I" host in fact appeals to young viewers' collective memory by reminiscing fondly about his own teenage experiences doing "grind-em up" dances at parties held away from the watchful eyes and ears of stern parents.

In effect, "Shades of Soul I" invited Latino viewers into the affective compact that *Soul!* was continually negotiating with black audiences, pointing to music—particularly the musical traditions of Africa—as a means of articulating black and Latino counterpublics. In contrast to a U.S. race discourse that focused on divisions based on tropes of visibility and blood, "Shades of Soul I" portrayed music as a bridge between social groups. At the same time, in representing different generations of Puerto Rican musicians, the episode insisted on the variety and diverse histories of sounds grouped together under catchall, racializing terms like *Latin*. Even for viewers unfamiliar with Puente and Colón, the differences between their bands become apparent as the hour progresses. The light-skinned Puente appears nattily dressed in a pin-striped suit and platform shoes, his hair combed into an Afro, while Colón takes the stage in more laid-back attire, wearing his hair longish and his shirt open at the collar.[53] Whereas Puente, the Juilliard-educated Rey del Timbal, presents himself in the mold of mid-century African American jazz performers Duke Ellington, Count Basie, and Lady Day, Colón, known to fans as el Malo for his album covers that played with the image of the Latin pool shark or criminal, affects a persona less dedicated to old-school showmanship.[54] And while Puente appears on stage with a band featuring an eight-person horn section, Colón directs a pared-down group with a leaner sound and chooses songs that self-consciously affirm the music's African and Afro-Caribbean antecedents.[55] The roots sensibilities of Colón's music are particularly audible in his second selection, "Aguanile," an intricately rhythmic song that references the orishas, or deities, of the Afro-Caribbean Santería religion.

Through the display on "Shades of Soul I" of old and new faces of Nuyorican music, Luciano validated a continuum of Latin musical creativity in New York. "We needed the young market," he recalls. "I didn't want to do a show that just paid homage to our parents. I wanted to do a show that paid homage to ourselves."[56] One of the younger viewers of "Shades of Soul I" was a teenager flipping through the channels on his family's TV in search of something to watch. Bobby Sanabria would grow up to be a respected educator and musician who played with Mongo Santamaría, but then he was living in the Melrose Projects in the South Bronx with his parents and sister. Although he had seen Puente perform live in front of his building, and he knew of Luciano through the Young Lords, seeing these around-the-neighborhood figures on Channel 13 was new, a sign that "somebody cared about us." More than forty years later, Sanabria still recalls the "beautiful way" the episode depicted his community in all its "different shapes, sizes, and colors." But mostly he recalls watching Puente—"our Muhammad Ali, our Malcolm X, our Duke Ellington" rolled into one.[57] In retrospect, Sanabria speculates that the pan-Africanist undertones of *Soul!* episodes like "Shades of Soul I" "did a lot to help connect the black community and the Hispanic [community]," forcing some young viewers to start asking why and how the two groups were separated. The episode featuring Puente and Colón also prompted Sanabria, who grew up listening to African American radio stations in New York like WBLS, to hear black musicians differently. When, a few weeks later in January 1973, he saw Earth, Wind and Fire—in an ensemble including Maurice White on timbales and Phillip Bailey on congas—he said to himself, "Wow, this band is like Santana."[58]

"Shades of Soul II," airing a week later, further advanced the notion of a linked soul culture between U.S. blacks and Latinos by bringing together a revered Cuban percussionist and a reinvented all-female trio whose sound and style demolished the raced and gendered musical boundaries erected between rock and R&B or soul. Broadcast without a host, so that musical performance dominated the hour, the episode opened with a brief introduction by the radio announcer Gerry B (for Bledsoe), who explained that "Shades of Soul II" would feature Mongo Santamaría and Labelle, two of the outstanding musical performers from the previous summer's "beautiful" Soul at the Center festival at Lincoln Center. Over the course of ten days and evenings, New York City's newest prestigious performing arts venue had opened its doors to a range of black musicians, dancers, and poets—many of whom, like Kirk, either had appeared or would appear on *Soul!*[59] Beyond having performers and producers in common, *Soul!* and Soul at the Center both aspired to bring the vibrations of black artists and their audiences to institutions that had previously shut their doors to them. Both the television show and the festival, that is, imagined black performance as a means of occupying and transforming culturally authoritative spaces, whether the technologically mediated landscape of public television or the formal and austere spaces of Alice Tully and Philharmonic Halls. As its name implied, Soul at the Center would decenter the aesthetic sensibility that enshrined European traditions at the expense of other forms of creative achievement, establishing the centrality of black artists and the black aesthetic in the development of both American and global culture.

In sampling the Lincoln Center festival for *Soul!*, Haizlip appropriated public television's practice of making high culture accessible to the television-watching masses. From *Great Performances* to *Masterpiece Theatre*, public broadcasting abounded with examples of programming that beamed the sounds, images, and august atmosphere of the concert hall into living rooms around the nation. In bringing Soul at the Center to television via "Shades of Soul II," *Soul!* thus riffed both on public television's uplift mission and the function of prestigious stages in validating black artistic achievement for white audiences. Soul at the Center was not an authenticating event, along the lines of John Hammond's famous Spirituals to Swing concerts at Carnegie Hall, which positioned seasoned African American musicians like Sister Rosetta Tharpe—one of whose last performances was at the 1972 festival—as interesting discoveries for primarily white, middle-class spectators. Nor was it quite like the Cuban percussionist Chano Pozo's 1947 Carnegie Hall cameo with Dizzy Gillespie, understood as a public affirmation of the Latino influence on jazz. Rather, the point of Soul at the Center was, as Haizlip envisioned it, to release the vibrations of black arts in Lincoln Center, permanently transforming both its hallowed halls and the consciousness of audiences present as witnesses.

In putting Santamaría and Labelle on the same bill, and in letting the musicians do the talking without the intercession of a host or interviewer, "Shades of Soul II" advanced the previous episode's thesis of the common Africanist roots of New World black musical practices. Indeed, in asking audiences to listen across different sonic registers of the diaspora, the episode might well have been titled "The Changing Same." Here were two groups that, on the surface, had very little to do with each other musically; yet they worked for audiences that were open to hearing them as members of the same family pursuing different musical expressions of different black experiences. (One explicit sign of this continuity was the inclusion of conga drums in the band backing Labelle.) The Cuban-born Santamaría, introduced by Bledsoe as "the Watermelon Man" because of his 1963 hit of the same name, had been a central player in the boogaloo and Latin jazz scenes in New York and Los Angeles, and was among the late twentieth century's most authoritative interpreters and innovators of Afro-Cuban percussion traditions. Santamaría's appearances at Soul at the Center and on *Soul!* came in the wake of the release of *Up from the Roots*, a 1972 album that reflected his determined reimmersion in African percussion practices after a series of commercially successful albums for Columbia Records. "Shades of Soul II" likewise found the three women in Labelle—Hendryx, Sarah Dash, and Patti LaBelle—in a period of creative transformation. By late 1972 they were no longer the Apollo Theater "Sweethearts" who had resolved to sell their hearts "to the junkman," nor did they resemble the color-coordinated group that sang an affecting version of "Over the Rainbow" on the October 1968 debut of *Soul!* Under the tutelage of their new manager, the British producer Vicki Wickham, they had cast off the model of "three girls, three gowns, sixties glamour" to embrace Hendryx's adventurous songwriting, a more liberated look, and the musical confidence to take on the material of British rockers like the Who and the Rolling Stones.[60] Both groups, that is to say, were committed to ongoing aesthetic and cultural experimentation, and both placed a high value on exploring black musical traditions, whether via Cuba from West Africa or via England from Memphis and Detroit.

On "Shades of Soul II," Santamaría goes first, leading a tight band through a set that spans musical styles and moods. There is tender bossa nova ("Estrada do Sol"), extroverted mambo ("Cuidado") and nostalgia-infused Cuban *guajiro* ("Sofrito"). In between songs, the drummer, who is seated at the center of the bandstand surrounded by his congas and bongos (figure 3.8), sporting a satin, purple-rose-hued vest over a funky shirt with an impressive collar, thanks the appreciative audience and introduces his band, whose members, hailing from Colombia, Venezuela, Cuba, Puerto Rico, and Harlem, are a diaspora in miniature. Notably, when he introduces songs, Santamaría offers their titles in English— perhaps as a nod to viewers unfamiliar with his music—but even these translations are attuned to the differences, cultural as well as linguistic, within U.S. black populations. For "Sofrito," a song named after the pan-Caribbean sauce that, in Cuba, includes onions, garlic, and peppers, Santamaría offers the English translation "Black-Eyed Peas and Rice," a "mistake" that conveys quite accurately the sense of *sofrito* as a staple food for U.S. Latinos of African descent.

The headliners of the evening, Labelle (figure 3.9)—dubbed by Bledsoe "three of the baddest sisters in the world"—offer a similarly eclectic

3.8. Mongo Santamaría on the congas, flanked by members of his band, during the "Shades of Soul II" episode.

set, combining Hendryx's compositions from the group's 1972 *Moon Shadow* album (the gospel-tinged "I Believe That I've Finally Made It Home" and the ballad "Touch Me All Over") with versions of Nina Simone's classic "Four Women" and the Who's "Won't Get Fooled Again." To clamorous applause, the women take the stage, decked in idiosyncratic, individualized ensembles. Hendryx wears an embellished white pantsuit with a rakish blazer; Dash a strappy, tiered dress, her relaxed hair pulled back into a bun; and LaBelle bright yellow culottes, shimmering blue eye shadow, and a tunic with billowing, kimono-style sleeves that lend drama to her dance movements. The women's display of different personas through their dress is consistent with their deconstruction of the girl-group norms: Dash once asked, "Why do black women all have to look alike because they're singing together?"[61] Indeed, in so emphatically not looking alike, Labelle claimed the prerogative of their white male rock peers to use style to express their individuality, however constructed. Furthermore, their different looks conveyed a range

3.9. The women of Labelle, from a November 1971 episode. From left to right: Patti LaBelle, Sarah Dash, Nona Hendryx.

of gendered expressions of black femininity, from Dash's more conventional prettiness to Hendryx's effortless butch chic and gay icon Patti LaBelle's self-assured embrace of sartorial excess.

In featuring LaBelle, Dash, and Hendryx on the show for the fourth time since 1968 and for the second time as Labelle, *Soul!* archives the women's creative work in a particularly generative period of their development, when they were actively seeking alternatives to the girl-group mode of performance. (In addition to appearing on the *Soul!* series opener, Patti LaBelle and the Bluebelles appeared on a 1970 episode with the football player Gale Sayers, the Unifics, and Roberta Flack; in late 1971, Haizlip again welcomed the women to *Soul!*, this time as

Labelle.) Most narratives of Patti LaBelle and the Bluebelles' transformation into Labelle in the late 1960s and early 1970s focus on Wickham's inspired mentoring of the group and the creative invigoration provided by its London sojourn. In contrast, *Soul!* documents Labelle's evolution in a manner that focuses attention on the agency of the black freedom movement on the group's feminist and queer self-fashioning as liberated black female musicians. This is not to dispute the accuracy of the narrative of change through England and Wickham, but rather to argue that the *Soul!* archive presents certain things that remain absent or unrepresented in this conventional narrative—in particular, the formative role of Black Power in creating the conditions of possibility for the group's pursuit of heterodox sounds and images. *Soul!*, in other words, allows us to see and hear the revolutionary quality of the group's performances well before the release of the justifiably celebrated 1974 megahit "Lady Marmalade" and their famous channeling of glam rock and gay subcultural style in a concert in that year at the Metropolitan Opera House (part of New York City's Lincoln Center complex), where they performed in silvery Afro-futurist spacesuits. Their display on "Shades of Soul II" has special relevance for black female and black queer viewers insofar as it offers black arts and Black Power—that is to say, masculinist political and cultural formations—as the sources of agency for feminist and queer projects that potentially call into question the idea that these formations are the only or primary modes of black radical visibility.

The articulation of freedom in Labelle's 1972 performance—freedom from gender and racial stereotypes and expectations and freedom to carry out aesthetic experiments and unapologetically pursue self-expression—is amplified and deepened in the group's remarkable performance of "Four Women." In the version on her 1966 album *Wild Is the Wind*, Simone's famously distinctive voice represents all four black female characters, including Peaches, whose ironically sweet name Simone draws out in the song's closing moments with a wrenching, hair-raising fury. In Labelle's version on *Soul!*, each of the three singers performs a single verse of "Four Women," occupying the small stage alone, and each extemporizes on her character, before all three women come together to perform the climactic "Peaches" verse in glorious unison. As

Aunt Sarah, a domestic worker (perhaps a slave), Dash uses her soprano to interesting effect, representing the laboring black female body in a vocal register that calls attention to the erasure of that body's femininity and sexuality. In the second verse, Hendryx—as Safronia, the daughter of a rich white man and the black woman he "forced . . . late one night"—substitutes her own name for her character's, bringing the reality of her own persona into jarring collision with the image of the high-living but lonely character she voices. In breaking the imaginary fourth wall of the lyrics and singing "What do they call me? They call me Nona," Hendryx signifies on the song's much-discussed realism (some thought Simone guilty of perpetuating stereotypes) and playfully subverts the notion of authenticity as an inherent quality of black women's vocal performance. Whereas Dash sings to a pared-down instrumental accompaniment and at a slow tempo, Hendryx performs in a more upbeat and rhythmically complex arrangement that connects "Four Women" to Santamaría's music. The sound gets funkier and more frenetic as Patti LaBelle performs the streetwalker character, "Sweet Thing." More than her bandmates, LaBelle embodies her character, changing her enunciation and posture and pretending to chew gum as she brags to the audience about the money she earns in an evening. "Sweet Thing is my name, walking the streets is my game," she rhymes, swinging her hips exaggeratedly to whoops and cheers that acknowledge and encourage her performance. "That's the way they do it, y'all," she calls back.

The energy is at a pitch by the time Dash and Hendryx join her on the stage for the final verse. By this time, the room is no longer still or silent with concentration—as it was for Dash's more intimate performance—but expectant with the combined energy of all three singers. The camerawork emphasizes the emotional tension in the studio by alternating between medium close-up shots of the three women on stage and a more distant view from the back of the room, so that the viewer at home has the impression of watching over and through the silhouetted heads of the audience members, who are several rows deep and sitting not more than five feet from the singers. After drawing out the song's climactic line, "My . . . name . . . is . . . Peaches," in a final chorus that accentuates rather than blends the difference in their voices, the women walk off the stage, and the camera offers an image (from the viewpoint of the stage) of audience members leaping to their feet, applauding as the band continues the funky groove.

Then, without a break in the music, Labelle returns to the stage and launches into "Won't Get Fooled Again," imagining Townshend's famous lyric as an anthem of race and gender—not only youth—liberation. The arrangement, which has Patti singing lead and Hendryx and Dash backing her up, signifies on the use of black women as backup singers in rock anthems, but their use of rich vibratos and gospel timbres in lines like "And I get on my knees and pray" draws a connection between the song's theme of refusal and the musical traditions of the black church. During an electric organ solo at the break, the women dance—not with girl-group uniformity but in a freestyle, spirit-driven fashion; and when they sing the title line, "We won't get fooled again," they gesture with arms perpendicular to their bodies and palms flexed, seemingly appropriating the Supremes' famous choreography to "Stop in the Name of Love" and, in so doing, commenting implicitly on the highly choreographed expectations for girl-group performers. Toward the end of the song, Patti leads the audience in a call and response of "we won't," recalling the sing-along to Kirk's "Blacknuss." Performed with the affective energy of "Four Women" still vibrating, "we won't" becomes a cry of resistance not only to the authority of the state and its leaders but to the forces that shape the lives of Simone's characters. Furthermore, it is the women who lead the song's call for revolution, with Patti singing out "Freedom, y'all" and rallying the audience to answer her. At one point, she steps off the stage, extending the microphone to a man in the front row who sings and dances with a sort of ecstatic abandon. "We won't, we won't, we won't get fooled again. We won't, we won't, we won't"—the song ends not with the spectacular pyrotechnics of smashed electric guitars, but with a fade-out, the volume diminishing as the show credits roll.

In Sam Greenlee's 1969 satirical novel *The Spook Who Sat by the Door*, a black man named Dan Freeman infiltrates the Central Intelligence Agency and uses the knowledge he gains on the inside to organize a group of black freedom fighters in his hometown of Chicago. For Freeman, who is something of a cross between Eldridge Cleaver and James Bond, television is irrelevant to the imminent revolution against white supremacy. At best, TV represents "the white fantasy world"; at worst, it aestheticizes the spectacle of the violent suppression of black protest for its "entertainment value." "Antonioni announced plans in Rome to do a Technicolor movie concerning the riots," the narrator wisecracks. "It would involve one man's agony in trying to decide whether to throw a brick at the police and the entire movie would take place in a kitchenette apartment. Marcello Mastroianni would play the lead in blackface."[62]

In contrast, when Freeman undertakes the political education of the Cobras, the youth gang who become his operatives in fomenting revolution, he turns to music. "They listened to Miles's records and to Lady Day, Pres, Monk, Diz and the rest, and began hearing things in jazz that they had heard in rhythm and blues," Greenlee writes, and "in the negative urge to strike out against oppression they had found something that freed them from their fears and the doubts about themselves and their color." "Man, it's all there if you listen," Freeman tells his youthful charges. "You can't find your history in the white man's books. If you want to know your history, listen to your music."[63]

We should not be surprised to hear Freeman talking in ways that recall Baraka—or, for that matter, Wonder or Scott-Heron, Haizlip or Hille, Kirk or Santamaría or Labelle. "Listen to your music" might have been the motto of *Soul!*—although unlike Greenlee's character, the show's producers, its guests, and its audiences were not prepared to give up on television as a tool of black education or liberation. As a rallying cry and a call to a heightened consciousness of black struggle, "black is beautiful" belonged as much to musicians and their audiences as it did to activists.

When Stokely Carmichael came out of his African exile to appear on *Soul!* in 1973, the former leader of the Student Nonviolent Coordinating Committee (SNCC) speculated that the revolution might be further along if African Americans had control of the U.S. mass media. Haizlip countered, "But we have Aretha Franklin and James Brown!" Neither the Queen of Soul nor the Hardest Working Man in Show Business appeared on *Soul!*: unlike Aretha's sister Carolyn (who appeared on the 1971 episode titled "Salute to Black Women"), they had the option of

3.10. Al Green in a moment of absorption, February 1972.

larger and more lucrative stages. Yet in suggesting that these musicians were important communicators who "belonged" to black people ("we have" them, Haizlip said), the producer also suggested that music and television might still offer what he called "encouragement" and Hille called "relief."[64] When the shy genius Al Green (figure 3.10) talked about wanting to emulate his hero, the gospel singer Claude Jeter, and then took the *Soul!* studio audience to church; when Gladys Knight and the Pips sang about the "Friendship Train," Williams testified that "Prayer Changes Things," and Ashford and Simpson urged listeners to "reach out and touch / somebody's hand" (in an episode lovingly remembered by Baraka's daughter Lisa Jones); when Wonder distinguished between soul as a means of pigeonholing black artists and soul as cultural expression located outside of market logics—all these were moments, temporally fleeting if affectively enduring, when *Soul!* indeed made good on Haizlip's summation: "It's been beautiful."

4 Freaks Like Us

BLACK MISFIT PERFORMANCE ON *SOUL!*

Harlem . . . is a community of nonconformists, since any black
American, simply by virtue of his blackness, is weird,
a nonconformist in this society.
—LeRoi Jones, "City of Harlem"

I am not a black nationalist but some of my best friends are.
—James Baldwin

In his biography of Betty Shabazz (figure 4.1), the historian Russell Rickford describes the years after the 1965 assassination of Malcolm X, during which his widow, grieving and injured by what she believed to be the many abuses of her husband's legacy, moved with her children to the New York City suburbs and avoided socializing. Shabazz was eventually coaxed "out of her seclusion," Rickford tells us, through the efforts of two groups of friends. One consisted of the "more established figures in Malcolm's progressive circles," a "crowd of writers, artists, and academics that included [James] Baldwin, Larry and Evelyn Neal, John Henrik Clarke, and John and Grace Killens." The other was a predominantly female group that Rickford describes as "younger and saucier": "Its members were self-made, well read, and college bred. They were artists, but they were not too artsy. They were heavy, though not as heavy as the old-guard Civil Righters or the New Left. Nor were they as ethereal as the black bourgeoisie. They were, in truth, misfits.

4.1. Betty Shabazz, on a *Soul!* episode honoring her late husband, Malcolm X, February 1972.

Stage and screen actress Novella Nelson was among them, as was poet Nikki Giovanni. At the center of the ring was Ellis Haizlip."[1]

The producer of *Soul!* had, in fact, deliberately befriended Shabazz in the late 1960s, escorting her to concerts and shows in the city and encouraging her to enjoy New York nightlife notwithstanding the pressures of her public role as a widow. As a result of this friendship—which, Rickford implies, was facilitated by Haizlip's status as a safe male companion because he was gay—Shabazz appeared on the second *Soul!* episode in September 1968 and was also featured on a February 1972 episode commemorating the seventh anniversary of her husband's death.[2] Indeed, when Shabazz shed her social reclusiveness to become part of Haizlip's circle, she not only acquired a new set of lively and urbane friends, but she also entered into a New York social, cultural, and intellectual milieu centered on the television show. Nelson, who met Haizlip in a chance encounter in Washington Square Park, had performed on the first *Soul!* episode and was thereafter a creative anchor of the program. (A photograph from a 1972 episode [figure 4.2] shows her in the midst of an intense off-camera conversation with Sidney Poitier and Harry Belafonte.) The actor Anna Horsford, another member of Haizlip's circle, recited poetry on *Soul!* and served as an associate producer; after the second season, she was also the face of the show in the opening title sequence. And Giovanni, *Soul!*'s unofficial house poet, did triple duty: she was also a consultant to Haizlip and an occasional host, conducting interviews over several seasons with Muhammad Ali, Miriam Makeba, Gladys Knight, Chester Himes, and, as I discuss below in this chapter, James Baldwin. All three women—as well as poets Jackie Early, Sonia Sanchez, and Saundra Sharp—were among the featured guests on a landmark 1971 "Salute to Black Women" episode (figure 4.3).[3]

Shabazz was not alone in being exposed to this extraordinary group of young, gifted, and black New Yorkers. When Haizlip came to produce *Soul!*, Horsford recently observed, "He exposed his circle of friends to the world."[4] It was a circle that Haizlip had been cultivating since his days at Howard University, where he had come into contact with students from Africa and the Caribbean, met left-wing faculty members, kept up with (like some of his peers) *The Daily Worker*, and generally

4.2. Novella Nelson talks with Harry Belafonte during a break in March 1972. Sidney Poitier leans in to listen.

absorbed the university's "climate of defiance."[5] Leaving Howard before graduation to pursue a career in the New York theater world, Haizlip found the job discrimination against African Americans so dire that he took to sending a photo of himself in letters to prospective employers.[6]

Denied access to Broadway, Haizlip—like other creative black people of his generation—turned to alternative venues and institutions to develop his talents. Haizlip cut his teeth at places like the Harlem YMCA, where he worked in the late 1950s as a production assistant under the brilliant and demanding Vinnette Carroll, and Equity Library Theater, a nonprofit institution on the Upper West Side where he learned to make shows on a shoestring budget—knowledge that would come in handy during his tenure in public broadcasting. Later, he honed his skills and garnered valuable experience in Europe, Africa, and the Middle East producing the touring productions of works including *Black Nativity* and *The Amen Corner*. In these and other settings, Haizlip developed an understanding of audiences for the performing arts and initiated or solidified relationships with a wide range of writers, actors, musi-

4.3. Poets recite on the "Salute to Black Women" episode, January 1971. Left to right: Jackie Early, Nikki Giovanni, Sonia Sanchez, and Saundra Sharp.

cians, dancers, and visual artists—from Baldwin, Cicely Tyson, and Alvin Ailey to the German-born Jewish visual artist Eva Hesse, with whom he briefly shared an apartment. At Equity Library Theater, he worked alongside a young white man, Patrick "Packy" McGinnis, the future operations manager of Alice Tully Hall at Lincoln Center, home of Soul at the Center and Soul '73. When Haizlip's friend Christopher "Kit" Lukas, director of cultural programming at Channel 13/WNDT, came calling in 1968, in need of a black TV producer for a new, Ford Foundation–funded venture, Haizlip was poised to put not only his experience but also his extended network to use. As Horsford suggests, he was able to put his talented friends on television, and to do so years—in some cases, decades—before white producers and audiences would discover them.

Although Haizlip's path from the Deanwood neighborhood of easternmost Washington, D.C., to 275 Fifth Avenue, his longtime New York address, was unique, in other ways, his formation was unexceptional. Like Haizlip, the members of his extended circle developed their artistic, cultural, and political sensibilities in a context defined by state-sanctioned discrimination and racial segregation, as well as Cold War–era backlash against the progressivism of the 1930s popular front. Yet these limiting circumstances provided fuel for careers defined by restless political exploration and creative rebellion. From their experiences of being relegated to stereotypical roles, black artists and intellectuals shaped in this historical moment came to reject the policing of their self-expression, insisting on black self-definition as a fundamental right. (As Nelson told the black female journalist Margo Jefferson in "Different Drums," a 1974 *Newsweek* profile that described her eclectic Greenwich Village cabaret act, "I'm evolving into song. But you don't have to play one role."[7]) Because they had been forcefully and dismissively shut out—from prestigious white universities, commercial publishing contracts, lucrative record and movie deals, and choice stage roles—they learned to pursue their work heedless or even contemptuous of mainstream approval or recognition. (Giovanni self-published her first volumes of poetry and garnered her early audiences through black social and cultural networks.[8]) And because they understood the rules of the commercial marketplace, they pursued their ambitions wary of commercial incorporation, all the while insisting on their value. (Although they were limited in the compensation they could expect on public broadcasting, no one on *Soul!* performed for free.) From the historical perspective of this generation of artists and cultural workers, the black arts and Black Power movements did not represent a shift into radicalism but a flowering of dissident expression, the seeds of which had been planted and nurtured in the seemingly tamer era of civil rights.[9]

The figures who constituted Shabazz's more established circle of friends were, in fact, among the most prominent theorists of this modern black countertradition. Baldwin, in particular, had been exploring the figure of the black misfit since his earliest published work in the 1950s. In his 1965 essay "Sweet Lorraine," composed on the occasion of the untimely death of Lorraine Hansberry, he wrote affectingly of his grief at losing the company of a person who shared his experience of loneliness—thereby suggesting the existence of a black counterpublic sphere where being black and a misfit (in this case, black and queer and a writer) might be a source of connection and solidarity. Baldwin would return to these themes in an even more intensely personal fashion twenty years later in "Freaks and the American Ideal of Manhood," an essay in which the mature writer looks back at the period when he left the known world of family and church to immerse himself in the interracial gay New York sexual subculture of the 1940s. Discovering that he feels freakish even among other sexual outlaws is painful and even terrifying for the young Baldwin, but it is also undeniably liberating, freeing him to fashion himself as a writer who bears privileged witness to the freakishness of U.S. society and culture.[10]

Baldwin's musings on the critical power of the outsider invite me in this chapter to contemplate the pleasures of *Soul!* as a television show that represented black diversity, nonconformity, and freakishness as the norm, part of the "changing same" of twentieth-century black misfittedness.[11] The preeminent representative of such misfittedness was, of course, "Mr. Soul." In an era that was generally lacking socially sanctioned avenues of cultural recognition for queer subjects, Haizlip quietly but insistently used *Soul!* to register the existence of gays and lesbians within the black collective. He did so, moreover, with an awareness of the ways this would inevitably draw attention to his own gender and sexual non-normativity. In minutes from a meeting of project advisors for a proposed program titled "The Sixth Period" (which eventually became the short-lived 1978 PBS classroom comedy-drama series *Watch Your Mouth*), the former *Soul!* host is noted to have observed that a black man "can be considered effeminate if he speaks very correctly." In the course of the group's discussion of how the character of a black male teacher in "The Sixth Period" should sound, Haizlip recalled that during his stint as *Soul!*'s host, "quite a few people, usually female, came up to me and said, 'You know, we really admire the way you speak.' And quite often males would come up and say, 'Man, why don't you talk some different way.'"[12]

The *Watch Your Mouth* meeting notes do not speculate on why male and female viewers of *Soul!* may have experienced Haizlip differently or how their perceptions of class might have shaped their sense of its significance. Nor do the notes comment on the relationship between black masculine authenticity and speaking in an admirable or "correct" manner, although in some quarters, radical self-fashioning among middle-class black men in the Black Power era entailed the adoption of a "working-class" argot.[13] Yet the story Haizlip tells is significant for establishing his awareness that some *Soul!* viewers associated his manner of speaking with sexual as well as class difference and, more importantly for this chapter's purposes, for demonstrating that he was unwilling to modify his vocal performance to assuage any anxieties it might have generated. The social audibility of the effeminate black gay man, Haizlip's story suggests, means that his sexual non-normativity had a cultural and affective presence on *Soul!*, even if it was unspoken and unrepresented. When Haizlip introduced the topic of black homosexuality in his interviews with *Soul!* guests, then, he was not only defying the social compact that demanded silence around the presence of so-called sissies, faggots, and bulldaggers in black communities, but also channeling and amplifying that which was always already audible in his spoken performance.[14]

An ecumenical progressive in an era of proliferating political factions and -isms, the producer fashioned *Soul!* as a big-tent political stage, a program that extended an equally warm welcome to revolutionary nationalists (Kathleen Cleaver), former Garveyites (Queen Mother Audley Moore), neo–civil rights leaders (Jessie Jackson and Shirley Chisholm), Black Power entrepreneurs (Tony Brown of the *Black Journal*), and cultural nationalists (Amiri Baraka and Neal) in the studio between 1970 and 1973. It was indeed one of the few programs on national television in the early 1970s to figure black radicals and black radical thought as worthy of serious engagement rather than blanket condemnation, caricature, or ridicule. The show constituted a stern rebuttal of television productions that painted political expression of Black Power in crude strokes, or capitalized on differences and disagreements among leaders to create an impression of collective disarray. *Soul!* implicitly called to account news programs that profited from the spectacle of brash young activists only to represent them as dangers to democratic civility and destroyers of mainstream goodwill toward civil rights. If mainstream programming portrayed the diverse political energies of the black Left within a melodramatic scenario that pitted the good protestor against the bad troublemaker, the deserving citizen against the misguided agitator, and the profane provocateur against the respectable artist, *Soul!* countered with a representation that refused to identify heroes and villains but looked instead for the good in different aesthetics, strategies, and ideologies.[15] If the generational narrative preferred by most TV producers was complicit with the erasure of black women in black arts and Black Power, *Soul!* beat back against this characterization of black political culture as an arena of Oedipal strife, bringing women more fully into the conversation.

Soul! made visible the tensions and debates in nationalist discourses, in the process testing viewers' own identifications with and affective investments in nationalist utopias.[16] As the episodes I describe in detail below vividly demonstrate, although nationalism on *Soul!* was vigorously interrogated, particularly for its subordination of women and demonization or suppression of homosexuality, it was also consistently represented as a historically valid framework within which a wide variety of black actors (including black women and black queers) thought and worked, rather than an inherently corrosive ideology external to black history and experience. And although the program probed the limitations of masculinist paradigms of the black experience, it did so while acknowledging the tremendous affective appeal of nationalism's narratives of male dignity and suppressed black genius (going all the way back to Loretta Long's and Barbara Ann Teer's appreciation for the Last Poets' "Lady Black" on the fifth episode of *Soul!*, discussed in chapter 2). Indeed, one of *Soul!*'s most significant aesthetic hallmarks was its extraordinary sensitivity to radical subjects and viewpoints that were not only excoriated, mocked, and misconstrued within mainstream TV representations but were also regarded skeptically within black mainstream representation and some quarters of the black Left. The best example of this may be the two *Soul!* episodes featuring Louis Farrakhan, who was greeted warmly by the show's host notwithstanding lingering suspicions on the part of many Black Muslims (including members of the Shabazz family) of his complicity in the assassination of his former mentor, Malcolm X.

Most of the talk segments with black political figures on *Soul!* were brief, complementing the music and other arts performances that were the heart of the program. But some episodes— including a special two-episode dialogue between Baldwin and Giovanni in December 1971 and hour-long specials devoted to Farrakhan and Baraka, both in fall 1972— gave viewers chances to listen in on extended, in-depth exchanges where what I am calling the misfit energies of the Black Power era were manifest.[17] In the "Baldwin and Giovanni" episodes, the two writers converse in highly personal terms about intimacy between black men and black women, even as they self-consciously enact such intimacy as a weird or misfit couple. Their impassioned dialogue, which reaches an emotional climax in Giovanni's trenchant feminist critique of Baldwin, sets the stage for "Farrakhan the Minister" and "Baraka, the Artist," *Soul!* episodes in which Haizlip openly questions the gender and sexual politics of the Nation of Islam (NOI) and cultural nationalists—which leads to moments of tension and irresolution, but also moments that theatricalize the ongoing quest for brotherhood in the face of difference. It is to these episodes, which bring to the surface the disruptive but also richly generative presence of the misfit within the black collective, that I turn before returning, in the conclusion of the chapter, to the question of the archives and to *Soul!*'s own misfittedness within even revisionist histories of the soul era.

"Baldwin and Giovanni," which aired in two consecutive episodes, is a conversation between two writers, one renowned for his groundbreaking fiction and essays, the other an up-and-coming poet and memoirist. Although Rickford accurately identifies Baldwin as an established figure, the most prominent literary spokesman of the civil rights movement was also a target for many younger 1960s radicals. *Soul on Ice*, the 1968 memoir by the Black Panthers' Minister of Information Eldridge Cleaver, is but the most infamous example of the homophobia marshaled by some on the black Left to caricature Baldwin's philosophical ambivalence about nationalism, fueled by his long-standing commitment to civil rights interracialism. Not all of Baldwin's critics would indulge in the violent rhetorical excesses of Cleaver, who accused "Negro homosexuals" of being "outraged and frustrated because in their sickness they are unable to have a baby by a white man."[18] Yet by the late 1960s, "Baldwin-bashing," often with a gay-bashing component, had become "almost a rite of initiation" within black nationalist circles, a means by which male intellectuals staged their own claims to ideological correctness and race and gender authenticity.[19]

Although Giovanni ardently disassociated herself from such homophobic rhetoric and distanced herself from the aesthetics of cultural nationalists, she was nevertheless popularly identified as a poet in the black arts movement and enjoyed enormous acclaim among the ordinary readers whom the movement held in esteem. Her first volumes, *Black Feeling Black Talk* and *Black Judgement* (sometimes written as "Judgment"), both from 1968, had sold remarkably well, and her 1971 album *Truth Is on Its Way*, a poetry and gospel mash-up featuring Giovanni with the New York Community Choir, had been such a smash that it had crossed over to the pop charts. (Her friend and admirer Ellis Haizlip contributed liner notes.) As a highly popular poet, Giovanni had her share of detractors. Some accused her of selling out, others of untoward self-promotion that revealed a greater concern with her individual stature than with the well-being of black writers as a whole. In her unflattering portrait in *Black Macho and the Myth of the Superwoman*, Michele Wallace would somewhat dismissively refer to Giovanni as the movement's "reigning poetess" and, more unkindly, call her a "black Rod McKuen." Wallace would even go so far as to accuse

Giovanni of recklessly encouraging other young black women to follow her example of giving birth out of wedlock.[20] Yet as Virginia Fowler, Giovanni's literary biographer, points out, the very qualities that could make Giovanni seem "counter-revolutionary"—her interest in individual self-expression, her "ego tripping" (to cite the title of a well-known poem), and her aggressive pursuit of an audience—also rendered her an unorthodox figure, a woman who resisted demands that she defer creatively as well as socially to her male counterparts.[21]

The complex dynamic of misfittedness and celebrity in both writers' personas adds a layer of complexity to the "Baldwin and Giovanni" episodes. Edited in New York but filmed in a drab London studio that was decorated with two chairs and a coffee table arrayed with drinks, ashtrays, and microphones, the episodes begin with the twenty-eight-year-old poet deferentially informing the author of "Everybody's Protest Novel" that she first read his groundbreaking critique of Richard Wright as a precocious first grader, and with Baldwin—a bit uncomfortable at being treated as an elder before his fiftieth birthday—commenting that he is "very proud" of her and her youthful cohort for what they have achieved in the black freedom struggle.[22] About fifteen minutes in, however, their dialogue becomes less predictable and more combustible, as the axis of difference shifts from age to age and gender. The spark is Baldwin's reflections on the plight of black men, which come up as he attempts to narrate his intellectual and political formation as the oldest child in a large and poor family headed by his violent and domineering stepfather. The key to grasping the condition of black Americans, Baldwin argues, lies in understanding men such as David Baldwin, who endured multiple humiliations in the workplace so he could be a "man" in his family. With the camera showing the tip of his cigarette burning to ash, Baldwin—attired in a black shirt and black pants and wearing bold silver jewelry—holds forth passionately about the "spiritual disaster" of his stepfather's life, crediting the black freedom movement with empowering a generation of black men to resist the sort of experiences that had destroyed him.

It is Baldwin's lengthiest and most fervent comment in their dialogue to that point, yet Giovanni, seen in a close-up reaction shot as he talks (figure 4.4), appears more piqued than sympathetic. Leaning in from

4.4. Nikki Giovanni listening to James Baldwin in the "Baldwin and Giovanni" episodes, as seen from the New York editor's monitor, late 1971.

her chair, she challenges Baldwin about being more concerned with the oppression of black men than that of black women and accuses him of "rationalizing" black women's subordination in the quest for black male affirmation. Turning to her own experience, Giovanni notes that her decision not to marry the father of her young son sprang from a wish to avoid replaying the role of her own mother, who had been locked in an unequal domestic arrangement. When Baldwin (figures 4.5–4.8) counters that young women of Giovanni's generation no longer have to be their mothers—just as Baldwin, it is assumed, does not have to be his stepfather and toil to fit a masculine ideal—Giovanni asserts that although nationalism may have benefited black men, it has not redressed gendered imbalances of power within black heterosexuality: "I have seen how the community, and even today in 1971, even today there are divisions based on those same kinds of problems, so that the black men say, 'In order for me to be a man, you walk ten paces behind me.' It means nothing. I can walk ten paces behind a dog. It means nothing to me, but if that's what he needs, I'll never get far enough behind him for him to be a man. I'll never walk that slowly." Granting

4.5–4.8. James Baldwin in the "Baldwin and Giovanni" episodes, as seen from the New York editor's monitor, late 1971.

the validity of Giovanni's experience, yet claiming the authority (which she has granted him) of someone who has lived longer and "seen it all," Baldwin reassures her that Black Power is only the most recent expression of black resistance in an ongoing and incomplete struggle. "What's valuable will remain," he says. "The rest will go."

Although their dialogue ranges over other issues, including the black church and the responsibility of the black writer, the critique of nationalism's recuperation of patriarchal gender relations hovers over it as a point of simultaneous agreement and contention. Both use their own families as templates for understanding the struggles of the collective, or the national family. When Baldwin counteridentifies with the injured masculinity of his stepfather, Giovanni counteridentifies with her mother, who traded away social agency for the sake of traditional domesticity. Remarkably, at various points over the course of the two episodes, they dramatize these multilayered differences in the form of a lover's quarrel, with Baldwin and Giovanni portraying a black couple who try to work out private differences that stand in for larger, public debates.[23]

These moments are marked not only by a physical closeness between the two speakers, who lean in toward one another, but also by a grammatical intimacy, as they shift into personalized modes of address. For example, when Baldwin returns to an earlier point he made about the difficulty, for black men, of playing the social role of "provider" within their families, Giovanni responds in the voice of a woman addressing her partner. "I demand that you be a man," she tells Baldwin, "and I don't think that's asking too much, because if I wanted a provision, I would get a camper . . . an Army surplus kit. I need a *man*." As the camera focuses on Baldwin, who regards her intently and with a markedly sad expression—perhaps because her performance challenges him to channel his own abused and abusive father—she adds, with extreme tenderness: "Sometimes you're not able to feed your family, sometimes you're not able to clothe your family, but do you then also deprive them of your manhood and of the input that a man has?" At one point while Baldwin is talking, a reaction shot shows Giovanni looking down at her hands, a gesture that embodies the resignation of a woman who has failed to make her lover understand her. At another point, in response to Giovanni's entreaty that Baldwin "fake it with me . . . for ten years, so we can get a child on his feet," he replies sadly, "If I love you I can't lie to you." To which Giovanni responds, with a small smile, "Of course you can lie to me. And you will . . . What Billie Holiday sang: 'Hush now, don't explain.'"

To tease out the complexity of this fractured and nonlinear exchange, culminating here in Giovanni's citation of the celebrated Holiday song—in which her lyrical persona arguably concedes power for love— would require more space than is available here. Much of what I have excerpted here from the televised conversation, moreover, was edited out of Baldwin and Giovanni's published *Dialogue*. Yet Giovanni provides a succinct metacommentary on their conversation. "It looks like a black man can't make it with a black woman," she says to Baldwin regretfully, late in the first episode. "If somebody looks at the two of us, man, we're the weirdest looking people on earth, 'cause you want your way and I want my way. But we're saying the same thing. And that's sort of a shame."

Giovanni's suggestion that she and Baldwin are "the weirdest looking people on earth" is striking, not only because it inserts the concept of weirdness into their dialogue, but also because it associates weirdness with heterosexual intimacy that labors under the weight of political tensions between the nationalist project of shoring up black masculinity and black women's demands for agency and equality. Indeed, although the 1965 U.S. government report *The Negro Family: The Case for National Action* (popularly known as the Moynihan Report) and its discourse of black social pathology remains beneath mention for both writers, Giovanni's observation articulates an incipient black feminist analysis that includes white supremacy, capitalism, and black patriarchal masculinity in its purview. Their performance, in other words, anticipates not only Baldwin's "Freaks and the American Ideal of Manhood" essay (for drawing attention to the freakishness of lovers who cannot love each other) but also, and more importantly, black feminist analysis that would come to fuller visibility in the late 1970s and 1980s in the work of women such as Barbara Smith, Audre Lorde, and the members of the Combahee River Collective.[24] In fact, neither writer seems to have the language in this moment to respond to Giovanni's insights about the "weirdness" of a couple who profess to love each other and who yet envision so differently the mechanisms for fulfilling their mutual desire for intimacy. Here is where the staging of their conversation in a makeshift studio resembling a spartan domestic space (or perhaps a hotel room) becomes important, as do the nonverbal signifiers of their shared affection, anguish, and frustration: from the tilting of their heads to the inhalation of their cigarettes.

In thus dramatizing—at the register of its spectacle as well as its content—a conversation between a real couple, the "Baldwin and Giovanni" episodes stage a performance of black heterosexual intimacy that was glaringly absent on commercial television in the early 1970s. Before the bickering but affectionate George and Louise Jefferson and *Good Times*'s James and Florida Evans came to embody black married life on American TV, the most popular black TV families—those of Diahann Carroll's Julia or Redd Foxx's Fred Sanford—were conspicuously devoid of intact couples; the lead characters of both *Julia* and *Sanford and Son* had dead spouses. Riffing on famous TV couples, we might indeed imagine "Baldwin and Giovanni" as the title of a post–civil rights black satire of the domestic sitcom, in which a dueling but well-matched queer couple discuss the writer's life, the role of the black artist, the enticements and pitfalls of nationalism, the ethics of love, and the challenges of black intimacy. (If this were not enough, "Baldwin and Giovanni" echoes the title of Baldwin's 1958 novel, whose protagonist David has an affair with an Italian man named Giovanni.[25])

However, Baldwin and Giovanni's dramatization of a couple is predicated on the unspoken fact of Baldwin's homosexuality, which saturates their discussion—both in the knowledge that audiences may have brought to the episodes and in Baldwin's body language and vocal performance, which is studded with "my dears" and "sweethearts" that read both as gestures of (potentially patronizing) tenderness for Giovanni and verbal signifiers of Baldwin's queerness. Homosexuality, or the existence of black homosexuals, comes up only at the very end of their televised conversation, when Giovanni is critiquing the uses of categories—"that junkie hype, that war hype, that whole homosexual hype"—to fashion some people as "better than others." "Do you know what I mean?" she queries Baldwin, who rolls his eyes, and answers, significantly, "Do I *not*. . . . People invent categories in order to feel safe. White people invented black people to give white people an identity. Cats who invent themselves as straight invent faggots so they can sleep with them, [performing an 'effeminate' male voice] without becoming a faggot themselves . . . [resuming his 'normal' voice] somehow."

Yet beyond this assertion, Baldwin is not merely silent on the issue of sexual misfittedness in his dialogue with Giovanni, but he works to ensure that their discussion does not challenge the reproductive, heterosexual norm of his stepfather's violent household. Beginning with the example of David Baldwin as a man who shouldered the responsibility of feeding nine children, James Baldwin repeatedly uses the figure of the child to imagine the future of black people in the United States. At one point, he confides to Giovanni that before he left the country to live the life of an exile, he had been involved with a woman whom he wanted to marry and have children with, but whom he left because of the looming negative example of David Baldwin's life. In so doing, he implies that his 1948 decision to leave his girlfriend and his native country was fueled primarily by the fear of not being able to play the role of a male provider, not by ambivalence about heterosexuality (as the later "Freaks and the American Ideal of Manhood" essay will indicate). Audiences are thus left to presume that racism alone, not racism in concert with homophobia and a desire to explore alternatives to heterosexuality, was the determining factor in Baldwin's self-exile.

The silence around homosexuality in "Baldwin and Giovanni" contrasts with its prominence as a topic of conversation in "Farrakhan the Minister," which aired in late October 1972. The NOI spokesman and spiritual leader of Harlem's Muhammad Mosque No. 7 had appeared on *Soul!* before, in a May 1971 episode that included Mongo Santamaría (in his second turn as a guest) and the Delfonics (some of whose members would later convert and receive their X's). But "Farrakhan the Minister" devoted its entire hour to Elijah Muhammad's second in command, receiving him with a respect bordering on reverence. Such cordiality was all the more notable given the tenuous position of the NOI in black political culture at the time. Although Farrakhan was invited to participate in such landmark events as the 1970 Congress of African Peoples conference in Atlanta and the 1972 National Black Political Convention in Gary, Indiana, many established civil rights and Black Power leaders viewed the NOI warily. Its emphases on moral rectitude, economic independence, and the development of autonomous black institutions placed it squarely within a nationalist tradition reaching back to Booker T. Washington, yet its critiques of black popular culture and popular artists, its advocacy of black separatism, and its theological grounding in a contemporary African American interpretation of Islam rendered it an anomaly among secular nationalist and pan-Africanist organizations, and its recruitment from the ranks of prisoners and drug addicts distanced it from middle-class civil rights groups. As the public face of the NOI, Farrakhan was, in a word, a misfit: a man widely admired for his uncompromising critiques of American society, whose authority as a spokesman was rooted in an organization viewed as unlikely to gain political traction among the masses of black people.

"Farrakhan the Minister" works to mitigate the strangeness of the NOI for a geographically diverse *Soul!* audience interested in yet unfamiliar with Black Muslims beyond Malcolm X.[26] Rather than pursuing questions that might lead Farrakhan to criticize civil rights leaders or organizations, drawing attention to painful rifts within the black polity, Haizlip queries him from the viewpoint of the middle-class convert that the NOI was seeking at the time. Can "black professionals," he asks, "be of service" to the NOI without giving up the pleasures of pork and nicotine? Must such converts follow all of its precepts, including those governing dress? What does getting one's X entail? Some of Haizlip's questions, while asked with an air of ingenuousness, touch on riskier issues, underscoring the gap between the NOI and more progressive black nationalist organizations like the Black Panthers. In this way, questions of gender enter the conversation early on. Why, Haizlip asks, do NOI women have to cover themselves, thereby drawing attention to their difference, while Black Muslim men may occupy public spaces relatively inconspicuously? What is the NOI's viewpoint on polygamy? Where does it stand on women's sexuality, outside of or within marriage?

The inviting set design of "Farrakhan the Minister," unlike the drab, suggestively domestic set of "Baldwin and Giovanni," fosters a relaxed, conversational ambience. The two men—Haizlip in a dark dress shirt and slacks, Farrakhan in a military-style tan suit complete with epaulets and an insignia bearing three stars—sit on modern leather armchairs separated by a small table bearing NOI symbols, including the red-and-white NOI flag and a large framed portrait of Elijah Muhammad. Members of the studio audience, including a few scattered children, are arranged in a circle around the small stage, some in rows, others at small tables repurposed from the Club Soul set; most are identifiable as Muslim through their attire and hairstyles (for once, Afros do not dominate the room). On the far back wall of the studio enormous letters spelling *soul* are illuminated in rainbow colors; at the center of the room, the men are spotlighted, with the audience dimly visible around them.

By previous agreement, Farrakhan opens and closes the episode with brief and, for the purposes of television, rather undynamic prepared statements, which he delivers standing up and facing the audience, in the manner of a political candidate; but most of the episode is structured around Haizlip's questions and Farrakhan's answers, each of which is a miniature oration, and each of which is received with a hearty round of audience applause. Throughout, Farrakhan appears smiling and in his element; at times, his bearing is almost beatific. Audience members mirror his self-assured contentment, sitting with upright postures and straight-ahead looks and interspersing the minister's commentary with supportive nods and audible interjections of "uh-huh" or "yes, sir!" that sonically evoke the black church, an irony in light of Farrakhan's later equation of Christians and junkies. This performance of minister and flock is echoed in a somewhat unusual display of physical affection between host and guest. More than once, as the audience applauds, Haizlip leans forward to slap palms with Farrakhan. At the end, the two engage in a sustained embrace.

Such physical intimacy between Haizlip and Farrakhan—notably absent in "Baldwin and Giovanni," despite the affective warmth of the writers' dialogue—conveys a mutual desire to enact solidarity in the face of what, by a certain reckoning, was the social and ideological chasm separating the two men. In his questions, Haizlip, his frequent on-screen cigarette conspicuously absent out of respect for Black Muslim prohibitions on tobacco, offers the minister several opportunities to expound on beliefs that would seem to directly implicate him and his misfit friends. Notwithstanding the discomfort this might provoke, the vibe between the two is extraordinary friendly. Indeed, "Farrakhan the Minister" foregrounds the spectacle of black fraternity: the natural animosity between two antagonistically constructed black male identities is easily overcome by Haizlip's verbal and embodied expressions of respect.

We can best discern the performativity of this warmth between the two men at the moment, about twenty minutes into the episode, when Haizlip questions Farrakhan about the NOI's recruitment of prison inmates, introducing homosexuality into their conversation.

> Very recently—and this probably gets back to the morality or immorality—we've seen quite a few incidents where prisoners—and I think it's a known fact that quite a few of the people who have been brought into the Nation of Islam have discovered their righteousness while incarcerated in a prison. And one of the things that most males, and now I understand from the news that's coming out a lot of females, have to deal with is homosexual relations in prisons. How can *they* serve the Nation of Islam, and does the fact that a man is a homosexual have anything to do that would negate his coming into the Nation and being dealt with by the Nation?[27]

Such forthrightness on Haizlip's part would be notable even if we were not able to contrast it with Baldwin's conspicuous silence about non-normative sexuality in "Baldwin and Giovanni." Indeed, it is particularly audacious, for although couched as a query about prisoners who presumably have little opportunity to satisfy their sexual needs with opposite-sex partners, it posits the existence of black gay men and lesbians, joining notions of practice and identity. Moreover, the question would seem to put the unspoken "secret" of Haizlip's own sexuality squarely into the open. Is Haizlip, a man regarded as effeminate for his "very correct" manner of speaking, outing himself in this moment, in the manner of someone asking about some embarrassing or shameful matter supposedly on behalf of a friend? Is the *Soul!* host asking how the NOI might "deal with" him? Or is he attempting to point up a contradiction within the NOI, which accepts converts from prisons yet regards homosexual acts—indeed, all sex not in the service of reproduction—as an anathema? To what degree might Haizlip be "queering" the NOI or its members, from ex-convict Elijah Muhammad to the most famous NOI convert from prison, Farrakhan's late teacher and role model, Malcolm X?

As though to underscore the destabilizing implications of this question, the camera initially displays Farrakhan's response through the image of Haizlip's reaction to it. "Let me say this, my dear brother," Farrakhan says to Haizlip, who maintains an impassive expression but leans forward slightly, "and to you in our viewing audience, the honorable Elijah Mohammad has been raised up by Allah not to condemn our people but to reclaim the fallen black man of America." The crowd shouts its approval. A second camera switches from this reaction shot to a medium shot of Farrakhan, who launches into a lengthy recitation of NOI teachings about homosexual "deviance" and the promise of Islam to restore black men and women to their heterosexual "nature." At one point, during a break for applause, Haizlip looks as though he might attempt another question, but instead he shifts his body slightly in his chair and gently clears his throat. Farrakhan continues:

> We didn't learn this freakish behavior in Africa [shouts of "No, sir!" from the audience]. You cannot find brothers in Africa walking around with broken [limp] wrists [he demonstrates with his own hands; shouts of "No sir!"]. You don't find women in Africa running with women. We *learned* that behavior in our sojourn in America [shouts of "Yes, sir!"]. So since we *learned* this behavior, we can unlearn this behavior. [Applause interrupts the minister, who puts his hands up, palms forward, signaling that he has not yet finished] . . . There is no such *thing* [he brings his fist down forcefully on the arm of his chair] as a homosexual that cannot be changed. There is no such thing as a lesbian that cannot be changed. Almighty God Allah is here to change us all up, again, into a new growth and to bring us back to the natural order in which we were created.

At this conclusion of his monologue, which lasts four and a half minutes, the minister sits back in his chair to bask in the audience's thunderous applause, while Haizlip extends his right hand for a palm slap that morphs into a soul handshake. Haizlip's microphone picks up his voice (it is not clear whether he intends to be heard) as he says to Farrakhan, "You're incredible. You are incredible." The applause continues as the camera switches to a jib-arm shot of the studio; from above, we see Haizlip raise his bent arms, palms open toward the minister, and lean forward, gently shaking his head from side to side.

I read Haizlip's gesture, just short of a bow, as an expression of combined admiration for and surrender to the virtuosity of Farrakhan's oratorical excursion, if not its thesis of homosexuality as a kind of freakishness. (The contemporary equivalent is the half-ironic expression "I'm not worthy," offered to a mock rival.) I mean *surrender* here in the sense of Haizlip's allowing himself to be moved by Farrakhan, to be receptive to the emotional appeal of his condemnation of white American culture and his prophetic vision of a future in which change is not only possible but also imminent. Likewise, when Haizlip utters the words "You are incredible," I take him to be conveying respect for Farrakhan's self-assurance and its effects on his listeners, who appear spiritually and emotionally buoyed up by the minister's performance. In applauding Farrakhan, Haizlip acknowledges the validation that his discourse of the natural black subject grants to the studio audience, as well as to *Soul!*'s viewers. The fact that this sense of community emerges in and through an aversion to homosexual "deviance" is not, therefore, beside the point, but neither is it determinative of the feelings of well-being and connectedness that Farrakhan's performance of self-assuredness mediates. Through this performance, which encompasses Farrakhan's words as well as his vibrations and physical bearing, black men can see themselves as powerful role models for black children, and women can see themselves as faithful wives and mothers of the black nation; as Muslims, both are able to experience pride in their rectitude and the strength of their faith.

On the surface, the handshake between Haizlip and Farrakhan would seem to require a certain self-censorship on Haizlip's part, in addition to the subordination of self that is inherent to role of an interviewer whose job is to get his guest talking. Yet we need not read the handshake as a capitulation to homophobia or even as a sign of frictionless ideological alignment. In his 1962 essay, "Letter from a Region of My Mind," Baldwin describes being surprised at his own receptiveness to Elijah Muhammad during a private dinner at the latter's South Side Chicago residence. Although Baldwin cannot embrace the Black Muslims' apocalyptic vision or their faith, he finds himself personally drawn to Muhammad, a man who elicits palpable joy in his disciples. Moreover, he is drawn to the emotional truth of the NOI's antipathy toward white people and finds that despite his political wariness of Muhammad and the NOI, he cannot write them off. Baldwin recounts this series of realizations with an acute awareness of the interests of white liberal readers of the *New Yorker*, the magazine in which his essay appears. That is, he fully anticipates that his refusal to condemn the Black Muslims and Muhammad will be seized on as a means of discrediting him, both as an individual and as a proxy for black intellectuals. But as much as he might chafe against Muhammad as an ideologue, Baldwin also chafes against the racialized policing of his discourse. He accordingly defends both his attraction to Muhammad and his entitlement to pursue subjects and affiliations likely to provoke anger among whites.[28]

Reading Haizlip's embrace of Farrakhan through the lens of Baldwin's defiant ambivalence as a black writer with access to prestigious white publications enables us to understand the *Soul!* host's response to Farrakhan (whose name, given to him by Muhammad, means "charmer") as a strategic display enacted with multiple publics in mind. As a performance of brotherhood despite personal and political differences in 1972, the men's handshake symbolically rebuts the narrative of the waning of Black Power in the wake of disunity, political repression, and economic or political co-optation. In so doing, moreover, it tacitly decries the investment of television in the spectacle of black male intraracial discord and disagreement. Yet paradoxically, to produce this counterrepresentation of black male solidarity, the episode must also bring to the surface tensions and contradictions about issues of sexual identity and sexual practice. When Farrakhan promises American black men with "broken wrists" a return to their original African "nature" through Black Muslim teachings, a certain notion of brotherhood is fractured, even as a homophobic version of black community—one constructed under the sign of the management of sexual misfittedness—is instantiated. The warm embrace of host and guest at the episode's conclusion manages the misfit energies introduced into the room by Haizlip, allowing "Farrakhan the Minister" to come to a happy ending; but it cannot, finally, resolve or eliminate them.

The issue of homosexuality also arises in "Baraka, the Artist"—not as a topic for homophobic sermonizing but as one piece in a larger conversation about the political and social imaginary of cultural nationalism framed by riveting spoken-word performances that open and close the episode (figure 4.9). In this way, viewers are introduced to Baraka as a writer, performer, and orator before they learn—from Haizlip's calculated, information-seeking questions—about the trajectory of his literary and political career, from his early interest in Richard Wright and Edgar Allan Poe to his work as a dramatist and founder of a Harlem theater collective, culminating in his move back to his natal city of Newark and his embrace of Kawaida, the Africanist philosophy associated with Maulana Karenga, leader of the nationalist group US Organization. We also learn about Baraka's recent political work, in particular his leadership of the Committee for a Unified Newark (CFUN), a local, pan-ethnic black political coalition; and his chairmanship of the Congress of African Peoples, a national umbrella group of black political organizations.[29]

Like Farrakhan, Baraka appears on *Soul!* quite literally wearing his politics on his sleeve. At one point, in response to Haizlip's observation that he is sporting a "new style of dress," the poet, seemingly embarrassed by the *Soul!* host's complimentary attention to his appearance, explains that the somber garment is a "nationalist dress suit" of African origin, designed by the president of Tanzania and functional for black American men put off by "the whole shirt-tie syndrome."[30] Visually, "Baraka, the Artist" recalls "Farrakhan the Minister" in other ways as well, employing a strikingly similar stage and lighting design. Instead of sitting in rows circling the stage, however, the studio audience for "Baraka, the Artist" is arranged at round tables that face it, lending the studio an air of a makeshift performance space or café. A small library of Baraka's volumes, possibly from the producer's own collec-

4.9. On "Baraka, the Artist" (November 1972), Amiri Baraka recites his poetry.

tion, replace the NOI coffee-table props of "Farrakhan the Minister," serving, for the uninitiated, as an instructive illustration of Baraka's literary achievements.

Yet whereas "Farrakhan the Minister" has a ceremonious air, reflected in the NOI leader's tightly controlled orations in response to Haizlip's gentle questions, "Baraka, the Artist" feels warm and intimate, even as it represents the writer as a revered figure. By Baraka's own account, he and Haizlip had a cordial relationship, so their on-screen conversations on *Soul!*—"Baraka, the Artist" was the poet's fourth appearance since 1969—lacked the "painful formality" of most TV interviews with black nationalist leaders. Haizlip was a few years older than the writer, but along with other relatively privileged members of their generation, they had inherited a shared "structure of feeling," Baraka recalled.[31] Haizlip was, in Baraka's eyes, a "cosmopolitan," a "quintessential New York black sophisticate"; but unlike some who wore their intellects like armor, the producer combined an acute awareness of the issues of the day with a disarming ability to "pass as an interested observer . . . knowing what you're talking about but at the same time being able to appear more or less objective." In 1972 Baraka was doing a lot of public interviews, but "*Soul!* was different because Ellis was different. Ellis made you feel that you were talking to somebody who knew what you were talking about . . . who understood and knew how to shape his questions and [the] answers he thought those questions would provoke."

As these comments suggest, the Baraka-Haizlip conversation—like the Baldwin-Giovanni dialogue and, albeit to a lesser degree, the Farrakhan-Haizlip interview—were mediated by a shared sense of black political commitment visible in the nonverbal elements of the performances, particularly in the facial and hand expressions and bodily miens that the television cameras intentionally sought out to add visual interest and detail to otherwise static spectacles. To return to a central argument of this book, the spectacle of collective black intimacy in *Soul!*—in this case, the spectacles of sympathetically aligned yet quite different black men and women talking to each other in a friendly but rigorous fashion, and in ways that did not end with punch lines—was, in and of itself, a key part of its message. Baraka remembered that "in that period there was a great deal more collective spirit in the Afro-American community because there was the whole civil rights [movement], so people felt linked more closely because we all felt ourselves in some ways involved in that struggle." To see these links enacted in *Soul!*'s conversational episodes and segments was a powerful experience for black audiences, not merely because such images were exceedingly rare on television, but also, and perhaps more important, because they galvanized and affirmed these links as they existed in the world beyond television.

In "Baraka, the Artist," the intimacy and shared political purpose of the collective is represented through the specific intimacy of Baraka and Haizlip. Appearing relaxed, Baraka strikes various contemplative poses as they talk, sometimes looking down as if concentrating, at other moments resting his elbows lightly on his knees, a little like Rodin's *Thinker*. Although he makes eye contact with the audience, in general his gaze demands less attention than Farrakhan's, contributing to a sense that spectators are privy to Baraka's interiority. Haizlip's conversational cues and questions also strike an easy and familiar tone. For example, right after he welcomes Baraka back to *Soul!* and recites the long list of his guest's achievements (reading from the back cover of *Spirit Reach*, Baraka's latest volume of poetry), Haizlip congratulates him on the recent birth of a son and inquires after the health of his wife, Amina Baraka.[32] At another point, about five minutes into the interview, Haizlip is more explicit about his personal acquaintance with Baraka. "I've known you for quite a number of years, and everything you've said today is very beautiful and very gentle," he observes. "What makes you so controversial?"

Even as Haizlip moves on to less ostensibly personal terrain, Baraka repeatedly reroutes the conversation toward the familiar and the familial, so that the writer's family becomes a primary topic of conversation, not merely a tool for breaking the ice. For example, when Haizlip inquires about the sustainability of CFUN in light of the historical vulnerability of black male leaders who threaten the white power structure, Baraka asserts that CFUN is "a family," not merely an organization, and goes on to answer the question about leadership in terms of intrafamilial legacy. "My wife is as articulate and involved with nationalism, pan-Africanism, and Ujama [a Kawaida principle] as I am," he notes, referring to Amina Baraka as an embodiment of the cultural national-ist ideal:

> I don't think there's that separation. I think that maybe in other gen-erations, there was a thing where husband did this [gesture with hand] and the wife was somewhere else. But that is incorrect. It's incorrect. Because first of all, the children are the ones who are going to carry on the struggle if you get cut down. And the women are the ones who teach the children, contrary to what anybody might think. . . . And if they somehow have a reactionary ideology based on them not being stride for stride with you, it means that you really can't make your next cycle the way you should, because there's a gap. And that's why brothers always say you can tell how revolutionary a people will be by how revolutionary the women are.

As Baraka talks, the eye of the camera scans the audience, which con-tains a notably large (for *Soul!*) number of children (figure 4.10). It lands first on the image of a female audience member holding a sleeping child and subsequently on a group of older children, who fidget as they listen. Such images would seem to illustrate Baraka's points, while adding vi-sual interest to the relatively static spectacle of the interview. (The cam-era similarly homes in on children in the studio audience at parallel mo-ments of "Farrakhan the Minister.") It comes as more a surprise when, a few minutes later, as Baraka is discussing the origin and manufacture of his nationalist dress suit, the sounds of an infant crying off-camera can be distinctly heard, persisting beyond a few quickly hushed squalls. The impromptu noise of the baby defies the convention of the studio space as a highly controlled sonic environment, where microphones strategically amplify certain sounds while muffling or silencing others. Not only does it indicate that the producers and director permitted very young children to attend the taping of the episode, although they could not be expected to conform to conventions of noiseless specta-torship, but it also suggests that the unrehearsed sounds of children crying or talking were to be incorporated in the aural design of the epi-sode. Anticipated or not, the fortuitous accident of the baby's crying af-

4.10. Children in the studio audience, probably during "The Young People's Show," March 1972.

fects the atmosphere in the room. Sonically, it transports viewers from the counterpublic space of the *Soul!* studio to the black counterpublic spaces, where unprompted sounds are more common—perhaps to an arts event or a political meeting, complete with women dragging sleepy or restless children along with them.[33]

Haizlip's response to Baraka's assertions about his wife's role in their nuclear family, as a miniature of the black national family, takes the form of an implicit critique. Echoing his questions to Farrakhan about homosexuals and homosexuality in the NOI, Haizlip inquires about the role of black women who are not wives or mothers in Baraka's vision of black radical politics. Can those women be protagonists of revolutionary struggle outside of their domestic roles? Agreeing with Baraka's premise that a nationalist political movement can succeed only if it includes women, Haizlip laughs slightly and then challenges Baraka in a more assertive tone: "But then that raises the other problem that in the society today, there's so many instances where the males are being ripped off by drugs, there's a great deal of homosexuality, there's an overpopulation of black women who do not have men to fulfill the necessary chores to support them. So how can you utilize and use them in your organization? Does it make it a polygamous situation, or is it a monogamous situation, or how do you as a family operate?"

Using unmarried heterosexual women as an example, Haizlip challenges Baraka's commitment to the nuclear family as the privileged social unit of revolutionary political struggle. Noting that many people—including, presumably, drug addicts and male homosexuals—are unable or unwilling to imagine themselves in such a construct, he points to the backward-looking deployment of both the family and motherhood in cultural nationalist discourses. Baraka shrugs off the issue of polygamy, noting that he and his wife are "very monogamous"—an assertion that draws a spontaneous reaction from Haizlip ("That's going to surprise a lot of people," he interrupts with a laugh). In any case, he says, polygamists have no time for politics: "Their revolution would be coming in that house, trying to deal with all the women."

Although Baraka makes a nervous and awkward joke of it, the question of polygamy is significant, not only because it inquires into the limits of nationalist idealizations of supposedly African social and sexual practices (looking back to Farrakhan's assertion that homosexuality is absent in African society and to their discussions of the Black Muslim family), but also because it so clearly points to the redundancy of women within cultural nationalist conceptions of revolutionary politics.[34] In imagining the lot of the black nationalist polygamist to be "deal[ing] with all the women," Baraka notably projects women as the wards of male nationalists, when in fact the domestic scene he conjures also clearly situates women as the caretakers of the nationalist home. Although Haizlip does not mention her, Giovanni—in her articulation of a desire for a future defined by new gender and sexual arrangements of the black family—is very much present in this moment. So, too, perhaps more obviously, is Haizlip, as a gay man excluded from the nationalist family's reproductive economy.

Where the publicity of black misfittedness is concerned, these moments when Haizlip questions the role of women in the nationalist family are significant for their articulation of a gendered critique of this family's resemblance to the bourgeois nuclear family—the very construction associated with the division of spheres that Baraka claims to have transcended. Although Baraka's praise of his wife might seem to suggest her political equality, in fact his discourse reveals how nationalism's elevation of women as teachers of children is predicated on placing these women in traditional domestic roles. In other words, the ideal of mothers as teachers envisions a highly gendered distribution of labor within domesticity, leaving imbalances of power in the black counterpublic sphere intact. Not only does Baraka's phrase about women keeping up "stride for stride" recall Giovanni's complaint that even radical black men insist on women's being "ten paces behind," but his vision of contemporary domestic arrangements, far from improving on the past, also reifies the distinction between feminized domestic labor and masculinized work and politics. However conversant with and involved in nationalist politics Amina Baraka is, her husband's comments do not indicate a public role for her as an activist except through her role as wife. Indeed, his assumption that "the children are the ones who are going to carry on the struggle" is notable for skipping over the political agency of black women, and it contrasts with the very public—indeed, iconic—roles of the female partners of imprisoned, exiled, or assassinated male activists, including Shabazz, Kathleen Cleaver, Myrlie Evers, Coretta Scott King, Lynn Brown, and Miriam Makeba, when she was married to an exiled Stokely Carmichael.

In fact, this part of the interview culminates in Baraka's most explicit conflation of the nationalist family with the bourgeois nuclear family. After expounding briefly on polygamy, Baraka reiterates his commitment to reproductive nuclearity within black revolutionary practice:

> Basically, it is revolutionary for a black man and a black woman to live together according to a black value system and raise a revolutionary family. In America, boy, that's revolution right there. [He looks to Haizlip, who nods gently and smiles, then looks down at his notes, as though preparing for a subsequent question.] Especially if you're raised up in a neighborhood where nobody's got a father. You might be the stranger on the block 'cause you've got a father and mother who live in the same house. That

was my situation. We were strange on our block 'cause all our people [he turns to audience] were still there [he points with a hand to an imaginary place].

What Roderick Ferguson calls the "unprecedented and often unconscious intimacies" of the "radical and the hegemonic" in 1970s black nationalist thought are on full display in this moment, as Baraka, drawing on his own memories of feeling like a misfit for having grown up in a middle-class nuclear family, argues that the path to revolution lies in the claiming of a normativity historically denied the black family.[35] In so doing, Baraka not only reinscribes single black women as redundant to the revolutionary family unless and until they partner and reproduce with black men, but he also shuts the door on alternatives that might include in the nationalist ideal those who are misfitted with the reproductive, nuclear ideal. A few minutes later, in the course of describing his idea for a new play, he returns to the point, telling Haizlip that the new work will be "about something that is quite normal . . . about black people achieving health, you know what I mean, and normalcy in our time." Although it originates in opposition to a legacy of othering, Baraka's articulation of black liberation with the recuperation of social norms comes perilously close to the discourse of the Moynihan Report, which made the case for viewing the misfitted Negro family as an object of liberal social welfare policy. Indeed, Baraka's own prescriptions for achieving such normalcy assume that the family can be rendered a tool of radical social renewal (for example, in disseminating a "black value system") without any alteration in form.

The moments of friction between Haizlip and Baraka in "Baraka, the Artist" are not as overt or disruptive as those in "Farrakhan the Minister," and therefore not as demanding of a reparative public display of brotherhood. Thus, they are allowed to remain as tensions that invite viewers, following Haizlip's example, to think about the ways their own families might or might not fit the nationalist norm and whether they aspire to normalcy as Baraka defines it. Interestingly, toward the end of the interview, Baraka offers an alternative vision of the black collective imagined as a confederacy of socially differentiated "tribes." In response to Haizlip's question regarding whether "outsiders" can contribute to

CFUN's work in Newark, Baraka is notably ecumenical: "We believe that black people in America have as many tribes as our brothers and sisters on the continent, and so we have to learn how to detribalize ourselves even while being tribed, begin to work with each other to work toward larger goals." Here Baraka's language registers an intriguing shift away from the discourse of the nuclear family. But by the time he introduces the metaphor of the tribe, the interview has run its course. Haizlip concludes in his usual fashion. "Imamu," he says, addressing Baraka with the Swahili word for "spiritual leader" (pronounced "ee-mah-mu"), "you're a very beautiful man, and I thank you."[36]

Giovanni's impassioned dialogue with Baldwin and Haizlip's respectful but critical interviews of Farrakhan and Baraka are generative performance texts for scholars interested in black arts and Black Power. As televised enactments of the sometimes strained relationships and unanswered questions between parties united in a common purpose and a shared critique of white supremacy, they illustrate that black expression in the early 1970s was far from uniform, although the categories through which we retroactively engage with this era often flatten out differences and alliances alike. In particular, *Soul!* provides examples of performance events in which varieties of black radical political thought are pointedly called to account for their embrace of normativity, whether in the form of the affirmation of black masculinity at the expense of black women, the repression of queer energies and identities, or the idealization of the black nuclear family. This may seem like an obvious point, but it is in danger of being lost in contemporary revisionist scholarship, which can inadvertently create the impression that nationalism—although a dominant expression of 1970s black radicalism—was not answerable to emerging queer and feminist critiques.

Soul!'s visual representations of Haizlip and Giovanni as deferential but also questioning interlocutors of three commanding male figures is crucial insofar as they offer spectacles of black heterodoxy and differences within the black community. Through its dialogue format, which encouraged dynamic, affectively infused performances, the program avoided the static representations of public-affairs programs (including

Black Journal), which favored moderated debates between the usually male representatives of different factions or organizations. In the case of the Baraka and Farrakhan episodes of *Soul!*, the audible and visible presence of the studio audience contributed to feelings of intimacy on the set and, more important, decentered the authority of the figures on stage, who might be interrupted by spectators' applause or the sounds of a crying baby. In the *Soul!* dialogues, a speaker's posture, her facial expression, the moment at which he sighed or took a deep drag on a cigarette, and the moment when he leaned in for a brotherly handshake were just as communicative as formal statements of position; in fact, they sometimes undercut or complicated the conflicts that surfaced in arguments between dissenting parties. In the "Baldwin and Giovanni" episodes, Baldwin's silences and evasions about his own queerness are complicated and undercut by the communicative performance of his voice and body (obscured in the text of the published *Dialogue*). And in "Farrakhan the Minister," Haizlip's deferential gestures toward and moments of physical intimacy with the NOI leader complicate, while surfacing, the submerged context of Haizlip's own status as *Soul!*'s gay male host. The agency of misfit energy and affect on the *Soul!* set underscores the value of the *Soul!* archive to our understanding of the intimacies and camaraderie possible despite or within difference—indeed, of the ways such difference might have itself been constituitive of a certain affect of togetherness.

Where cultural histories of black arts and Black Power are concerned, *Soul!* is not only an archive of what Vertamae Grosvenor called the "invisible community" of black nonconformists, including Haizlip and Giovanni; it is also a misfit enterprise, in the sense that it does not fit neatly within twenty-first-century scholarly narratives of cultural resistance to patriarchy and homophobia.[37] As I have argued, Haizlip's handshake with Louis Farrakhan, which might appear to perform the *Soul!* host's capitulation to queer invisibility, actually enacts a much more complex dynamic, in which camaraderie (what I have called *brotherhood*) is shot through with critique, refusal, and resistance, and in which the encounter with the homophobic subject is an opportunity to counter homophobia and prompt an acknowledgment of gay men and lesbians in the black community. The analytical rubric of black misfittedness enables us to recognize how freakishness was itself a site of contestation, variously embraced as a source of creativity and paradoxical social agency and rejected as a deviation from imagined norms of identity and family.

Soul!'s status as a misfit enterprise derives, finally, from its culturally eccentric location on public television, a medium only now being recognized as a significant site of black radical political and aesthetic undertakings in the 1960s and 1970s. If *Soul!* demonstrates television to have been a platform for more diverse performances of blackness than previously acknowledged, it also compels us to reconsider powerful nationalist views of the medium of television as hopelessly compromised by virtue of its embeddedness in market logics and social relations. Although operating in a context that afforded limited or highly controlled visibility to diversity in the black political culture of the 1970s, Haizlip and the team of misfits who created *Soul!* labored to provide a stage for a variety of identities, ideologies, and energies. Their work remains a powerfully affecting archive of performers and performances that moved, and continue to move, to different drums.

5 The Racial State and the "Disappearance" of *Soul!*

Sometimes it is necessary in the
evolution of things to disappear.
—Ellis Haizlip

For its creators and viewers, *Soul!* was a heady experiment in what might be achieved when black people gained authority over their representation on television. It reflected and refracted the ideas of its producer and frequent host, Ellis Haizlip, who curated shows that earned the trust of black audiences by giving them what the poet Camille Yarbrough terms the "breathing space" to "look at each other."[1] On *Soul!*, culture was not a realm of instruction or a commodity to be acquired, but a dynamic terrain where racially defined Americans, denied access to traditional public spheres, worked out issues of identity and strategies of resistance in music, conversation, dance, literature, drama, and visual arts. *Soul!* gave TV viewers in far-flung locations the opportunity to see and hear an array of performers, artists, and intellectuals neglected by—or patently unwelcome on—commercial television, depicting them in relaxed settings with a receptive studio audience. Before the late 1960s, public broadcasting had tended to define its public narrowly, but *Soul!* used the medium of noncommercial television to establish a black counterpublic space, a vibrant oasis in the TV wasteland. As Haizlip noted at the outset of the pair of *Soul!* episodes featuring an intimate and at times heated conversation between James Baldwin and Nikki Giovanni, "one of the miracles of this universe that we deal with is the way it can use something as cold and gray and as impersonal as an electron . . . to bring you an experience as warm and as rich and as human as the program you are about to see."[2]

The *Soul!* "miracle" ended on March 7, 1973, with "To the People, Thank You," a live, hour-long episode devoted to staff reminiscences and the reading of poems and tributes from viewers. Seated on stage with members of his production staff, Haizlip explained that after five seasons on the air, one locally in New York and four as a national program, the show was being forced to suspend operations after the announcement by the Corporation for Public Broadcasting (CPB) that it would not renew the show's funding for the 1973–74 season. Although Haizlip did not elaborate, the termination of CPB support had been in the works since at least January 1973. The same day "To the People, Thank You," aired, the CPB Board of Directors issued a resolution noting that it would hold $305,000 in reserve for "Black programs" of the "highest obtainable quality," but signaling an intention to break with precedent and fund, instead of *Soul!*, what it described as "the promising program concept and format for a proposal called *Interface*."[3] *Black Journal*, the other black program carried by PBS, had also been on the chopping block, but its defunding was forestalled by pressures brought to bear by Tony Brown, its politically savvy executive producer and host. A public campaign and back-channel lobbying on behalf of *Soul!* failed to produce the same result. With the loss of government and foundation funding, and with Channel 13 unable to pay for *Soul!* out of its own production budget or to find a corporate sponsor, Haizlip had no option but to shut down operations. For a program that had celebrated, even as it interrogated, the construct of the black community, the homage to viewers was an apt finale.

This chapter investigates *Soul!*'s demise, rooting it in the decline of U.S. public broadcasting in the late 1960s and early 1970s. When Channel 13/WNDT's director for cultural programming, Christopher "Kit" Lukas, submitted a proposal to the Ford Foundation for a "black *Tonight* show" in early 1968, he was motivated by the personal realization that the New York metropolitan area's chief noncommercial TV outlet could no longer continue to claim to serve the public while excluding black people from meaningful employment or representation. However, he did not arrive at this position, or at his optimism about public television as an instrument of racial justice, in a vacuum. Well before members of the Kerner Commission publicized their 1968 report asserting that racially biased representations in the mass media contributed to black Americans' social alienation, civil rights activists had protested against racial stereotyping on television and called for an end to discriminatory hiring policies. Lukas was part of a generation of white broadcasters who looked to noncommercial television as a site for the expansion of democracy in mass media. With the passage of the Public Broadcasting Act in 1967, the federal government seemed poised to promote this vision, holding out the promise of regular and robust support for the sort of feisty, alternative programming that members of the Carnegie Commission had seen as the primary mission of noncommercial television.[4] In cases where government funds were seen as likely to be slow to materialize, the Ford Foundation stepped in to provide resources to help local TV stations and production centers create politically progressive and aesthetically daring programs for minority audiences without delay.

As it turned out, however, the window of opportunity for publicly funded television targeted specifically at black viewers and created with the input of black producers was exceedingly narrow. Even with national profiles and solid ratings among black households despite competition from the networks, *Soul!* and *Black Journal* were vulnerable, as state and private investments in both racial justice and public broadcasting shifted in the period immediately after 1968. By the start of the 1973 TV season, Richard Nixon, famously hostile to the news media, had begun a second term as president; the black freedom movement had suffered significant losses in leadership and momentum; and the CPB, the ostensibly neutral agency responsible for administering federal funds for public television, had spent the better part of its brief existence embroiled in struggles with a White House bent on shutting down programming perceived as critical of the president or his policies. In an independent development, the Ford Foundation had begun to shift its philanthropy away from public broadcasting and toward other social needs, including the seeding of black studies programs at colleges and universities. In New York City, the patching together of the public TV station WNDT, home to *Soul!*, and NET, the independent production center where *Black Journal* originated, resulted in the creation of a new, hybrid entity, WNET, which increasingly looked to corporations and wealthy individual donors for its bread and butter. Starved of long-range federal funding, enmeshed in political struggles that put it on the defensive, and embarking on a path toward de facto privatization through corporate sponsorship, public television at this point was no longer the fertile ground for progressive programming that it had been only a few years earlier.[5]

Soul! was a foreseeable casualty of this period of political and racial retrenchment in American life. Not only was Haizlip's show caught up in the White House campaign to rid public media of liberal and leftist voices, but it was also subject to the new logic of what Michael Omi and Howard Winant call the "racial state." Emerging in response to the threats posed by the civil rights, black arts, and Black Power movements, this new state formation sought to blunt the radical edges of antiracist social movements through strategies of "absorption," whereby moderate or cosmetic changes in policy forestalled deeper transformations of the social order.[6] In the realm of television, racial-state absorption dictated a largely cosmetic, or representational, approach to racial justice, in which images of an integrated public sphere were substituted for structural transformations, including the actual integration of public television.[7] The CPB's decision to fund *Interface* in 1973 registers the effectiveness of these strategies, insofar as the government could reaffirm its support for racial integration while silencing programming it either did not appreciate or deemed radical. Indeed, by implying that in its specific address to a black viewing public, *Soul!* was a relic of the segregated past—or at least a past of racial crisis that the nation had worked to surmount—the CPB could paradoxically position itself as a champion of progress.

Focusing closely on the last several months of *Soul!*, this chapter pursues three main sets of concerns. First, I trace the circumstances that led to the demise of *Soul!* in spring 1973, starting with Nixon's campaign to rid the airwaves of publicly funded news and public-affairs programming and culminating in the CPB's early 1973 defunding of *Soul!* and *Black Journal*, two WNET shows that attracted negative attention for their embrace of radical black politics and aesthetics. Here I tread familiar ground, but I inflect my discussion with a distinctive focus on *Soul!* as an auxiliary casualty of this era, because as programming that subsisted largely on government funding, it was profoundly vulnerable to state rollbacks. A second concern of the chapter is to explore the resistant response to these decisions by Haizlip and his program's allies. Joined by advocates for *Black Journal*, defenders of *Soul!* challenged the authority of the majority-white CPB board to decide what was in the interests of black television viewers. It denied the political neutrality of the CPB's embrace of *Interface*, claiming that, contrary to what the corporation alleged, its support of a "cross-cultural" program was intended to consolidate its power over black programming while escaping charges of racism. The third concern takes me from the realm of public political theater to the televised campaign to save *Soul!*, and to Haizlip's formulation of a prophetic discourse of *Soul!*'s survival via its vibrations in time and space. *Soul!*'s final episode, while serving an elegiac function, also enacted this prophetic vision, celebrating the power of black performance to move and inspire audiences long after the *Soul!* studio went permanently dark. I end the chapter with Haizlip's notion of "disappearance" as a strategy of survival, a paradoxical notion that underscores the immaterial effects and affects of black performance.

Although it would be reductive to ascribe the demise of *Soul!* to the Nixon presidency, the notion, while incomplete, is not altogether without merit. The backlash against the counterculture, solidified by Nixon's ascendency as a president who campaigned on a platform of restoring law and order to the proverbial streets, would see the strengthening of forces bent on scrubbing the airwaves of liberal and leftist content in the name of restoring law and order to the media as well. The president's assault on TV programming that was opposed to his administration was, of course, a highly subjective operation, to the point where some observers have argued that Nixon irreparably politicized news and public-affairs broadcasting in a way from which it has never recovered.[8] But the presidential attacks against liberal or leftist critique on television were also highly effective, particularly where financially dependent public broadcasting stations were concerned.

Indeed, although the architects of the CPB had sought to safeguard it from political interference, Nixon's contention of liberal bias in public television news and public affairs, and his profound distrust of the liberals and leftists whom he believed exercised disproportionate power over the media, took firm root in the social imagination at large. To the degree that they invoke specters of artists run amok, liberal elites disdainful of average Americans, and wasteful government support for antiestablishment arts enterprises, the culture wars of the 1980s and 1990s reprised rather than reinvented Nixon's late 1960s and early 1970s attacks, in which public television was a prime—and supremely vulnerable—target.

Other political leaders detested the news media, but "Nixon was the first to turn personal hostility into public policy and to use his Administration to try to neutralize the critical media," observes James Day, who served as president of New York's Channel 13/WNET between 1970 and 1973.[9] As Day and a host of others have documented, from virtually the moment of his inauguration in 1969, Nixon, working with Vice President Spiro Agnew and various White House officials, engaged in a furious effort to wrest power away from the so-called Eastern establishment types whose critical viewpoints he found subversive of his administration.[10] The White House took aim at both commercial and public television; where the president's ire at TV news broadcasters was concerned, it mattered little that compared to the three major networks, noncommercial television had relatively minuscule audiences and presumably limited ability to adversely affect him. Yet commercial television was somewhat insulated from intrusion by the executive branch, whereas public television—which subsisted on grants and government monies—was susceptible to direct and indirect deployments of presidential power, and Nixon and his allies eagerly seized any opportunity to bend public TV to their will. During the years that *Soul!* aired, Nixon devoted considerable and sustained energy to altering the landscape of public television. Although the developing Watergate scandal would eventually derail his presidency—and in a supreme irony, draw record-breaking audiences to gavel-to-gavel public television broadcasts of the Watergate hearings—by the time of his August 1974 resignation Nixon had largely succeeding in "de-fanging" (as one journalist put it) government-supported TV news operations and, with them, public television itself.[11]

Where the war against public television news coverage was concerned, the Nixon White House worked with an air of imperial entitlement. "Our position," as Peter M. Flanigan, assistant to Nixon, put it matter-of-factly in a late 1969 memorandum to the president, is that "government funding of CPB should not be used for the creation of anti-Administration programming or for the support of program-producing organizations which use other funds to create anti-Administration programs."[12] Two years later Clay Whitehead, newly appointed director of the Office of Telecommunications Policy (OTP)—assisted by Antonin Scalia, then the OTP's general counsel—provided a more politically refined template for the government's campaign. "The immediate goal is to eliminate slanted public affairs programming on public television as thoroughly and quickly as possible," Whitehead wrote in a draft memorandum to the president dated November 15, 1971. "The longer range and more fundamental goal is to reverse the current trend of CPB toward becoming a BBC-like fourth network supported by public funds, which inevitably would reflect the taste, politics, and morality of the national artistic and intellectual elite."[13] The effort to shut down "slanted" public-affairs programming, defined as programming critical of the executive branch, was thus both a starting point and a proxy for a more ambitious and more general effort issuing from the Oval Office to limit the access of progressive artists and intellectuals to public broadcasting.

The OTP urged Nixon to proceed with caution. Whether or not they watched public television—then occasionally still referred to by its older and stodgier name, *educational television*—most Americans considered it a boon to democracy and appreciated its existence. As one draft memorandum to the president noted, "the current concept of Federal funding creates a dilemma—striking at public broadcasting generally puts us in the posture of being against 'Sesame Street,' high school equivalency programs, drug abuse programs, television drama, and the like."[14] Nixon might be able to make the case that public broadcasting had gone too far in its political affiliation with liberals, but he would have to do it without seeming to be an enemy of Big Bird, moral and educational reform, and *Masterpiece Theatre*.[15] Meeting the president's objectives was complicated by the fact that public television, far from being a "BBC-like fourth network," was not one "thing" in one place controlled by one set of people beholden to one set of funders. Rather, it was a multifaceted and decentralized entity, a motley collection of parts receiving funding from various sources to produce programming that some, but not all, public television stations aired.

Ultimately, the OTP adopted a two-pronged approach: while the president used his executive authority to appoint political allies to the CPB's board, Whitehead was dispatched to make the administration's case to broadcasters. In October 1971 Whitehead used a keynote address to the professional organization representing public broadcasters to announce the federal government's plan to withhold support for national news or public-affairs programs via cutbacks in CPB appropriations. The White House, he announced, was concerned about the autonomy of smaller stations obliged through their PBS affiliation to air what it considered left-leaning news and public-affairs shows emanating from East Coast production centers.[16] Disingenuous as this was—White House memos reveal only political concerns about the president's standing, not philosophical qualms about centralization—it at least appealed to the antifederalist principles that undergirded the hodgepodge system of public broadcasting in the United States. Supporters of *Soul!* had mustered similar arguments about local self-determination in their early arguments for a black show for public television in New York City. In a subsequent appearance on National Public Radio, Whitehead offered less varnished reasoning for a cutback in federal support for the CPB, telling the interviewer: "There is a real question as to whether public television, particularly the national federally funded part of public television, should be carrying public affairs, news commentary, and that kind of thing . . . the commercial networks, by and large, do, I think, quite a good job in that area."[17] According to this strained logic, with its sham plaudits for commercial news operations, the White House was battling to end redundancy in TV programming, not noncommercial television's airing of liberal or leftist viewpoints.

Not surprisingly, Whitehead's antagonizing speech did not earn the administration friends among broadcasters or the print journalists who wrote about the TV industry. In a *New Yorker* piece that voiced what many felt, Michael Arlen deemed Whitehead's radio statements "arrogant" and accused the president of trying to stifle political opposition in an election year. Arlen also disputed Whitehead's praise for the "good job" of commercial broadcasters, who in fact devoted less than 5 percent of their airtime to news programming. What the nation needed, Arlen argued, was not less news and public affairs on public television, but more, to counter "the inadequacies and Administration-directed deferences of commercial television."[18] Other observers noted the inherent contradiction of the White House's decision to use executive branch powers to "liberate" public broadcasting from undue interference or centralized control.[19] Still others, hoping for a compromise with the White House, understood Whitehead to be telegraphing the possibility of a deal: a tacit promise of the president's support for long-range CPB disbursements, something public broadcasters desperately wanted, in exchange for fewer programs like NET's *Banks and the Poor*, a muckraking 1970 documentary about the corrupt politics of the banking industry that enraged members of Congress. The idea was that if liberal broadcasters would agree to tone down their approach, they might win assurances of money for other sorts of projects. For those inclined to make such a deal, the trick would be to concede just enough to the White House to serve their future self-interest.[20]

In part because of the disorganization of public broadcasters, Nixon's tactics for bringing public television into line with his interests largely succeeded. At the same January 1972 meeting at which it voted to defund *Soul!* in favor of *Interface*, the CPB's board, which included several Nixon appointees, decided "not to fund news, analysis, or political commentary" for the coming fiscal year. For programs that it did not totally defund, the board tied the amount of its grants to a stipulation that stations work to acquire matching funds from outside sources—imposing unrealistic pressures on stations without mature development operations and hastening the trend toward the de facto privatization of their programming.[21] Six months later, much to the chagrin of broadcasters who thought that they would receive a quid pro quo if they absorbed these blows without protest, the president vetoed a bill authorizing multiyear funding for the CPB, even though both houses of Congress had overwhelmingly supported the bill. (The veto ultimately led Whitehead, who had also supported the bill, to resign.) Although the president would soon be appearing a great deal on public television, in extensively watched live broadcasts of the Watergate hearings, by 1974 public broadcasting was in a substantially weaker position than it had been when he first took the oath of office.

Where does *Soul!* fit into this larger picture of a White House intent on neutralizing, if not abolishing, news and public affairs shows and controlling criticism of administration policy on public television? On the face of things, as a program tallied in the cultural-affairs ledger of industry spreadsheets, *Soul!* was marginal in the official showdown between public television and the Nixon White House.[22] The same gendered and classed logic that led public TV executives to separate cultural affairs from public affairs, and to regard the former as less intellectually demanding or consequential than the latter, led government officials to take notice of *Black Journal*—deemed "balanced against us" by Patrick Buchanan, a special advisor to Nixon—while overlooking *Soul!* as "entertainment."[23] Of course, the line between public and cultural affairs was distinctly blurry. An internal memo from late 1971 serves to illustrate the broad swath of "public affairs" programming the White House had in mind. It cites antiwar coverage of Vietnam on Bill Moyers's *This Week,* an episode of the WNET show *Free Time* that "had Bobby Seale discussing Black Panther involvement in Attica," and episodes of the WNET-produced *Great American Dream Machine,* one including Paul Jacobs, who ran for public office in California in 1968 on a ticket with Eldridge Cleaver and another featuring an "anti-establishment song and dance number by Jane Fonda."[24] Yet while *Soul!* routinely broadcast musical performances that were more subversive than Fonda's, and Haizlip over the years had hosted dozens of figures from the black Left, I found no archival evidence that suggests the show was ever on the OTP's radar.

However, as the only two black programs carried through PBS interconnection, a complicated system that gave station managers veto power over programming they deemed undesirable, *Soul!* and *Black Journal* were threatened by ideological enthusiasm emanating from the White House for local autonomy over public television programming.[25] A 1971 survey circulated to public broadcasters found that the managers of PBS member stations generally disliked both programs, finding them irrelevant to their viewing publics. "We receive much negative comment about both while having no reaction that would indicate that Blacks either watch or like the programs," reported one such manager (identified in the report as white), who voiced concern about whether the shows were "appropriate" for his locality.[26]

Moreover, because public television audiences associated culture with programs like *Masterpiece Theatre*, they were often affronted by shows such as *Soul!* that presented provocative contemporary performances. "Few viewers complained about the Boston Pops," reflected the former CPB President John Macy Jr., "but the more frenetic music of the counter-culture caused ripples of dissent in some quarters."[27] Over the years, station managers registered particular displeasure with the language of many of the poets who appeared on *Soul!*, prompting Channel 13/WNET to send out weekly alerts if episodes contained problematic words; ironically, the most commonly flagged term was "nigger," used by writers in an ironic manner or to cite other people. Looked at in the light of this book's argument about the affective compact that *Soul!* forged with viewers, the anxiety of station managers over provocative language appears to be a proxy for their anxiety about the self-assured, often confrontational delivery of the writers themselves, as well as the spectacle of the studio audience's passionate appreciation of their performances.[28] It was not words in and of themselves that caused displeasure—although there were plenty of arguments to be made for the inappropriateness of certain words—but the power displayed by those who voiced the words.

Thus, although *Soul!* seems not to have been actively targeted by the White House, it was by no means safe from the campaign to rid the airwaves of leftist or liberal programming. Unlike *Sesame Street*, *Soul!* did not have Big Bird to make it bulletproof; nor, for that matter, did Haizlip have the political clout of Brown, who also served as dean of Howard University's School of Communications, located just a couple of miles north of the centers of political power in Washington. Haizlip had long feared that Brown's public-affairs show threatened *Soul!* because broadcasters might think the two WNET productions redundant. As early as February 1971, Haizlip had written to Lukas, his immediate supervisor, to express concern that the merger of NET and WNDT, in bringing the two programs under one roof, was "programming us into a confrontation with 'Black Journal.'"[29] At the time, Channel 13 President Ward Chamberlain wrote off Haizlip's worries that *Black Journal* was in line for preferential treatment, but in retrospect it is clear that Haizlip correctly understood that because entertainment was a realm of ambivalence, both for public television and for black people, *Soul!* would always be regarded as the more expendable of the two programs.

Haizlip also had a different relationship to institutionalized power than Brown. When Brown took over as executive producer and host of *Black Journal* in late 1970, he was gently but publicly criticized for producing a "slicker," more self-promoting product than his predecessor, the widely admired William Greaves; behind the scenes at WNET, there were fears that Brown was intent on making *Black Journal* his program.[30] The producers' differences were reflected in their different responses to the threatened loss of CPB funding. When *Soul!*'s producer sensed his program was endangered, he reached out to Huey Newton.[31] In contrast, when Tony Brown got wind of PBS programming recommendations for the 1973–74 season that imperiled the standing of both *Black Journal* and *Soul!*, he brought his concerns both to Samuel Holt, PBS's coordinator of programming, and to Henry Loomis, the recently installed CPB president. In a late November 1972 letter, Brown offered his congratulations to Loomis while encouraging him to look favorably on the "impact and viability of Black Affairs programming" as the CPB worked through its funding decisions.[32] His brief but tactical letter received a prompt reply. "I want to assure you that, as a producer of one of public television's major series, you will have my ear, whatever your experience has been with others," Loomis wrote. "Programming support for the specialized audience which you have developed through BLACK JOURNAL is something which receives considerable attention at CPB and something to which I am personally committed."[33] A month later, Brown would be telling the *New York Amsterdam News* that Loomis and Thomas Curtis, president of the CPB's board, "are trying to destroy anything that doesn't suit their political ideology. Or their racist ideology."[34]

Not only did Brown wield more influence than Haizlip with public broadcasting officialdom and operate more shrewdly in his dealings with the CPB, but *Black Journal* also attracted a wealthier and better educated audience than *Soul!* According to a late 1972 study, *Soul!*, while on the whole more popular than *Black Journal* and notably successful at appealing to grandmothers and their grandchildren in equal numbers, also attracted a greater share of "ghetto viewers," to use the language of contemporary pollsters. Although this positioned the show well in terms of public broadcasting's mission of enlightening a broad swath of the public, it put *Soul!* at a distinct disadvantage when it came to fund-raising. Letters such as an undated one sent to Haizlip from Betty Lawson of the Bronx alluded to the lack of affluence of some of *Soul!*'s most ardent fans. "I have never been a contributor (financially) because I haven't the means," she wrote. "My support has always been present morally though."[35] Moral support, of course, was not enough to sustain a TV program, particularly at a time when the state was increasingly shifting the burden of funding public broadcasting to the private sphere, where familiar and seemingly apolitical shows raked in the most dollars. According to Jack Willis, former director of programming at WNET, although there was support for *Soul!* among station executives who recognized its unique contributions, the show was a tough sell for Channel 13's development office, which looked to white benefactors from Westchester and other wealthy New York City suburbs to keep the station afloat.[36] The general feeling was that, in an era of severely restrained public funding, the station could ill afford to invest its meager production budget in shows that neither generated their own revenue nor attracted significant numbers of dues-paying station members.

Notwithstanding these vulnerabilities, WNET executives seem to have counted on the renewal of CPB funding for *Soul!* for 1973–74, based on the program's track record and alignment with public broadcasting's mission as defined by the Kerner Commission. In its fifth season, *Soul!* still evidenced considerable creative vitality. In the weeks and months leading up to the CPB announcement, it had aired a memorable "Wonderlove" episode devoted entirely to Stevie Wonder, as well as episodes featuring the Spinners, Al Green, and the national television debut of Earth, Wind and Fire. Around Christmas, Nikki Giovanni had reprised her enormously successful collaboration with the New York Community Choir. Intimate conversations with Louis Farrakhan ("Farrakhan the Minister") and Amiri Baraka ("Baraka, the Artist") had given viewers opportunities to ruminate on a range of challenging issues, from black economic self-development to the gender and sexual politics of cultural nationalism.

For Channel 13 executives as well as for Haizlip, then, the CPB decision to award all of the funds set aside that fiscal year for "black programs" to *Interface* came as an unanticipated provocation. It would have been one thing had the CPB, in slashing support for news and public affairs, gone after *Black Journal*—although as Tony Brown argued, the White House argument of the "redundancy" of public TV news operations did not pertain to a show that was unique in its black perspective on the news. But in transferring money that would have gone to support the WNET productions to *Interface*, a show produced by WETA in Washington, the CPB was specifically repudiating both the New York station and black programming formed in the crucible of 1968, in favor of a new program whose chief recommendation appeared to be its integrationist interpretation of public broadcasting's post-Kerner mandate. Like *Soul!*, *Interface* had a black producer, the respected TV journalist and—ironically for Brown and Haizlip—*Black Journal* veteran Tony Batten. Yet unlike *Soul!*, it would not focus exclusively on black and Latino guests or style itself as a show for a black counterpublic. Although CPB sources were elusive in their descriptions of the show—owing in part to the fact that Batten had not yet produced a pilot—on this one point they were quite clear: *Interface*, as its name suggested, upended the post-1968 paradigm of black public TV programming in favor of a new paradigm of post-civil rights, post-race dialogue.

By throwing its support behind an untested show, the CPB board clearly relayed the desire of the state to eradicate programs associated with black radicalism and weaken WNET, a "known" center of public broadcasting's Eastern establishment. This did not stop CPB officials from assuring irate WNET executives that the judgment on *Soul!* had been politically neutral. "We love the program. We'd love to have them find somebody to fund it," Keith Fisher, CPB's executive vice president, told Tom Shales, a *Washington Post* reporter.[37] When pressed by Ralph Metcalfe, a member of the Congressional Black Caucus—a group drawn into the battle by Brown—CPB President Loomis was similarly evasive. "In an effort to diversify the kind and source of minority programming earlier this year we requested proposals from many different production sources," he wrote to the Democratic representative from Illinois. "Through our normal process of proposal evaluation we determined that . . . 'Interface' was most interesting."[38]

Although cordial, Loomis's letter was at pains to minimize the tension between routine bureaucratic procedure ("our normal process of proposal evaluation"), with its implicit adherence to objective standards of merit, and the CPB's specific interest in distancing itself from black radicalism and Channel 13 ("an effort to diversify the kind and source of minority programming"). Undergirding it is what I call *racialstate reasoning*, in which *Soul!*, a program popular with black viewers, was challenged by means of a quasi-government agency's seemingly impartial discourse about these same viewers' best interests. We can see a similar mode of thinking at work in the testimony of PBS President Hartford N. Gunn Jr. before the Senate Subcommittee on Commerce (the committee charged with oversight of the CPB) later that summer. With respect to the challenge of how best "to serve audiences too long ignored by all television broadcasters," Gunn offered a series of questions: "Should we adopt a somewhat separatist approach, and develop programs exclusively by, exclusively for, and exclusively about a particular target group? Are minorities and women best served by general audience programs which show them interacting with the so-called white establishment in non-stereo-typed racial ethnic or sexual roles? Is a program which deals with problems facing the urban poor a 'minority program' regardless of the racial balance of the reporters? These are questions on which reasonable people disagree."[39] Echoing Loomis's language about the "normal process" of bureaucratic evaluation, in his testimony Gunn drew on an idealized notion of the public sphere as a site of robust civic encounter, in which the disagreements of "reasonable people" register the health of the polity. Recalling Loomis's insistence on the CPB's commitment to diversity in programming, Gunn positioned PBS as a benevolent organization that recognized the vexing issues of representation confronting minority citizens. Yet in his testimony, Gunn—like Loomis—obscured the power of the CPB board, which had the ultimate authority to determine the answer to his questions. Indeed, his appeal to reasonable debate and argument was moot, since the issue had already been definitively decided. Neither debates over racial representation nor decisions about the allocation of federal monies for minority programming in public media transpired in a public sphere to which all citizens enjoyed equal access. Rather, they took place in a stratified society, in which those with the greatest investment in certain outcomes were also the least likely to have power to decide them.

I want to be clear here that I am not suggesting that interested parties had no cause to question *Soul!*'s format or its particular mode of address. Over the years, sympathetic observers had indeed questioned the wisdom of the approaches taken by "first-generation" black TV shows like *Soul!* and *Black Journal*. In 1974 *Freedomways*, a highly regarded quarterly of the black freedom movement, devoted a special issue to "The Black Image in the Mass Media," which included several pieces that pointedly questioned the mission as well as the efficacy of *Soul!* and other shows touting themselves as being by and for black people. As the media scholar Tommy Lee Lott notes, no less eminent a figure in the black media world than the documentarian St. Claire Bourne believed *Interface* to have been a "step away from the first generation's flaw of addressing African Americans about issues related only to black people."[40] The dilemmas and contradictions of minority representation could hardly have been solved by a single set of underfunded programs that first drew breath in 1968. That said, I do want to insist on the disingenuousness of broadcasting officials who framed the question of *Soul!*'s future as a matter of the urgency of integration and openness to varieties of black self-representations, when in fact what they seem to have objected to were the particular modes of blackness that the program circulated and mediated.

The embrace by PBS and the CPB of racial-state reasoning—that is, their claiming of common cause with minority citizens as a strategy of imposing their own interests—provoked a related conundrum for Haizlip and his allies, who were put in the position of having to respond to charges of advancing an outmoded politics and aesthetic. As Omi and Winant note, racial-state reasoning is, by definition, difficult to contest, insofar as it operates through strategies of absorption and incorporation.[41] In an additional complication, Haizlip faced the task of contesting the CPB decision on *Interface* without producing an ungainly and potentially disastrous spectacle of internecine conflict among black TV producers. (Indeed, both he and Brown would accuse the CPB of using *Interface* to drive a wedge between them, thereby weakening all minority programming.) The White House had conducted its crusade against liberal and progressive news and public affairs programming quite openly, with no apparent fear of alienating key constituencies. In contrast, the defunding of *Soul!* and, initially, *Black Journal* by the CPB board took place under the banner of promoting innovation and progress.

As Gunn's testimony before Congress implied, the country had moved on since 1968. Should not media representations of black people thus also move on? If racial integration was now the consensus of the liberal state, should not public television shows reflect this new norm of public policy in their form and aesthetic, abandoning the "somewhat separatist" approach of *Soul!* and *Black Journal*? Haizlip had long maintained that offering performers a black framework for their work was not tantamount to separatism, arguing that "an attempt to integrate white performers or other cultural themes [in *Soul!*] could only dilute the purpose and effect of the series."[42] Yet the accusation of separatism was hard to shake off and potentially alienated nonblack supporters of the show. Not only did it label *Soul!* and *Black Journal* as programs working in an outmoded black political formation, but it also branded them as antagonistic to integration and thus to the liberal public-sphere ideal.

In statements to the press following the spring 1973 announcement on *Interface*, Haizlip negotiated this tricky terrain by focusing on issues of power instead of representation. Rather than engage the unwieldy question of how best to represent minorities on television, he cast doubt on the government's commitment to opening up mass media to black people. Who defined the legitimacy of the various approaches to programming for women and minorities, and whom did these approaches alternatively benefit or threaten? Using the rhetoric of equal citizenship, he appealed to the economic productivity of black citizens to make the case that they had the right to define the terms of their representation on public television. "The tragedy of it all is that Blacks didn't have any voice in how the CPB distributed the $215 million available for public television," he told *Jet* magazine. "This is the taxpayers' money. If the Corporation for Public Broadcasting can fund the white programs for millions of dollars, it is an absolute insult that Black programs can't even be [funded] for $650,000"—a number representing the combined budgets of *Soul!* and *Black Journal.*[43] In hearings held that fall before the CPB board, the civil rights activist Jesse Jackson—who had recited his poetry on a 1972 *Soul!* episode with the singer Merry Clayton—made a similar argument. "The fundamental question is whether our access to the public airwaves is a civil right," he asserted. "We as black people have a distinct point of view," he said, melding the discourses of Black Power and civil rights, "and our tax investment in public broadcasting obligates public broadcasting to hear us."[44]

As Haizlip's and Jackson's comments demonstrate, even after the CPB extended an additional year of funding to Brown's show, supporters of *Soul!* and *Black Journal* addressed the CPB decision on black programming in a unified voice. In spring 1973 the Friends of Black Journal, a national group reported to have eighty chapters around the country, issued the statement titled "Soul! Cancelled, Black Journal in Danger: A Blackgate in Public Television," punning on President Nixon's mounting troubles stemming from the discovery of a break-in at the Watergate Hotel. Noting that authority over black programming rested in the hands of "15 political appointees," only one of whom—Gloria Anderson, a chemistry professor at Atlanta's Morris Brown College—was black, the group's members questioned whether black people could expect a fair and thorough airing of their interests within an "institutionally racist structure."[45] At the same time, carefully disregarding Tony Batten and his intentions, the statement interrogated the bona fides of *Interface* as a black program, predicting that its format would endear it instead to white viewers drawn to its image of an integrated public sphere. "There are only two categories of programming on public television," the National Friends of Black Journal contended: "(A) Black programs and (B) White programs. White programs are duplicated in profusion. Children's programming is funded into the millions and every conceivable white topic and event has a permanent platform for its expression. Blacks must struggle along for crumbs and fight one another for funding in the old classic plantation style."[46] Haizlip made a similar statement to the *Washington Post*, accusing the CPB of pursuing "a policy to destroy all black programming."[47] By 1974, he told *Jet*, "black programs on public TV will have been successfully and skillfully removed."[48]

Although privately Haizlip may have held WNET partly responsible for *Soul!*'s termination, publicly he avoided statements critical of his employer or its commitment to the show it had supported for five seasons. Likewise, WNET maintained a face of public support for *Soul!*—with the station president John Jay Iselin accusing the CPB of reversing course on a previous commitment to funding the program, and with an unnamed "spokesman for WNET" telling *Broadcasting* that, where *Soul!* was concerned, "We're going to fight them [the CPB] on this one."[49] But while WNET management may have deeply resented what it understood to be the CPB's betrayal of *Soul!* and its rebuke of the station's liberal or left-leaning politics, station executives also knew that the Nixon-era climate of distrust for public broadcasting, combined with the Ford Foundation's turn to other philanthropic projects, rendered them more dependent than ever on individual donations (membership fees) and corporate underwriting. *Soul!* had been "for sale" once before—in 1969, when the Ford Foundation left it high and dry. In the political climate of 1973—in the midst of executive branch retrenchment on liberal reform, national consolidation of a notion of racial integration that minimized structural inequalities, and, more locally, Channel 13 members' preference for established public-broadcasting brands (such as *Masterpiece Theatre*) and programs in support of high-arts traditions—it was unlikely that a private entity would come through with the money to keep *Soul!* on the air.

Haizlip's sense of the CPB's abandonment of principles enshrined just five years earlier in the Kerner Report proved prescient. In a markedly ironic twist, less than a year after *Soul!* was terminated, the CPB embarked on a new round of inquiries into noncommercial television's "systemic inadequacy in serving" minority audiences. At Loomis's direction, in December 1973 the organization commissioned a panel, headed by Anderson, to study whether "the interests and needs of minorities have been neglected in public broadcasting."[50] Not surprisingly, that study found the needs of minority viewers were undercut by the color-blind principle of the autonomy of local stations, and it ultimately blamed the previous board for prompting *Soul!*'s cancellation and provoking a crisis about *Black Journal*. Thus did public broadcasters enter into a new cycle of hand-wringing over the problems that *Soul!* and other first-generation shows had been called on to address.

As important as the traditional public-sphere battle for *Soul!* was, Haizlip also saw the impending cancellation of the show as an opportunity to ignite the *Soul!* community. Since the program's first season, when it was broadcast only locally, it had been a regular practice of the *Soul!* host to encourage audience members to write to the studio with their feedback, ideas, and questions. These requests served the practical purpose of giving production staff a chance to alter the set between acts, but more important, they fostered viewers' sense of belonging to an imagined *Soul!* community, in turn providing Haizlip and his staff with the sort of qualitatively rich feedback lacking in official, commissioned surveys of the program's audience. Many of the surviving viewers' letters from early 1969—when *Soul!* confronted its first existential crisis in the loss of an anticipated second year of grant funding through the Ford Foundation's Project for New Television Programming—expressed pleasure with particular musical performances or episodes, but even more of the letters conveyed gratitude for, or even relief in the fact of, *Soul!*'s very existence. In a commercial television landscape that many described as indifferent or hostile to black people, *Soul!* appealed to these viewers as a weekly source of challenging, compelling, and relevant programming. Its existence signaled the value of black audiences as part of the *public* of public broadcasting. And unlike broadcasters invested in the distinction between cultural and public affairs, the viewers who wrote to *Soul!* in 1969 found entertainment to be a source of pleasure as well as of valuable information and ideas.

The routine calls for audience feedback took on a new urgency in early 1973, as details emerged about the program's likely loss of CPB funds, and as Haizlip entered into tense discussions with John Jay Iselin, the new president of WNET. Believing that Iselin was sabotaging *Soul!* by making changes to the Channel 13 broadcast schedule (thereby rendering it harder for the program's fans to find it), Haizlip set out to make a point by overwhelming the Channel 13 mailroom, once again using his bully pulpit to exhort *Soul!* viewers to send in statements of support.[51] As in 1969, viewer testimonials—handwritten, typed, and telegrammed; some colored by children; some sent on behalf of neighborhood or community groups; some from viewers who identified themselves as white or Jewish—poured in and continued to arrive through the early summer, although episodes broadcast in rerun were prohibited from containing such appeals (presumably because by then the fate of *Soul!* had been decided). In all, Haizlip estimated, *Soul!* received nearly 100,000 individual expressions of support. A spokesman for WNET told *Broadcasting*, an industry publication, that the program's live March 7 episode alone—its last—prompted 20,000 of these messages.[52]

In the end, the outpouring of viewer support for *Soul!*, which carried an implicit threat that viewers could be mobilized to picket the CPB—did not persuade CPB officials to rethink their funding priorities or reexamine their notions of minority representation.[53] From a political perspective this is not surprising, given the intensity of the early 1970s backlash against 1960s social movements, as exemplified in the White House campaign to eradicate news and public-affairs programming on noncommercial stations. Yet the efficacy of viewer letters and other testimonials on behalf of *Soul!* need not be framed solely or even primarily in terms of their ability to change the hearts and minds of officials or derail the implementation of racial-state logics. Rather, these testimonials collectively constitute a black public counternarrative of *Soul!* The political agency of this counternarrative consisted of a refusal of the state's authority to define *Soul!*'s meaning, let alone adjudicate its value for its black viewers. Indeed, one of the character-istics of this counternarrative was its vivid sense of *Soul!* as a program that had worked indelible changes on its audience. From this point of view, although *Soul!* was officially ending, the program would continue to have effects, through its place in the memories and sensibilities of those it had touched.

Although Haizlip lacked Brown's political connections, in focusing his energies in early 1973 on the viewer campaign for *Soul!*, he might thus be seen as possessing a keener appreciation of both racial-state logics and the power of what Fred Moten and Stefano Harney have called the "undercommons," the space or place of critique associated with "fugitivity" and fugitive subjects—those who refuse their inter-pellation by the state.[54] Haizlip had always seemed to understand the relationship of *Soul!* to its institutional benefactors, including Chan-nel 13, as one of necessary and inevitable tension, not unlike the rela-tionship of black activists and artists to their white patrons since the days of Phillis Wheatley. At the moment of *Soul!*'s defunding, when the state was defining and defending its interests in moving on from the radicalism of 1960s and early 1970s social movements, he may well also have understood that the struggle for *Soul!* lay elsewhere than in the lobbying of broadcasting officials, the picketing of CPB offices, or the issuing of defiant statements to the press. This is not to downplay the significance of these endeavors, traditional expressions of politi-cal agency in the liberal public sphere, but to argue that they ought to be seen alongside an overlapping yet distinct struggle for *Soul!* waged within the very black counterpublic spaces that the program had a hand in mediating. It is to argue that continued funding for the show was but one manifestation—a particularly narrowly constructed and time-bound one—of a larger struggle that neither began with *Soul!* nor would conclude with it.

It is in light of this notion of a struggle for *Soul!* that goes beyond a petitioning of the state and is embedded in the longer black freedom struggle that I approach the final *Soul!* episode, titled "To the People, Thank You"—and with it, Haizlip's notion of the historical necessity of the program's "disappearance." As Haizlip announced at the outset of the hour-long live show, in light of the CPB decision, the *Soul!* production staff had decided "that it was time that we sort of reminisced a bit, and that we began the root of documenting our own history, because we know from what we see in the media, from the response we've had from the people, that *Soul!* will be included in the television history of this decade when things go down."[55] "When things go down" is a phrase that might signify the writing of history—the putting of things down on paper—or might be read as a tantalizing and suggestive colloquialism for social revolution. From the viewpoint of the latter interpretation, "when things go down" is evocative both of 1973—when it was still possible to refer to future social revolution without the distancing irony of post–civil rights discourse—and of new social formations and social relations, of history as it would be written in an imagined future. Following from this introduction, the episode both looked backward to *Soul!*'s beginnings and forward to its future legacy. There was a video clip from the very first *Soul!* episode of Patti LaBelle and the Bluebelles singing "Somewhere over the Rainbow," the singers' matching gowns and bouffant wigs or hairdos exuding an air of antique charm at a distance of only five years, a visual reminder of the aesthetic and political changes since 1968. Closing the circle, Haizlip read a telegraph received earlier that day from LaBelle and her then-husband Armistead Edwards, whose message—"Although it's over, it's not the end. Black seeds keep on growing"—encapsulated the evening's wistful but unbowed mood. Also featured were a brief tribute to the saxophonist King Curtis, the *Soul!* musical director who had died suddenly in 1971; readings by Haizlip of passages from the works of the novelist Charles Wright; and a lively round-robin reading by members of the *Soul!* staff of a selection of viewers' poems, clearly inspired by the many *Soul!* episodes spotlighting poetry.

In the course of the show, Haizlip also took time to call out the names of "all of these beautiful people who have given me all these vibrations," from co-workers to friends to family. The list extended from *Soul!*'s original and current directors, Ivan Curry and Stan Lathan, and its longtime hair stylist, floor manager, sound man, announcer, control-room technicians, and secretarial staff to Langston Hughes, the writer whom Haizlip acknowledged as "a great inspiration" and "the father of all this." The tribute to Hughes as a progenitor of the television show fit nicely with the evening's theme of "documenting our own history," linking *Soul!* to an ongoing legacy of black cultural representation that specifically addressed itself to black people, and did so in a self-consciously accessible manner. It also hinted at a submerged genealogy of black queer culture and social networks as an important, if unacknowledged, thread linking the New Negro era to the era of black arts and Black Power.

Although he spent much of the final episode thanking others, Haizlip drew on a single viewer's letter to express audiences' collective gratitude for five years of *Soul!* shows. The writer was "Ruth McLean, a loyal fan,"[56] and Haizlip read her letter—addressed to "Ellis and Staff"—in its entirety, which took several minutes. By reading McLean's letter aloud, Haizlip entered it into the *Soul!* archives, much as the reading of a document in court enters it into the official record. In this way, he enacted his intention of rendering the end of *Soul!* as the beginning of a process of self-documentation.

McLean opened her letter by acknowledging that she had initially been a reluctant viewer of *Soul!*, having expected a program on "educational (yuk!)" TV to feature pedantic lectures on dry topics, like "musicology in Eastern Africa," "or worse still . . . a bunch of Negro intellectuals rambling on about the comparison of the first Reconstruction with the then-contemporary political scene." (Knowing laughter from the studio audience followed the producer's reading of these lines.) But she came to appreciate *Soul!* as a "friendly" and "relaxed" weekly visitor to her home, delivering "images of myself" in the form of a wide range of guest performers, and McLean cited by name Wilson Pickett, the Last Poets, Roberta Flack, Barbara Ann Teer, Bill Withers, Amiri Baraka, Marion Williams, Nikki Giovanni, and "that fantastic lady who taught me how to make a natural facial." "Until your show, I didn't even understand the creative possibilities of a TV camera," she wrote, noting that via *Soul!* she found herself "awakened" by "subjects I thought would put me to sleep." Over time, even WNET, a station she had previously avoided, came to seem not "so bad." In a strikingly lyrical section, McLean explained the meaning of the phrase "there is no alternative to *Soul!*," a phrase she repeated three times in the letter. "I'm not trying to say that I won't ever see black people on TV" again should *Soul!* be canceled, she averred. "While we are everywhere eating soup and cleaning our own floors and ovens and hosting comedy shows with white guest stars and being guest stars on shows with white hosts, and intellectualizing about problems trying to sound profound, it's just that I won't see black people creating, searching, and acting instead of . . . researching and reacting. There is no alternative to Soul."

McLean's letter spoke eloquently to the qualities of *Soul!* that were most highly prized and sought after by Haizlip. Through the metaphor of being roused from sleep, she validated his thesis that performance quickened the consciousness of the attentive audience member, offering insight as well as a pleasurable aesthetic experience. In describing *Soul!* as a trusted friend who has "physically come to my house in person to visit," she endorsed the show's defiance of educational TV's convention of imagining viewers as students and *Soul!*'s attempt to produce a felt sense of intimacy between viewers and TV representations. And in her testimony to the power of a diverse group of *Soul!* guests to provide "images of myself," she confounded simplistic notions of minority representation as a narrowly self-affirming mirror, attesting to TV spectatorship and listening as complex practices of negotiation, identification, and disidentification.[57]

In its allusions to other television programming, moreover, McLean's letter subtly refuted the racial-state reasoning of the arbiters of public television and their pursuit of the integration of representation. In her letter, McLean expressed her critique in the form of a contradiction, in which "we are everywhere" on television yet somehow still not empowered to determine the manner of "our" representation—that is, both everywhere and nowhere at once. In 1973 an American could turn on a television and find black people depicted as consumers, representative in their ordinariness ("eating soup and cleaning our floors and ovens"—as on TV commercials), or portrayed as celebrities, living proof of the nation's liberalism and its progress on racial issues ("hosting comedy shows with white guest stars"—a likely reference to Flip Wilson's popular program). Yet neither of these images of blackness—neither the black subject as a generic American consumer nor the black subject as extraordinary embodiment of the American dream—satisfied McLean's desire, which she characterized in terms of *Soul!*'s representations of black people "creating, searching, and acting": being, outside of the imperative of being for the state or for capitalism. In other words, neither image offered resistance to the absorption of the black subject within racial-state logic or its use as a means of shoring up American nationalist self-regard for progress on racial issues.

Although we cannot know for sure what prompted Haizlip to select McLean's letter to read on air from among the thousands he had received, we can nevertheless infer from her missive's refrain a resistance to incorporation and accommodation that I have associated with Haizlip's strategy of taking the question of *Soul!*'s future directly "to the people" instead of conceding to CPB bureaucrats. Haizlip had been advancing the themes of McLean's letter—survival in the face of loss; the refusal to be limited to or defined by dominant representations; the stubborn belief in alternatives, even when none existed—during the course of several episodes leading up to the March 7 show. For example, toward the end of "Wherever We May Be," the evocatively titled February 1973 episode featuring Stokely Carmichael, the self-exiled former leader of the Student Nonviolent Coordinating Committee (SNCC), Haizlip informed his guest that *Soul!* "probably won't be here much longer." When Carmichael asked why, implying that there might be political stones yet unturned in the fight for the show's survival, Haizlip demurred. "Maybe it is our evolutionary process that's necessary," he mused, speaking at once to Carmichael and to *Soul!*'s viewing audience. "And it's been beautiful. We will find a way to communicate and get our message through."[58] The following week, on an episode titled "Alone Again" that featured the singer Esther Phillips (figure 5.1) and a spirited staged reading of Toni Cade Bambara's short story "The Johnson Girls," Haizlip expanded on his notion of *Soul!*'s demise as part of a necessary "evolutionary process," which did not preclude its ongoing ability to "communicate." About forty minutes into the episode, following Phillips's performance of Gil Scott-Heron's "Home Is Where the Hatred Is" and the Billie Holiday–Arthur Herzog classic "God Bless the Child," Haizlip took a moment to update viewers on the progress of *Soul!*'s efforts to regain its funding. He thanked them for their ongoing support, briefly reviewed the show's history and the role of the CPB, and urged those watching to continue to send in letters and other testimonials.

5.1. Esther Phillips and a friend relaxing backstage, February 1971.

"Sometimes it is necessary in the evolution of things to disappear," he noted, closely echoing the language he had used with Carmichael. "We will continue to communicate."

In these and other comments offered during *Soul!*'s final weeks, Haizlip addressed audiences in a prophetic register, echoing the language of the era's black liberation theologians, who articulated traditional Christian concepts of deliverance and redemption to present-day struggles for social justice. Locating *Soul!*'s own troubles in the context of a much longer arc of history, he went beyond assuring viewers of the program's inclusion in the chronicles of late twentieth-century television, casting the imminent "disappearance" of *Soul!* as one chapter in the narrative of black political and social development ("the evolution of things"). According to these measures, the last episode of *Soul!*, for all of its finality, was not an ending but one step in an ongoing process (like the "black seeds" about which LaBelle and her husband had written). The CPB could take away the money necessary to produce *Soul!*, but it did not control the black cultural and spiritual wealth that the show had displayed and nurtured; nor did the state have purchase over

Soul!'s audience, in and through whose consciousness and memory the show would live on. Furthermore, in his repeated reassurances to viewers that *Soul!* would "continue to communicate," Haizlip suggested that the immaterial qualities of the program—the knowledge and feelings it had produced; and the aesthetic pleasures, surprises, and challenges it had offered—could not be squelched by the withdrawal of the material means of the production—the "cold and gray" electrons.

There was something prophetic, too, in Haizlip's embrace of "disappearance" as a necessary strategy of survival. Recalling the fugitiveness of black diasporic peoples, from the captive Africans of the Middle Passage and the maroon communities of Haiti to the 1960s radicals who had chosen or been forced to take refuge underground, disappearance, in the sense in which the producer used the term, was more akin to vanishing from sight than it was to ceasing to exist. If the lessons of Ralph Ellison's *Invisible Man* or even Hughes's early poem "I, Too" were to be taken seriously, then disappearance might be a strategy of regeneration, of the consolidation of resources in anticipation of more opportune circumstances.[59] As a student of live performance, Haizlip knew well that materially fleeting events—such as concerts and theatrical productions—nevertheless might have enduring afterlives. Disappearing was what performances, by their very nature, did; their evanescence was indeed constitutive of their affective power. In suggesting that it might be necessary for *Soul!* to disappear, then, Haizlip was reframing the program's 1973 cancellation as an opportunity both to reflect on what the program had accomplished and to create space for new projects and new visions responding to changing conditions of possibility. As the producer's allusion to an "evolutionary process" hinted, allowing *Soul!* to disappear did not have to amount to yielding to those who, from the outset, had wanted the TV program to go away. Rather, it might be part of a natural process of adaptation to changing times and new racial climates.

A *Soul!* tribute in the British music magazine *Melody Maker*, co-authored by Labelle manager Vicki Wickham, put a related spin on *Soul!*'s demise, noting that the program's unique position on American public broadcasting also rendered it uniquely susceptible to the withdrawal of government support. "The show is basically music but it envelops all sorts of entertainment and communication," the article explained for British readers. "Thus, 45 minutes in concert with Harold Melvin or Billy Preston may coincide with the view of activist Stokely Carmichael or Muslim leader Louis Farrakhan of the nation [*sic*] of Islam. Its asset, however, is also its handicap in a sense. It pays for its freedom by being dependent on donations, grants, and funds, and after five years on the air the money has run out."[60]

It is with this idea of *Soul!*'s disappearance in mind that I circle back to Haizlip's concept of vibrations. Like *soul, vibrations* was a common expression of the era, a term for designating interpersonal affects and energies, as when Brian Wilson of the Beach Boys sang about "picking up good vibrations" from an object of desire in the group's epic 1966 ode to summer romance. In addition to being of interest to writers like Vertamae Grosvenor (figure 5.2)—a frequent *Soul!* guest who is best known as the author (as Vertamae Smart-Grosvenor) of *Vibration Cooking: or, the Travel Notes of a Geechee Girl*—vibrations appealed to avant-garde musicians from Sun Ra (with whom Grosvenor had briefly performed) to John Cage, who were drawn to the creative possibilities of thinking about music as an effect of the vibration of sound waves in space and, in the case of listening to music, in contact with human bodies. Cage, for example, had been fascinated with the notion of the atmosphere or air as a dynamic sonic environment, both heard and unheard by human ears. In his compositions and performances he had probed the notion of bodies as organic machines capable of both producing and receiving vibrations; during explorations in the 1950s, he visited Harvard University's anechoic chamber, a space designed to resist sonic resonance so that scientists could perfect the capabilities of various weapons systems.

Sun Ra had taken his explorations of vibrations in a more overtly political direction than either Cage or Wilson, conceptualizing black music as a means of detoxifying a sonic atmosphere poisoned by racism and other forms of domination. In Ra's dense and sometimes opaque theorizations, human beings were instruments capable of giving off the wrong or the right vibrations, of producing sounds with the potential

5.2. Vertamae Grosvenor, author of *Vibration Cooking: or, the Travel Notes of a Geechee Girl*, during her turn as *Soul!* guest host, April 1971.

to amplify or diminish sonic discord. For these musicians, as well as for other artists of the period, the concept of vibrations was a way of conceptualizing sound as simultaneously audible and inaudible, material and immaterial, ephemeral and persistent. The turn to vibrations opened up new vistas for musicians who saw in these complexities ways of thinking about music beyond conventional notions of music making, listening, or even hearing.[61]

Haizlip conceptualized vibrations along similar lines, using the word to designate the affective ambience enacted by particular people or events, and associating it with art's—and especially music's—ability to bring people together through shared aesthetic experience. *Vibrations* referred to music's soul-stirring as well as body-stirring capacities, and to its insistently diasporic quality of communicating across national borders and linguistic traditions. Not unlike Sun Ra, who understood the social environment as an inherently sonic one, Haizlip had been drawn to thinking about musical vibrations in terms of their ability to shape and infuse social relations by producing warm and welcoming—or cold and impersonal—environments; such notions had been essential to his design of *Soul!* as a show centered on music. In so doing, as I have argued throughout this book, he recognized both the power and the limitations of conventional modes of political education and persuasion. Music could be "more valuable than a three-hour lecture"[62] on Black Power precisely because it communicated in an affective and embodied register, not just in a rational or an intellectual one.

In his comments to journalists covering Soul at the Center (figure 5.3), the 1972 Lincoln Center performing arts festival that was an outgrowth of the television show, Haizlip used the figure of vibrations to talk about his hopes that performance, despite its inevitable and defining evanescence, would leave enduring impressions—that is, both affective and material marks. Alluding to the marginalization of African Americans in the U.S. cultural imaginary, he told a *New York Times* reporter that he expected Soul at the Center to "leave vibrations . . . that will make it impossible for culture to be defined in New York without black people."[63] Similarly, in his brief but striking "Note from the Producer" that was included in festival programs, Haizlip characterized Soul at the Center in terms of a broader ambition to change popular perceptions of symbolically saturated civic spaces. Recalling how, as a nine-year-old Washingtonian, he had witnessed Marian Anderson's historic 1939 concert on the National Mall, and how that event had awakened in him a sense of the right of black people to claim the grand spaces of the racially segregated federal city as their own, he described Soul at the Center in terms of its ability to affect Alice Tully and Philharmonic Halls well into the future. "I do hope," he wrote, "that we are able to fill some of these dignified and solemn buildings we are being offered with vibrations so strong, so mean, that never will another enter without acknowledging our presence here."[64]

Haizlip's ambition of filling Lincoln Center with the vibrations of black performance reverberated richly with his hopes for *Soul!*, as a program that might also leave a mark—both on the history of television and on ordinary viewers, who would carry its vibrations forward in memory. How can something both disappear and continue to communicate? The concept of vibrations was a means through which Haizlip conceptualized the paradoxes of historicity, temporality, and

5.3. Ellis Haizlip in the plaza at Lincoln Center, summer 1972.

performance. And although it has not (yet) been the case that *Soul!* has been especially well remembered in the annals of U.S. television, public broadcasting, or the black arts and Black Power movements, Haizlip's conviction of the necessity of the occasional disappearing act as a strategy of refusal presents us with a resonant metaphor for thinking about cultural survival in an era notable for its emergent narratives of color blindness and the postracial state.

Conclusion

Those first early Black television programs set the
pace and showed what can be achieved. It is imperative that
those ideas and ideals, reinforced with new ones, rise again,
phoenix-like out of the ashes of white media racism, which
stands as the electronic extension of the great malaise—
national, institutionalized racism.
—Sheila Smith Hobson,
"The Rise and Fall of Blacks in Serious Television"

So we remember Ellis as we remember the
times when we were winning. When revolution
was the main trend in the world today!
—Amiri Baraka, "The Soul Brother"

The postmortems of minority public television programs of the era
immediately after 1968—most of which, like *Soul!,* were defunded or
terminated for other reasons within five years of being launched—
began as early as 1969. How is it that the late 1960s could have contained the conditions of possibility of programs like *Soul!* as well as
the conditions of possibility of such programs' demise? Such was the
question being posed by the editors of *Freedomways,* which devoted
its third issue of 1974 to "The Black Image in the Mass Media." Picking up on the themes of the letter by the *Soul!* viewer Ruth McLean,

which Haizlip read aloud in the program's final broadcast, the editors proposed that the new images of black people in contemporary movies, plays, and television shows were, in "the final analysis, old images . . . refined and put into new packages," creating "the illusion of heightened democracy, social equality, and establishment acceptance of Black 'Culture.'"[1] Sheila Smith Hobson, producer of the public-affairs program *Like It Is*—a survivor of this period—that aired as a local show on WABC in New York City, made a strikingly similar claim in her leading essay in the issue of *Freedomways*, arguing that although black people "will never again be invisible on the home screen and in this society," the challenges of black representation on television and in other media had therefore shifted rather than been resolved.[2] Or, as McLean had put it in her letter to Haizlip, by spring 1973 black people were simultaneously everywhere on television—in advertisements, sitcoms, and at the helms of their own network variety shows—and nowhere, in the sense that television had incorporated black images while leaving black TV producers (creative workers in the largest sense) and viewers behind.

The questions that haunted the contributors to *Freedomways* in 1974 also haunt this book and are evoked in its title, *It's Been Beautiful*. If the visibility of black people on television has no necessary or stable relation to social change—if, in fact, such visibility may render racism itself more "sinisterly subtle," as Hobson put it—then what, if anything, were shows such as *Soul!* good for?[3] Conversely, if Haizlip was right in forecasting the program's disappearance as a necessary part of an ongoing struggle—what Amiri Baraka, at the time of the producer's death, characterized as "our jagged rise and fall and rerise and refall, up and down the racial mountain"—then how might we conceptualize the program's enduring vibrations? What does it mean, as Baraka asked in 1991, that "we are still looking for our Soul to return to the media"?[4]

One way of approaching this paradox is to note the changing fortunes of black performers, particularly the musicians who consumed a majority of *Soul!*'s airtime, in the period between spring 1968 and summer 1973. In the original Ford Foundation grant application that led to *Soul!*, WNDT's Christopher "Kit" Lukas made an argument for the new program rooted in the observation that television—both commercial and noncommercial—lacked outlets for black performing artists. But by the time Haizlip and the other members of the *Soul!* team, many of them soon to be off WNET/Channel 13's payroll, were putting the finishing touches on Soul '73, a reprise of 1972's Soul at the Center festival at Lincoln Center, they confronted a new set of difficulties born out of the mainstream success of many of these very performers.

By 1973 audiences for black musicians had spread from the so-called chocolate cities where people of color were concentrated to the vanilla suburbs. Although black and Latino performers still faced considerable hurdles, young white people's growing acceptance of them meant that these performers were increasingly included in established cultural programming. Haizlip acknowledged as much in a meeting with Lincoln Center staff after Soul '73, whose program had included acts like War, Eddie Palmieri, Billy Preston, the Mighty Clouds of Joy, and the Spinners. George Wein's ten-day Newport Jazz Festival in New York (an outgrowth of the original Newport Jazz series) "causes great competition . . . as 90% of the artists of N.J. are black and the festival runs very close to" the Lincoln Center event. Although the meeting notes do not provide specific details, they record the fact that three of the performers or groups who appeared at Soul '73 actually withdrew from previous commitments to Wein to accept the invitation of Haizlip and his coproducer, Gerry Bledsoe.[5] However, the Newport festival, attempting to keep abreast of changing audience demographics for and definitions of jazz, drew other acts that had previously appeared on *Soul!*, including Roberta Flack, Stevie Wonder, Rahsaan Roland Kirk, and Jimmy Witherspoon. And the Pointer Sisters, who were scheduled to appear at Alice Tully Hall, canceled their Soul '73 engagement when they got a last-minute chance to appear on *The Flip Wilson Show*. The *New York Times* wryly noted that a July 1973 "Jazz and Soul on the Island" event—part of the Newport Jazz Festival in New York—was bringing some of the festival's biggest acts, including Duke Ellington, Aretha Franklin, Donny Hathaway, and Tito Puente, not to the Caribbean or even to Rhode Island, but to Uniondale, Long Island, home of the Nassau Coliseum.[6]

Yet to stop here—with the idea that the successes of the civil rights movement, in bringing about the integration of mass media representations and creating ways for white audiences to embrace black performers, ushered in a period that rendered "black" television shows or performing arts festivals redundant—would be misleading. As this book has argued, the goal of *Soul!*, especially once Haizlip refined Lukas's original vision for the program, was never reducible to visibility or image—or even, to return to Hobson's critique, to the amelioration of black people's material well-being, however much the *Soul!* staff also may have had that well-being in mind when they produced episodes. As an enterprise that emerged during a transitional moment in the black freedom movement, when new actors were critiquing the scope and tactics of the earlier civil rights generation, *Soul!* was both too modest and too worldly to imagine that a television program could heal the world, and too cognizant of what Baraka called the "Sisyphus syndrome" of African American history to imagine progress outside of a dialectic that demanded constant labors of reimagination and reinvention.[7] The last episode's tone of gentle but defiant resignation, and Haizlip's vague but pointed promises that the show would "continue to communicate," constituted an embrace of the notion that "evolution" was inevitable and that loss was an element of survival.[8]

One of *Soul!*'s crowning achievements was its ability to communicate the structures of feeling that were associated with a golden age in black American history, when it was too soon to know when this particular trip up the mountain would end and how it would turn out. *Soul!* galvanized a black audience that could not be taken for granted but had to be encouraged and cultivated over time. "I can recall Nikki Giovanni's emergence, her first show, and the response that resonated through the telephone and people calling each other and talking about it after having seen the show," recalls Harold Haizlip, the producer's cousin, an educator who also hosted *Soul!* early in its first season. "You just had a sense that here was a person that *we* could claim, who was one of us talking about us to us, not to the exclusion of others—perhaps to the edification of others. But the message and symbolism were all about validating the black community in all of its difference."[9]

In its showcasing of artists and intellectuals who were conduits of such collective self-validation, *Soul!* enacted the era's sense of possibility and beauty despite material restraint and abiding evidence of ugliness in American society. More than specific performers or specific conversations, viewers tuned in each week to see and hear sounds and images that fed their sense of being part of a larger project of black self-redefinition to meet the evolving challenges of the present. "For all the talk I heard about Black Power, *this* was Black Power," remembers Walter Fields, one of the program's viewers. On *Soul!*, unlike on other TV shows, Fields saw "black people being confident, intelligent, and having full control over their destiny."[10]

The fact of specific black performers' appearances on *Soul!* were, from this perspective, less important than what the performers did when they took the stage and how audiences both in the studio and in the various locations where the show was consumed "interreacted" with them. *Soul!* was a showcase, but it was neither a museum of past achievement nor a televised appeal to traditional public broadcasting audiences to belatedly recognize the contributions or existence of black culture. Indeed, the restlessness of Haizlip's vision, and the producer's openness to multiple approaches of imagining soul, allowed the show to change over time, as he and his staff sought out new sources of creative energy or took risks in bringing artists and intellectuals of different sensibilities and styles into conversation. The fact that all of this happened on public television, the bastion of culture in the vast TV wasteland, was all the more fitting and renders *Soul!*'s achievements all the more meaningful.

Soul! created a television space where black people—imagined to include Latinos of various hues who were seeking alternatives to whiteness, black women marginalized by nationalist conceptions of both the public and private spheres, and black gays and lesbians rendered as "unnatural" or "freakish"—could see, hear, and almost feel each other. This is not to characterize *Soul!* as a utopian enterprise untainted by internal disputes, or to say that its makers ever imagined public television as a safe harbor. Yet neither did the producers of *Soul!* underestimate the opportunity to imagine what public television could be and do if it assumed a black public. *Soul!* was also an important nerve center of New York City's black political and cultural networks of the late 1960s and early 1970s. The *Soul!* set in midtown Manhattan—and various satellite locations, including Haizlip's Fifth Avenue apartment—functioned as a hybrid of Spirit House, Baraka's Newark-based black arts community theater and arts space (home to experimental performances by Sun Ra and many others), and the Factory, Andy Warhol's meeting place for artists and musicians—with Haizlip (figure C.1), the queer man at *Soul!*'s center, as its muse and its primary social connector.[11]

Through the social networks that the program sustained, *Soul!* enabled the careers of actors, dancers, documentarians, writers, and fashion designers as well as, closer to home, TV camera operators, directors, production associates, writers, set designers, booking agents, hair dressers, and secretaries. Thanks in part to the platform that *Soul!* provided, Giovanni would become one of her generation's most enduring and popular poets and Stan Lathan, following a circuitous path that led from New York to Hollywood, would come to coproduce HBO's *Def Poetry Jam*, a show that channeled Haizlip's program in its celebration of poetry. Arsenio Hall, hired to do magic tricks on a 1971 episode after the author and performer Vertamae Grosvenor recognized the teenager's talents, would of course make history in 1989 as the host of his eponymous late-night variety program on the Fox cable network (an act he is repeating as I write). Yet, in an irony that should cause us to question the notion of a straight arrow of progress—or a notion of careers that proceed from triumph to triumph—Hall's run was derailed when controversy erupted over a 1994 guest appearance by Louis Farrakhan, the Nation of Islam leader, whom Haizlip had warmly interviewed on *Soul!* more than twenty years earlier.

A full account of the legacies of *Soul!* and the changing conditions of television, popular culture, and U.S. racial politics would take up several other volumes. However, it seems fitting to end this book by acknowledging that despite many and loud pronouncements to the contrary, we are living in a period that resonates with an earlier moment's vibrations—its achievements as well as its unresolved challenges. "It's been beautiful," Haizlip said, by way of putting a period to the television show and a soul—and *Soul!*—era that was also on the wane. But as his work reminds us, soul was and is never far from the center.

C.1. Ellis Haizlip posing outside at Lincoln Center, summer 1972.

Acknowledgments

My deepest thanks and admiration go to the makers of *Soul!* As a researcher, I have been continually impressed by the willingness of people who are total strangers to me to talk about subjects near and dear to their hearts. I especially thank those who provided the foundation for this book by graciously agreeing to speak to me about their work with Haizlip and the program, or their memories of watching it: Ilunga Adell, the late Amiri Baraka, Nick Besink, Edward "Sonny" Bivens, Alonzo Brown Jr., Kephra Burns, Ward Chamberlain, Ivan Curry, Carlos de Jesus, Leslie Demus, George Faison, Walter Fields, Nikki Giovanni, Loretta Greene, Vertamae Grosvenor, Harold Haizlip, Thomas Allen Harris, Anthony Heilbut, Nona Hendryx, Alice Hille (LaBrie), Charles Hobson, Mae Jackson, Al Johnson, Florence Ladd, Stan Lathan, Loretta Long, Louis Massiah, Patrick McGinnis, Donald McKayle, Carman Moore, Valerie Patterson, Alvin Poussaint, Bobby Sanabria, Cheryl Sanders, Sherry Santifer, Sarah-Ann Shaw, Andrew Stern, Roland Washington, Florene Wiley, Jack Willis, and Camille Yarbrough. I must single out for special thanks four special people—Anna Horsford, Felipe Luciano, Christopher "Kit" Lukas, and Novella Nelson—for encouraging, guiding, occasionally correcting, and implicitly trusting me. I literally could not have pursued this research without their assistance. Although I bear full responsibility for this work, I have tried to honor the special place of *Soul!* and Ellis Haizlip in their hearts. I hope I have done justice to their memories here.

Among the many "makers" of *Soul!* is Chester Higgins, whose beautiful photographs immeasurably enrich this book and inspire the words on its pages. Before this collaboration with Chester became a reality, he welcomed me into his home and shared his personal archives and recollections of *Soul!* I am honored and humbled to have Chester as a contributor to this book and can only hope that the written text "sings" even a bit like his magnificent images.

Above all else, writing takes time, and I would like to thank the organizations that provided me with the great gift of time to research and write this book. My deepest gratitude goes to the National Endowment of the Humanities and the John Simon Guggenheim Memorial Foundation for year-long fellowships, without which I might still be working on this book. I am deeply obliged to them for their belief in this project. The Columbian College of George Washington University (GWU) also generously supported my leave from teaching and service.

Although writing is a solitary practice, in fact writers are never really alone. The list of people who have kept me company, literally and intellectually, during the writing of this book is long. It includes Sarah Banet-Weiser, Daphne Brooks, Jayna Brown, Garnette Cadogan, Ramzi Fawaz, Ruth Feldstein, Farah Jasmine Griffin, Paul Gardullo, Herman Gray, J. Jack Halberstam, Matt Jacobson, Jennifer James, Meta D. Jones, Jason King, Josh Kun, Andrea Levine, Antonio López, Kip Lornell, Maureen Mahon, Melani McAlister, Charles McGovern, E. Ethelbert Miller, Jim Miller, Fred Moten, the late José Esteban Muñoz, Mark Anthony Neal, Ann Powers, Sonnet Retman, Gus Stadler, Jenny Stoever, David Suisman, Karen Tongson, Sherry Tucker, Alexandra Vazquez, Oliver Wang, and Calvin Warren. Robin Edgerton and Eric Weisbard were sources of crucial information about *Soul!* in the earliest stages of this project; they exemplify the spirit of intellectual community at its best. I have learned much from Meghan Drury and Elizabeth Pittman, my former GWU graduate students, and I am indebted to Marilena Zackheos, also a GWU PhD, who took on the tedious task one semester of compiling data on *Soul!* episodes. I could not have gotten through the arduous, if exhilarating, process of selecting a few dozen of Chester's images from several hundred contact sheets without the eagle eye, expert opinion, and good cheer of Amy Albert.

The Black Sonic Feminisms Seminar at Princeton University in 2013 was an especially nurturing and inspiring experience for me, and it occurred at a crucial time in the writing of this book. Thank you so much to Daphne Brooks for supporting feminist scholarship on black popular music culture, and to Nina Eidsheim, Farah Jasmine Griffin, Emily Lordi, Mendi Obadike, Imani Perry, and Salamishah Tillet for their acute critical intellectual engagement and their supportive camaraderie.

Thank you to Bill Bragin and Jennifer Sternheimer of the Lincoln Center for the Performing Arts for organizing a wonderful Soul at the Center fortieth anniversary event there in summer 2012, and thank you to the inspiring Felipe Luciano for agreeing to participate. Thank you to filmmaker Melissa Haizlip, for her encouragement and shared obsession with *Soul!*

Many people have facilitated my access to materials—an act of faith in an age when materials easily find their way on to the Internet. I offer my deepest thanks to Virginia Fowler, Alice LaBrie, and Kit Lukas for opening up their personal collections—especially Kit, who graciously invited me to his home to sort through materials, and who was instrumental in getting this project off the ground. Various archivists, librarians, and collectors have assisted me enormously along the way: Thank you to Harry Weinger (Universal Music); Deborah Willis (New York University); Joe Basile, Robin Edgerton, Winter Shanck, and Wayne Taylor (Channel 13, WNET); Alston Gonzalez, Jennifer Morris, and Tanajala Penn (Anacostia Community Museum); Paul Kelly (Rock's Backpages); Thomas Connors, Michael Henry, and Karen King (National Public Broadcasting Archives); Idelle Nissila, Mary Ann Quinn, and Judy Russo (Ford Foundation Archives); Don Chan, Judith Johnson, and Marian Skokan (Lincoln Center for the Performing Arts); Diane Paradiso (WPA Film Library); Steve Behrens (Current.org); and Ruta Abolins (Walter J. Brown Media Archives and Peabody Awards Collection).

I researched and thought about his book (mostly thought about it!) during a term as chair of the English department at GWU. I thank my colleagues in English and American studies at GWU for giving me an intellectually lively and personally supportive home base for my work. Thanks especially to Constance Kibler, the English Department manager, who made administrative work bearable and even fun, and to Jeffrey Cohen and Robert McRuer, my able predecessor and successor, for your patient and good-humored support.

My sincere thanks go to Ken Wissoker at Duke University Press, music lover extraordinaire, for supporting this project from its inception, and to Elizabeth Ault and Danielle Szulczewski at the press for guidance through the publication process. Jeanne Ferris was a wonderful copy editor—a gift in this age of shrinking budgets for publication.

It is a convention to save the dearest for last. To my parents, Marlene Wald and Max Wald, thank you, as ever, for your abiding love and support. To Scott Barash: How handy for me that my beloved partner in life, in addition to his many other wonderful qualities, possesses a quasi-encyclopedic knowledge of 1970s music! You never cease to impress me. My love for you, and for our beautiful son Zachary Adam Barash, is profound and enduring.

Notes

Introduction

1. New York public television station WNDT was the precursor to WNET, which was formed out of a 1970 merger of WNDT and New York production center NET; both before and after the merger, the station was known to viewers as Channel 13, or simply "Thirteen." In this book, I use "Channel 13" to refer to both entities—since that is how most viewers referred to the station—and reserve "WNDT" for references to the source of *Soul!* broadcasts before 1970.

2. Thanks to Garnette Cadogan for his insights into *Soul!*'s popularity in Jamaica.

3. Lisa Jones, "Hot Buttered 'Soul,'" *Village Voice*, March 12, 1991.

4. Readers will note that I alternate between using the terms *black* and *African American* in this book. Sometimes my choice is pegged to a sense of historical authenticity; I generally use the term *black* because *African American* did not come into wide circulation until after the historical period this book covers. At other times, I mean to draw attention to the historical moment of my own writing and highlight the historical contingency of collective self-naming as a dialectical enterprise. All quoted material reproduces the language of the original work cited.

5. See Ouellette, *Viewers Like You?*; Heitner, *Black Power TV*; Ledbetter, *Made Possible By—*; Lott, "Documenting Social Issues"; Abdul, *Famous Black Entertainers of Today*.

6. Fearn-Banks, *Historical Dictionary of African-American Television*.

7. Charles Hobson and Sheila Smith, "The Living Arts," *Tuesday*, March 1970, n.p. (clipping courtesy of Alice [Hille] LaBrie, from her personal collec-

tion). Hobson was a producer of *Inside Bedford-Stuyvesant*, a production of New York's WNEW that aired locally from 1968 to 1970. Sheila Smith (later Sheila Smith Hobson) was one of the original producers of *Like It Is*, a local black public-affairs program produced by WABC in New York that aired from 1968 to 2011. As I discuss in chapter 1, some white Channel 13 officials were uncomfortable with *Soul!*'s mix of talk and entertainment, wanting the show to focus more on public affairs. A somewhat different contemporary critique of *Soul!* is represented by James Haskins, a black writer, who questioned whether access to television was restricted to black entertainers. See Haskins, "New Black Images in the Mass Media."

8. Fred Ferretti, "Harris Polls Weigh Effects of Ethnic Programming," *New York Times*, July 4, 1969. See also Heitner, *Black Power TV*, 168. For a critique of the assumptions that underwrite audience surveys, see Ang, *Desperately Seeking the Audience*. On the difficulty of theorizing extradiegetic "aspects of cultural reception" among black consumers of visual media, see Stewart, "Negroes Laughing at Themselves?," 656.

9. Interview with Sanabria. Thanks to Channel 13's Wayne Taylor for helping me connect with Sanabria and other *Soul!* fans who posted comments on the station's website.

10. Interview with Washington.

11. Interview with Patterson.

12. Interview with Fields.

13. Williams, *Marxism and Literature*, 128, 132.

14. Lisa Jones, "Hot Buttered 'Soul.'"

15. Roland Washington recalls being impressed that the male lead singer of Soul Excitement! was permitted to take the stage in 1969 wearing a vest with nothing underneath (interview with Washington).

16. Quoted in Lisa Jones, "Hot Buttered 'Soul.'" In her study of women poets and the black arts era, Cheryl Clarke, inspired by a poem of Gwendolyn Brooks, envisions "Mecca" as a metaphor for this as-yet uncharted place, one which is "as much to be struggled toward as struggled for." Clarke, *"After Mecca,"* 2.

17. Works that have particularly shaped my thinking include R. Ferguson, *The Reorder of Things*; Muñoz, *Cruising Utopia*; Gould, *Moving Politics*; and Iton, *In Search of the Black Fantastic*.

18. Thanks to Herman Gray, the source of this phrase, in correspondence with me. This inquiry would not be possible without the indispensable works of Gray and other television scholars who have demonstrated the limitations of representational paradigms. See especially Bogle, *Primetime Blues*; Gray, *Cultural Moves* and *Watching Race*; Harper, "Extra-Special Effects"; Keeling,

The Witch's Flight; Lott, *The Invention of Race*; Torres, *Black, White, and in Color*.

19. Minow, "Television and the Public Interest."

20. The phrase "black seeds" is from a telegram sent by Patti LaBelle and her husband to Ellis Haizlip on the occasion of the program's final broadcast in March 1973. I discuss Haizlip's on-air reading of the telegram in more detail in chapter 5.

21. Interview with Nelson.

22. Ellis Haizlip, "A Proposal to the Corporation for Public Broadcasting for a Series of Black Cultural Programs," 1975, appendix C, "SOUL!," 1, folder 2, box 19, Ellis B. Haizlip Papers, Anacostia Community Museum Archives, Smithsonian Institution, Washington, D.C. (hereafter Haizlip Papers).

23. Studies of television that deeply inform or influence this study include Acham, *Revolution Televised*; Bodroghkozy, "'Is This What You Mean by Color TV?'"; Bogle, *Primetime Blues*; Gray, *Watching Race* and *Cultural Moves*; Harper, "Extra-Special Effects"; Lentz, "Quality versus Relevance; MacDonald, *Blacks and White TV*; Ongiri, *Spectacular Blackness*; Torres, *Black, White, and in Color* and *Living Color*; and Williams, *Television*.

24. See Tynan, "Fifteen Years of the Salto Mortale."

25. *The Flip Wilson Show* aired on NBC from 1970 to 1974.

26. Quoted in Robert Berkvist, "Dig It or Forget It," *New York Times*, September 15, 1968.

27. Sutherland, *The Flip Wilson Show*, 105.

28. On *American Bandstand*'s history of racial exclusion, notwithstanding the claims of its host Dick Clark that the show helped integrate television, see Delmont, *The Nicest Kids in Town*.

29. See, for example, Ledbetter, *Made Possible By—*; Ouellette, *Viewers Like You?*; Barsamian, *The Decline and Fall of Public Broadcasting*; L. Brown, *Television*; Day, *The Vanishing Vision*; and Hoynes, *Public Television for Sale*.

30. "Racial state" is a concept I derive from Omi and Winant, *Racial Formation in the United States*. I discuss the notion of the "racial state" at greater length in chapter 5.

31. "Face of public unity" is a phrase I take from Squires, "Rethinking the Black Public Sphere," 452. See also Baker, "Critical Memory and the Black Public Sphere," 16.

32. I thank Daphne Brooks for pressing me to think of the *Soul!* era as "transitional"—a concept supported by the work of Iton, *In Search of the Black Fantastic*. Calvin Warren's work prompted me to consider this book's investments in cultural politics in light of recent Afro-pessimist scholarship, such as Sexton, "The Social Life of Social Death."

33. On this point, see J. Hall, "The Long Civil Rights Movement and the Political Uses of the Past," which notes the ways the period after the passage of the 1964 Voting Rights Act and the 1965 Civil Rights Act has been retroactively rebranded as a declension from the "classical" phase of civil rights, even as this period saw the flowing of black feminist expression. Iton, *In Search of the Black Fantastic*, uses the phrase "post–civil rights" to designate the period after 1965, which he similarly sees as marked by disruptive fragmentations suppressed in the pre-1965 period.

34. For a work that similarly takes on black nationalist truisms and has deeply influenced my thinking, see R. Ferguson, *The Reorder of Things*.

35. Wallace, *Black Macho and the Myth of the Superwoman*.

36. Alan Dale, "New York Gets Its Own Soul Show," *R 'n' B World*, October 3, 1968. In its first season of broadcast, *Soul!* aired live on Thursday nights and was reaired on Sunday nights. With national distribution beginning in 1970, the day and time of weekly *Soul!* broadcasts depended on local station schedules.

37. *Soul!* #304, "Farrakhan the Minister," October 25, 1972.

38. Henderson, "The Forms of Things Unknown," 66.

39. Baker, *Blues, Ideology, and Afro-American Literature*, 82.

40. Ellis B. Haizlip, "Note From the Producer," Lincoln Center Presents Soul at the Center program, July 23–August 5, 1972, n.p. Lincoln Center for the Performing Arts Archives.

41. Ellis B. Haizlip, untitled proposal for "Black Experience Revival," submitted to Lincoln Center, February 22, 1972, n.p. Lincoln Center for the Performing Arts Archives.

42. See, especially, Baraka, "The Changing Same." On Afrofuturism, see *The Last Angel of History*, dir. John Amkofrah (First Run/Icarus Films, 1995). Although it does not engage directly with Sun Ra, Muñoz's *Cruising Utopia* advances ideas of utopian transport that are very much in an Afrofuturist vein that I associate with Ra and other experimental musicians. These similarities are illustrative of the rich scholarly associations among African American studies, Latino studies, performance studies, and queer theory.

43. My thinking about the erotic in relation to knowledge and power is shaped by black feminist theory, especially Lorde, *Sister Outsider* and *Zami*.

44. Haizlip's cousin, Cheryl Sanders, a minister and divinity school professor, likens Haizlip's intellectual, cultural, and spiritual formation in the Church of God (Holiness) in Washington, D.C., to Baldwin's formation in Harlem's storefront Pentecostalism (interview with Sanders).

45. I thank Cheryl Sanders for talking to me about Haizlip's relation to spirituality and religion. Felipe Luciano also made important observations

on this theme at a Soul at the Center symposium at Lincoln Center in August 2012. Anthony Heilbut's essay "The Children and Their Secret Closet," in *The Fan Who Knew Too Much*, is an invaluable piece on the queer roots of gospel music: Heilbut convincingly argues that the church in the civil rights era nourished queer expression, although it did not always explicitly acknowledge the queerness of that expression.

46. Quoted in Hobson and Smith, "The Living Arts."

47. Channel 13/*Soul!*, display advertisement, *New York Times*, May 1, 1969, 95.

48. Quoted in Barbara Delatiner, "Soul TV Not Black and White," *Newsday*, September 13, 1968.

49. I discovered Haizlip's producer's note while researching the gospel musician Rosetta Tharpe's 1972 appearance at Lincoln Center in the Soul at the Center festival.

50. The names of those I interviewed for this book appear in the acknowledgments. When I cite from particular interviews, information is provided in the endnotes and the list of interviews cited in the bibliography.

51. Most extant episodes of *Soul!* are available through the PBS Collection in the library's Motion Picture, Broadcast and Recorded Sound Division. (The same episodes are available for commercial leasing through the WPA Film Library.) A few are part of the Haizlip Papers, and one from 1968 (the fifth episode) is part of the Walter J. Brown Media Archives and Peabody Awards Collection at the University of Georgia. Several *Soul!* episodes may be streamed through the Thirteen.org website.

52. Thanks to Herman Gray for suggesting this idea of *Soul!*'s erasures as performative.

53. Dave Itzkoff, "Johnny Carson, Now Quipping Online," *New York Times*, August 11, 2010.

54. I am thinking here of Edwards, *Charisma and the Fictions of Black Leadership*. Heitner notes that *Black Journal* under Tony Brown took a more conventional approach to representing gender, the family, and sexuality than *Soul!* did (*Black Power TV*, 143).

55. Beginning in the late 1950s, COINTELPRO infiltrated and attempted to discredit a range of individuals and organizations, from King to the Black Panthers. See Betty Medsger's *The Burglary* for recent scholarship on COINTELPRO activities.

56. Ang, *Desperately Seeking the Audience*, 105. Timothy Mitchell's work has particularly influenced my conceptualizations of the state. See Mitchell, "Society, Economy, and the State Effect."

57. Killens, "'Our Struggle Is Not to Be White Men in Black Skin.'"

58. Stokely Carmichael and Charles V. Hamilton note, "A popular slogan of the 60's said, 'The Revolution will not be televised.'" See *Black Power: The Politics of Liberation in America*, 194. A survey of the television studies literature of the past two decades finds Scott-Heron's phrase creatively adapted in the titles of at least two full-length works concerned with television and social change: Spiegel and Curtin, *The Revolution Wasn't Televised*, and Acham, *Revolution Televised*. Amanda Lotz riffs cleverly on Scott-Heron's phrase in *The Television Will Be Revolutionized*, her study of postnetwork television.

59. My thinking here is influenced by Anthony Reed, *Freedom Time*, José Muñoz, *Cruising Utopia*, and Fred Moten, "Blackness and Nothingness." *Soul!*'s utopianism derives from its radical critique of the "here and now."

60. Blue and Murphree, "'Stoke the Joke' and His 'Self-Appointed White Critics.'"

61. *Soul!* #319, "Wherever We May Be," February 7, 1973. All transcriptions from *Soul!* episodes in this book are mine, reflecting my own sense of punctuation and formatting. Unless indicated otherwise, the sources of the tapes in the WNET Collection, Library of Congress, Washington, D.C. The date of broadcast usually refers to WNET; the same episode may have aired on a different day on other local public broadcasting outlets.

62. King, "Toni Braxton, Disney, and Thermodynamics."

63. *Soul!* #319, "Wherever We May Be," February 7, 1973.

64. Muñoz, *Cruising Utopia*.

65. Baraka, *It's Nation Time*.

66. Berlant, *Cruel Optimism*.

67. My understanding of vibrations intersects with that of Muñoz, *Cruising Utopia*, 1–9. See also Dolan, "Performance, Utopia, and the 'Utopian Performative'" for a take on the suspension of time and space in theatrical performance.

68. Undated letter from Ellis B. Haizlip to "Thomas," folder 15, box 1, Haizlip Papers.

1. Soul! and the 1960s

1. For a recent example, see Bodroghkozy, *Equal Time*. See also Torres, *Black, White, and in Color*.

2. Quoted in Bodroghkozy, *Equal Time*, 2.

3. United States National Advisory Commission on Civil Disorders, *Report of the National Advisory Commission on Civil Disorders*.

4. Executive order no. 11246. 30 C.F.R. 12319. Titled "Equal Employment

Opportunity," this executive order, signed on September 28, 1965, is the commonly cited source of the phrase "affirmative action."

5. This point is based on an observation made by the pioneering African American TV journalist Sarah-Ann Shaw (interview).

6. The autonomy of PBS member stations, beginning in 1970, meant that there was no counterpart, on PBS, to the national prime time of commercial networks.

7. Tommy Lee Lott makes a similar claim about *Black Journal*'s aesthetic negotiations of the Kerner Report ("Documenting Social Issues," 72).

8. Although I use adjectives like *black, white, minority*, and *mainstream* to describe audiences, I want to acknowledge the limitations of these terms. The discourse of race in the archive of *Soul!*'s prehistory is largely a discourse of black and white, although the term *minority* sometimes explicitly includes Latinos (referred to as Hispanics) and, less frequently, Asian and Native Americans.

9. Thomas Lask, "New Goals and New Ways," *New York Times*, January 17, 1973.

10. Fred Ferretti, "Harris Polls Weigh Effects of Ethnic Programming," *New York Times*, July 4, 1969.

11. Feretti, "Harris Polls Weigh Effects of Ethnic Programming."

12. United States National Advisory Commission on Civil Disorders, *Report of the National Advisory Commission*, 1–2.

13. United States National Advisory Commission on Civil Disorders, *Report of the National Advisory Commission*, 10.

14. Cited in Appiah and Gates, *Africana: Civil Rights: An A-to-Z Reference of the Movement That Changed America*, 233.

15. L. Johnson, "The President's Address to the Nation on Civil Disorders," 724.

16. United States National Advisory Commission on Civil Disorders, *Report of the National Advisory Commission*, 2. The second point, made initially in the report's summary, was repeated—with a slight difference in wording—in its subsequent preface: "Those few who would destroy civil order and the rule of law strike at the freedom of every citizen. They must know that the community cannot and will not tolerate mob *action*," ibid., 31 (emphasis mine).

17. John Herbers, "Study Says Negro Justifies Rioting as Social Protest," *New York Times*, July 28, 1968.

18. After it filed its final report, Johnson defunded the Kerner Commission and distanced himself from its commissioners, as well as its findings about government responsibility for black discontent. See Kevin Mumford, "Harvesting the Crisis," 208.

19. L. Johnson, "Remarks upon Signing Order Establishing the National Advisory Commission on Civil Disorders," 725.

20. "TV and the Riots," Congressional Record, Senate, S14075-14077, October 3, 1967.

21. Hickey, "Do TV Cameras Add Fuel to Riot Flames?," 10. The full text of the *TV Guide* article was entered into the Congressional Record, Senate, S14075-14077, October 3, 1967.

22. Hickey, "Do TV Cameras Add Fuel to Riot Flames?," 12.

23. "TV and the Riots," Congressional Record, Senate, S14075, n.a.

24. Hickey, "Do TV Cameras Add Fuel to Riot Flames?," 9. Hickey quoted the journalist Max Lerner: "Americans seem to have struck a Faustian bargain with the big media, by which they have received total and instant coverage and have in turn handed themselves over to the vulnerable chances of crowd psychology and of instant infection" (9).

25. Gould, *Moving Politics*, 14.

26. Lott, "Documenting Social Issues," 72–73.

27. United States National Advisory Commission on Civil Disorders, *Report of the National Advisory Commission*, 10, 204.

28. United States National Advisory Commission on Civil Disorders, *Report of the National Advisory Commission*, 386. On realist representation as a remedy for historical injury, see Harper, "Extra-Special Effects."

29. United States National Advisory Commission on Civil Disorders, *Report of the National Advisory Commission*, 20.

30. All quotations from Ouellette, *Viewers Like You?*, 85.

31. For a time, it was even hoped that television might solve the problem of "separate but equal" schooling identified in the Supreme Court's 1954 *Brown v. Board of Education* decision, thus deferring the need for social integration. See Perlman, "Television, Racial Inequality, and 'Carpetbagger Justice.'"

32. Arnold and Garnett, *Culture and Anarchy*, 5.

33. Ouellette, *Viewers Like You?*, 173. In the 1970s, the term *minority* was also often applied to women.

34. Meyer, "ETV and the Ghetto," 24. According to a note at the beginning of the article, it was "an outgrowth of the 'Report on ETV in the Ghetto' submitted to Vice President Hubert Humphrey by Richard J. Meyer and Chalmers H. Marquis." In 1970, after the merger of WNDT and National Educational Television, Meyer became vice president of the education division of the newly consolidated station WNET.

35. Frederick Breitenfeld Jr., "It's Not Easy," in National Association of Educational Broadcasters, *Broadcasting and Social Action: A Handbook for Station Executives*, 1–3. Washington: The Association, November 1969.

36. Interview with Horsford.

37. Quoted in Robert Berkvist, "Dig It or Forget It," *New York Times*, September 15, 1968.

38. "Ford Chooses Panel to Award TV Grants," New York Times, May 15, 1968.

39. Ford Foundation Annual Report for 1968, 75, Ford Foundation Archives, Rockefeller Archive Center, New York, NY (hereafter Ford Foundation Archives). Thanks to Mary Ann Quinn, archivist at the Rockefeller Archive Center, for her research assistance. See also Matt Messina, "Series on Negroes Set," *New York Daily News*, June 11, 1968.

40. Unsigned, undated, and untitled information paper submitted to Ford Foundation trustees, PA 68–683, Ford Foundation Archives.

41. "Television Reviews," *Variety*, n.d. (clipping courtesy of Christopher "Kit" Lukas, from his personal collection).

42. George Gent, "TV: Voices of the Negro," *New York Times*, June 27, 1968.

43. Gent, "TV: Voices of the Negro."

44. Lukas, "Memories of Ellis Haizlip and Enlightenment." As its title suggests, Lukas's piece ascribes his own "enlightenment"—that is, his education in black culture and black politics of the late 1960s—to Haizlip. The title is a telling inversion of the ETV discourse that saw (white) programming about (European high) arts as a means of "enlightening" its black audience. In his essay, Lukas refers to himself as the "godfather of *Soul!*"—a phrase that acknowledges his part in the creation of the show but displaces parentage to Haizlip.

45. Jack Gould, "If It's 'Public,' Does It Have to Be Dull?," *New York Times*, December 8, 1968.

46. Day, *The Vanishing Vision*, 191.

47. WNDT (Educational Broadcasting Corp.), Ford Foundation Project for New Television Programming, Program Proposal, April 25, 1968, cover sheet. PA 68–683, Ford Foundation Archives.

48. WNDT (Educational Broadcasting Corp.), Ford Foundation Project for New Television Programming, Program Proposal, April 25, 1968, 3, PA 68–683, Ford Foundation Archives.

49. Ouellete (*Viewers Like You?*, 85) quotes the social psychologist Harold Mendelsohn, keynote speaker at the CPB programming and promotion conference in 1970, arguing that public broadcasters should produce shows with "sufficient 'entertainment relief' to attract the target audience to these deeper educational messages."

50. WNDT (Educational Broadcasting Corp.), Ford Foundation Project for New Television Programming, Program Proposal, April 25, 1968, 3, PA 68–683, Ford Foundation Archives.

51. Quoted in Barbara Delatiner, "Soul TV Not Black and White," *Newsday*, September 13, 1968. Devorah Heitner makes a similar point (*Black Power TV*, 125).

52. The quote, attributed to former Boston public TV (WGBH) general manager David Ives, is cited in Shaw, "The History of *Say Brother*."

53. Killens, "'Our Struggle Is Not to Be White Men in Black Skin.'"

54. For a very different reading of Killens's *TV Guide* piece, see Harper, "Extra-Special Effects." I do not agree with Harper's claim (as I read it) that Killens's phrase "white men in black skin" is only or primarily a claim about the racial authenticity of TV representations. My sense is that Killens's critique of representation is inseparable from his critique of the means of production.

55. Winston, "Racial Consciousness and the Evolution of Mass Communications in the United States."

56. Allen, *Black Awakening in Capitalist America*, 153.

57. K. Ferguson, *Top Down*, 3. Bundy's speech, "Action for Equal Opportunity," was delivered at a meeting of the National Urban League in Philadelphia.

58. Greenlee, *The Spook Who Sat by the Door*, 183.

59. Heard, *A Cold Fire Burning*, 35–36.

60. H. Brown, *Die, Nigger, Die!*, 142. In her recent study *Top Down*, K. Ferguson argues that the Ford Foundation domesticated Black Power ideology through its involvement in many of Black Power era's hallmark projects. Rooks's *White Money/Black Power* traces the role of white philanthropy, primarily the Ford Foundation, in the institutional history of African American studies.

61. Quoted in Delatiner, "Soul TV Not Black and White."

62. Rooks, *White Money/Black Power*, 8.

63. "A.B.C. Will Televise a Series on Racism," *New York Times*, May 15, 1968.

64. WNDT (Educational Broadcasting Corp.), Ford Foundation Project for New Television Programming, Program Proposal, April 25, 1968, 1, PA 68–683, Ford Foundation Archives.

65. Letter from J[ohn] W. Kiermaier, President, Channel 13, to Fred Friendly, the Ford Foundation, April 25, 1968, 1, PA 68–683, Ford Foundation Archives.

66. Memorandum from Howard R. Dressner to McGeorge Bundy, June 17, 1968, 1, PA 68–683, Ford Foundation Archives. The description of "Where It's At . . ." is from an untitled attachment to the memorandum detailing grantees. In a June 12, 1968, letter from WNDT's John W. Kiermaier to David M. Davis, television program coordinator at the Ford Foundation, Kiermaier notes that during the panel to discuss Project for New Television Programming proposals, concerns were raised about the proposal's suggestion of inviting "real teen-agers" on the show to discuss topical issues. "I believe it would be in the

spirit of the meeting and the grant commitment if you would suggest to your producer that he discuss this point in detail with Ralph Ellison," Kiermaier writes. "There seemed to be considerable feeling that such things as high school debating teams mentioned in the proposal might not really be 'Where It's At.'" N.p., PA 68–683, Ford Foundation Archives.

67. Lukas, "Memories of Ellis Haizlip and Enlightenment."

68. Haizlip later told the writer Raoul Abdul that *Soul!* "was primarily *my* idea. It was quite a bit different from what the station had hoped to see" (quoted in *Famous Black Entertainers of Today*, 76–77).

69. Du Bois, *The Souls of Black Folk*, 205.

70. Quoted in Delatiner, "Soul TV Not Black and White."

71. Quoted in Delatiner, "Soul TV Not Black and White."

72. Quoted in Delatiner, "Soul TV Not Black and White."

73. Richard Flohil, "Soul!," *Toronto Daily Star*, February 18, 1970.

74. Interview with Brown.

75. Interview with Haizlip.

76. Letter from John W. Kiermaier to David M. Davis, television program coordinator, January 10, 1969, 1, PA 69–344, Ford Foundation Archives.

77. Ellis B. Haizlip, "Note from the Producer," Lincoln Center Presents Soul at the Center program, July 23–August 5, 1972, n.p. Lincoln Center for the Performing Arts Archives.

78. *Soul!* #304, "Farrakhan the Minister," October 25, 1972.

2. The Black Community and the Affective Compact

1. Brennan, *The Transmission of Affect*.

2. Hall, "Encoding/Decoding."

3. Letter from Sylvia Spence, director of public information at Channel 13, to David M. Davis, television program coordinator at the Ford Foundation, September 6, 1968, 1–2, PA 69–344, Ford Foundation Archives, Rockefeller Archive Center, New York, NY (hereafter Ford Foundation Archives). Haizlip had also recommended radio advertising, although records suggest that little or no money was left over for radio after the print campaign.

4. Meeting with Channel 13/WNDT regarding "Soul!", memorandum from David M. Davis, television program coordinator at the Ford Foundation, to Fred Friendly, Ford Foundation advisor on television, September 6, 1968, n.p., PA 69–344, Ford Foundation Archives. In the same communication, Davis raised concerns about whether station officials were conceding enough authority to Haizlip. "My only qualm at the moment is that they may not give the show enough black control and thus not achieve the kind of relevance that

this series ought to have. This is intuitive and personal on my part and gets into the area of content which we will stay out of."

5. Meeting with Channel 13/WNDT regarding "Soul!", memorandum from David M. Davis, television program coordinator at the Ford Foundation, to Fred Friendly, Ford Foundation advisor on television, September 6, 1968, n.p., PA 69–344, Ford Foundation Archives.

6. Quoted in Robert Berkvist, "Dig It or Forget It," *New York Times*, September 15, 1968.

7. I am influenced here by Griffin, "When Malindy Sings," 103.

8. Quoted in Berkvist, "Dig It or Forget It."

9. Monson, *Freedom Sounds*; Wilson, "The Heterogeneous Sound Ideal in African-American Music."

10. Quoted in Berkvist, "Dig It or Forget It."

11. Dede Compagno, "The Ellis 'n' Alice Show," *Image: Channel 13 Program Guide* 7, 8 (June 1970), 12.

12. Moten and Harney, "The University and the Undercommons."

13. "Apollo Musicman to 'Soul' TV'er," *Billboard*, August 31, 1968, 33.

14. Barbara Delatiner, "On Television," *Newsday*, September 13, 1968.

15. Newspaper accounts give the title of the English ballad variously as "Johnny We Hardly Knew Ye" (or "You"), "Johnny I Hardly Knew You," or "When Johnny Came Marching Home." The former versions are said to have British roots, the latter to have derived from the U.S. Civil War. In either case, the song gives voice to a woman who is welcoming home a severely disabled war veteran. Nelson referred to "Johnny I Hardly Knew You," the source of my title here (interview).

16. Interview with Nelson.

17. Quoted in Barbara Delatiner, "Soul TV Not Black and White," *Newsday*, September 13, 1968.

18. Interview with Nelson.

19. Kelley, *Freedom Dreams*.

20. Brooks, "Nina Simone's Triple Play," 177.

21. George Gent, "The Smotherses Protest TV Cuts: 7 1/2-Minute Trim by C.B.S. Charged by Comedians," *New York Times*, October 2, 1968.

22. For more on censorship of the *Smothers Brothers* show, see Bodrogh-kozy, *Groove Tube*, 123–63; Ozersky, *Archie Bunker's America*, 33–39. Although its homage to hippie and drug counterculture were seen as irreverent, Ozersky correctly notes that "what really got the show in trouble was its antiwar orientation" (36).

23. A *New York Times* TV listing for the program advertises the poet Ed Bullins as a guest, but not Clayton Riley. It is likely that Bullins was originally

booked to do the show and that Riley was called in as a last-minute substitute. This example illustrates the difficulty of using published print sources to accurately account for the content of live television programs.

24. Quoted in Thomas, *Listen, Whitey!*, 17. This account of Douglas's recollection of watching the Last Poets on television does not refer specifically to *Soul!*

25. Although the fifth episode of *Soul!* didn't win the award, a copy of it became the property of the Peabody administrators and thus survives in good condition today. The Peabody Award Collection is part of the Walter J. Brown Media Archives and Peabody Awards Collection at the University of Georgia.

26. Interview with Poussaint.

27. Interview with Stern.

28. Rickford, *Betty Shabazz*, 313.

29. Interview with Horsford.

30. Interview with Nelson. Nelson usefully observes as a black gay man at the time, Haizlip would have been an expert in the subtleties of communicating: in particular, of making himself understood without speaking and of putting others at ease so they felt free to speak.

31. Writing for the Channel 13 program guide, Nikki Giovanni called *Soul!* the "baddest Black show on television" and noted, "The first year producer Haizlip hosted it and became the love object of Black people from Harlem and Riker's Island, to the wilds of Pennsylvania and the beans of Boston" (Giovanni, "Soul Impressions," *Image* 8, January 1971, 12).

32. Haizlip's coproducer Andrew Stern recalls that he had accompanied Haizlip to scout out the Last Poets in Harlem, and that a condition of the show was their not using the word "motherfucker" on the air (interview with Stern).

33. "Diahann's Show Is Sponsored," *Daily Defender*, May 28, 1968.

34. Although the WNDT debut of *Soul!* (September 12, 1968) and the first national presentation of *Julia* (September 17, 1968) were separated by only five days, this fact has by and large escaped scholarly attention, in part because of the ways that scholarship separates commercial and noncommercial programming

35. Episode 5 of *Soul!* "points the way toward a new kind of television, transcending the tired stereotypes of showbusiness in an electric union with the best of this community." "Dep.," "Tele Follow-Up Comment," *New York Variety*, October 30, 1968, 45.

36. PA 69–344, Ford Foundation Archives.

37. The Ford Foundation, Project for New Television Programming, Program Proposal, January 10, 1969, PA 68–683, Ford Foundation Archives.

38. Letter from John W. Kiermaier, president of Channel 13, to David M. Davis, television program coordinator, Ford Foundation, January 10, 1969, 1, PA 69–344, Ford Foundation Archives.

39. Kiermaier to Davis, January 10, 1969, 1, 2.

40. Jones, *Blues People*.

41. Rooks, *White Money/Black Power*, 3.

42. Fred Ferretti, "Harris Polls Weigh Effects of Ethnic Programming," *New York Times*, July 4, 1969. In July 1969 the newly formed CPB publicly released the results of two Harris polls that studied black viewers of public broadcasting.

43. Letter from John W. Kiermaier, president of Channel 13, to Fred Friendly, Ford Foundation advisor on television, September 23, 1969, Ford Foundation Archives. PA 68–683, Ford Foundation Archives.

44. "Dep.," "Tele Follow-Up Comment."

45. Lukas, press release.

46. According to David Peck, while *Soul!* aired in repeats, Christopher Lukas at Channel 13 courted Mobil Oil Corporation, which was on the verge of giving the station money for *Soul!* until it decided to fund a new show called *Masterpiece Theatre*, jokingly known by some critics as "Master Race Theatre" ("Soul!," unpublished, unpaginated manuscript received January 1997, courtesy of Alice [Hille] LaBrie, from her personal collection). Interview with Lukas.

47. Haizlip's on-air appeal is noted in a letter from a *Soul!* viewer to the Ford Foundation, May 5, 1969, PA 68–683, Ford Foundation Archives. Confidentiality prohibits me from citing the author of the article.

48. Untitled and undated document summarizing *Soul!*, presumably submitted by Channel 13 to the Ford Foundation in support of a second round of funding from the Project for New Television Programming, 4, PA 68–683, Ford Foundation Archives.

49. Editorial, "Help for SOUL!," *Amsterdam News*, May 17, 1969.

50. All citations are from letters in the personal collection of Christopher "Kit" Lukas, which he graciously shared. Many of these letters have been posted online as "Letters Written in Support of Soul!, 1968–73," on the Thirteen .org website. Accessed July 27, 2014. See http://www.thirteen.org/soul/about -soul/letters-written-in-support-of-soul-1969-73/.

51. PA 68–683, Ford Foundation Archives.

52. WNDT Annual Report, July–December 1968, 4.

53. Quoted in Channel 13/WNDT press release, July 3, 1969, 1. From WNET Collection, Library of Congress.

3. *"More Meaningful Than a Three-Hour Lecture"*

1. Clayton Riley, "That New Black Magic," *New York Times*, May 17, 1970.

2. Quoted in Compagno, "The Ellis 'n' Alice Show," 12.

3. On music as an archive of black female expression, see Brooks, "'All That You Can't Leave Behind.'" On Hurston's notion of performance as "embodied cultural documentation," see Brooks, "Sister Can You Line It Out?"

4. Baraka, "The Changing Same," 209, 191.

5. Staple Singers, "I'll Take You There," *Be Altitude: Respect Yourself* (Memphis: Stax Records, 1972).

6. Occasionally, according to Alonzo Brown Jr., the production team would do stop tapes, which would give them time to change scenes and adjust the microphones for different performers. During breaks in the taping, Brown recalls, members of the studio audience were treated to a buffet including Anna Horsford's mother's famous salmon croquettes. "This made *Soul!* the hottest ticket in town," Brown said (interview).

7. Abdul, *Famous Black Entertainers*, 75.

8. Abdul, *Famous Black Entertainers*, 75.

9. Anderson, "'Calling on the Spirit.'" Many writers have addressed these issues. See especially Vogel, *The Scene of Harlem Cabaret*; Heilbut, *The Fan Who Knew Too Much*.

10. Childress, "The Soul Man," 68–69.

11. Zinn and Arnove, *Voices of a People's History*, 431.

12. On the Smothers Brothers' show's presentation of music, see Brodroghkozy, *Groove Tube*, 147.

13. Interview with Nelson.

14. Interview with Curry. Curry recalled the spontaneity of some of the show's early musical performances. In a January 1969 episode, for example, the duo Peaches and Herb were performing a "lovely ballad," and while the camera was in the middle of a "fat close-up," Herb took off his singing partner's earring "and started blowing" into her ear. Since the show was broadcast live, there was no time to edit out this erotic gesture.

15. Interview with Hendryx.

16. Interview with Johnson.

17. Interviews with Luciano.

18. Austen, *TV A-Go-Go*, 45. See also Warwick, *Girl Groups, Girl Culture*.

19. "Music on television," as Simon Frith writes, "involves a combination of presence and distance that is significantly different from the music experience of radio, records or live performance" ("Look! Hear!," 288).

20. Quoted in Ellis Haizlip, "A Proposal to the Corporation for Public Broadcasting for a Series of Black Cultural Programs," 1975, Appendix C, "SOUL!," 1, folder 2, box 19. Ellis B. Haizlip Papers, Anacostia Community Museum Archives, Smithsonian Institution, Washington, DC.

21. "Higher Ground" is a track from Wonder's album *Innervisions* (Tamla Motown, 1973).

22. Quoted in Compagno, "The Ellis 'n' Alice Show," 12.

23. I am, of course, unable to provide an exhaustive account here. For more, see Austen, *TV a-Go-Go*; Weingarten, *Station to Station*; MacDonald, *Blacks and White TV*; Bogle, *Primetime Blues*.

24. Neal, "Sold Out on Soul," 117–18.

25. The "People Get Ready" performance is available on *Movin' On Up*.

26. Richard Flohil, "Soul!" *Toronto Daily Star*, February 18, 1970.

27. Quoted in Loza, *Tito Puente and the Making of Latin Music*, 224.

28. Quoted in Kruth, *Bright Moments*, 237.

29. Quoted in the liner notes, Charles Mingus, *The Clown* (Atlantic SD-1260, 1957).

30. Quoted in Kruth, *Bright Moments*, 247–49.

31. Interview with Brown.

32. According to WPA Film Library records, *Soul!* #501 (sometimes listed as 301) featuring Kirk and the Vibration Society, was taped on September 22, 1972, although it did not air until October 1972. In his interview with Kirk, Haizlip notes that the musician prefers the phrase "not seeing too well" to "blind." All transcriptions that follow from this episode are my own.

33. Thanks to Daphne Brooks for making the connection between Kirk's chair act and sit-ins.

34. Quoted in Kruth, *Bright Moments*, 167. Kirk's Vibration Society drummer, Rober Shy, recalled that his boss "caused a riot" in a Baltimore club during a 1973 performance that inspired patrons to attack their own chairs.

35. *La concha* is a slang term for the female genitals. In this sense, Kirk's playing of the conch shell is also an assertion of black male power through sexual symbolism.

36. Scott-Heron, *The Last Holiday*, 267.

37. Ellison, *Invisible Man*, 17–29.

38. Frith, "Look! Hear!," 286.

39. Thanks to Ned-Stuckey French and Leigh Edwards at Florida State University for offering comments that have forced me to clarify my claims here.

40. I recognize the inadequacy and imprecision of the phrase *Latin music*. Yet I use it here in a historical sense because it is the phrase used by Puente,

Luciano, and Colón in the "Shades of Soul I" episode, which aired at a time when the catchall term *salsa*, itself a subject of debate, came into wide usage among musicians, record labels like Fania Records, and fans alike.

41. Baraka, "The Changing Same."

42. Cantanga (or Kantanga) is a southern Congolese province.

43. The December 19, 1968, episode of *Soul!*, devoted to "the Latin Soul Beat and African Music," was filmed on location in Puerto Rico and included performances by the Puerto Rican performer Carla Pinza, the band Los Pleneros, and the composer and guitarist Cruz Martinez. A 1971 episode featured the writer Victor Hernandez Cruz, a member of the influential Umbra Poets Workshop, then based on New York's Lower East Side. (I was not able to find copies of either of these *Soul!* episodes, and so rely here on press releases.) In 1974, after Umbra relocated to the San Francisco Bay area, it published a special "Latin Soul" issue of the journal *Umbra*, which included works by both Hernandez Cruz and Luciano. See Wilkinson, "'To Make a Poet Black,'" 328; Hernandez, "Latin Soul," 333–34.

44. Ogbar, "Puerto Rico en mi corazón," 159.

45. Ogbar, "Puerto Rico en mi corazón," 159.

46. Because Luciano was in a relationship with a member of the *Soul!* production staff, he was also an occasional visitor to the *Soul!* set. For more on Luciano and Puerto Rican poetry, see Wilkinson, "'To Make a Poet Black.'"

47. *Latin Roots* made a particularly strong impression on young English-speaking Puerto Rican listeners. See Jottar, "Central Park Rumba," 13 and 25, note 38.

48. *Soul!* #507 (sometimes listed as 307), "Shades of Soul, Part I," November 22, 1972. The date of broadcast reflects WNET listings; the episode might have appeared on other dates in other markets. All transcriptions that follow from this episode are my own.

49. Cited in Loza, *Tito Puente*, 224–25.

50. The well-received *Our Latin Thing*, directed by Leon Gast, while shot on a shoestring, is credited with increasing the global visibility of salsa. See Larry Rohter, "It Happened One Night at the Cheetah," *New York Times*, August 19, 2011.

51. Interview with Luciano, June 2.

52. Vazquez, *Listening in Detail*, 27.

53. In Puerto Rican Spanish, according to Bobby Sanabria (interview), Puente would have been called a *grifo*, the term for a person with light skin and kinky hair.

54. On the cover of the 1968 album *The Hustler*, Colón and his band members are pictured as pool sharks, and on 1971's *La Gran Fuga* (The big break),

the trombonist appears on a fake FBI wanted poster, signifying on his status as a musical upstart but also evoking the famous most wanted poster of Angela Davis, which appeared the same year.

55. Berrios-Miranda, "Salsa Music as Expressive Liberation," 166–67.

56. Interview with Luciano, July 7.

57. Interview with Sanabria.

58. Interview with Sanabria.

59. The 1972 Soul at the Center lineup included Kirk, Santamaría, and La-belle as well as previous *Soul!* guests Marion Williams, Taj Mahal, and the Jerry Butler Revue. Other Soul at the Center performers had never appeared on the show. They include the band War, Nina Simone, and the singer and guitarist Sister Rosetta Tharpe.

60. LaBelle with Randolph, *Don't Block the Blessings*, 153–54. My reading of Labelle on *Soul!* is influenced by Retman, "Between Rock and a Hard Place," and Neal, *Songs in the Key of Black Life*, 79–100.

61. Quoted in Carson, Lewis, and Shaw, *Girls Rock!*, 129.

62. Greenlee, *The Spook Who Sat by the Door*, 30, 172.

63. Greenlee, *The Spook Who Sat by the Door*, 111.

64. Haizlip made reference to music and culture as "encouragement" in *Soul!* #304, "Farrakhan the Minister," October 25, 1972. Hille's description of *Soul!* as "one-hour of relief once a week" is quoted in Hobson and Smith, "The Living Arts."

4. Freaks Like Us

1. Rickford, *Betty Shabazz*, 311, 313.

2. The *Soul!* episode list on the Thirteen.org website lists Shabazz as a guest on a May 1971 "Malcolm X Memorial" episode and records this episode as being rerun to commemorate his birthday in February 1972. However, PBS promotional materials dated May 3, 1971, omit Shabazz from the list of per-formers slated to appear on *Soul!* that month, and other records show her as appearing in early 1972. See http://www.thirteen.org/soul/about-soul/soul -episode-guide-1968-1973/.

3. Based on Nikki Giovanni's own recollections, Virginia Fowler also refers to a "circle of friends" that included Haizlip, Shabazz, Nelson, Horsford, and others (*Nikki Giovanni*, 57). Fowler notes that Giovanni and Haizlip had a fall-ing out about *Soul!* roughly six months before it went off the air, in late sum-mer or early fall 1972. Giovanni mentions *Soul!* in somewhat critical terms in her memoir, *Gemini*.

4. Interview with Horsford.

5. Interview with Ladd.

6. Examples of these letters are in the Ellis B. Haizlip papers, Anacostia Community Museum Archives, Smithsonian Institution, Washington, DC (hereafter Haizlip Papers).

7. Jefferson, "Different Drums," 87.

8. *Soul!*'s and Giovanni's creative deployment of a range of social and cultural networks to publicize their work represents an unheralded and important use of "social media" before the digital era.

9. For a book that strongly influences my thinking on this radical tradition, see Moten, *In the Break*.

10. Thanks to Fred Moten for pointing me toward "Freaks and the American Ideal of Manhood."

11. Baraka, "The Changing Same." The *Soul!* misfits are the relations of J. Brown's *Babylon Girls*; Brooks's agents of "Afro-alienation effects" (*Bodies in Dissent*); Peterson's eccentric nineteenth-century black feminists ("Eccentric Bodies"); E. Johnson's "quares" ("From Black Quare Studies"); Vogel's Harlem cabaret denizens (*The Scene of Harlem Cabaret*); Lorde's "sister outsiders" (*Sister Outsider*); Muñoz's "disidentifying" subjects (*Disidentification*); and Royster's musical eccentrics (*Sounding Like a No-No*). Royster, similarly notes that "eccentric performances are fueled by contradictory desires for recognition and freedom" (8–9).

12. Quoted in transcription, Project Advisor Committee Conference, "The Speech Class," November 1, 1975, 127. Ellis B. Haizlip Papers, folder 1, box 19, Anacostia Community Museum Archives, Smithsonian Institution, Washington, D.C. Others experienced Haizlip's voice in terms of its warmth. "It was a voice that had a southern tone to it, but it was warm," recalled Baraka years later (interview). "It was a voice that made you comfortable, like somebody who you could talk to."

13. Self, *All in the Family*, 33.

14. Using the black church as an example, E. Patrick Johnson argues that in social contexts in which sexual difference is rigorously policed, black queer identities are "always already socially visible" despite the "complicity of silence" around them (the quoted material represents my transcriptions of Johnson's presentation) ("Camp Revival"). Indeed, in some communities, such as church communities in which homosexuality is regarded as a sin, the ostentatious refusal to talk about sexual difference functions, paradoxically, as a form of recognition of the presence of queer subjects in the community. On gay visibility and audibility in gospel music culture, see Heilbut, *The Fan Who*

Knew Too Much, 3–91. Neal ("Nickolas Ashford and the Cult of Black Manhood") explores the ambiguous sexuality of the male member of the famous husband-and-wife duo.

15. Smith, "Television and the Tactics of Black Revolution."

16. Heitner, *Black Power TV*, 126.

17. As I hope is clear, I do not use *misfit* in a pejorative way. Rather, I invoke it—following Rickford (*Betty Shabazz*)—in recognition of the ways that the historiography of black arts and Black Power may insist on categories of affiliation that do not "fit" all of the diverse actors in these movements.

18. Cleaver, *Soul on Ice*, 127–28.

19. Gates, *Thirteen Ways of Looking at a Black Man*, 41. Emily Bernard writes that "it is meaningful to recognize how central these denunciations of James Baldwin were to the establishment of a kind of racial authenticity for those who perpetuated them" ("A Familiar Strangeness," 264).

20. Wallace, *Black Macho and the Myth of the Superwoman*, 166–67.

21. Fowler, *Nikki Giovanni*, 27.

22. *Soul!* #53, "Baldwin and Giovanni, part I," December 15, 1971, and *Soul!* #54, "Baldwin and Giovanni, part II," December 22, 1971. As explained in the introduction, all quotations from this and other *Soul!* episodes are from my transcriptions, Readers should note that Baldwin and Giovanni's co-authored work *A Dialogue* does not reflect the entirety of their conversation as it was broadcast on television. Presumably, moreover, the TV broadcast is an edited version of the conversation that was captured on film in London.

23. Devorah Heitner similarly observes that "it is striking that two prominent intellectuals who were not living traditional heteronormative roles in their adult lives playacted a married couple in the discussion about the heteronormative family" (*Black Power TV*, 139).

24. Ward, "The Third World Women's Alliance," 120.

25. Thanks to Daphne Brooks for this observation about the proleptic coincidence of the name Giovanni in Baldwin's novel.

26. At the time of the broadcast, the NOI was expanding and reaching out to the black middle class. The organization's purchase of a former Greek Orthodox church on Chicago's South Shore for $4 million attracted much attention that year, as did Farrakhan's participation on a panel of black political leaders convened for a special ninety-minute call-in episode of *Black Journal*, titled "Is it Too Late?"

27. *Soul!* #304, "Farrakahn the Minister," October 25, 1972.

28. Baldwin, "Letter from a Region of My Mind." For a thoughtful commentary on Baldwin's meeting with Elijah Muhammad, see Joseph, *Waiting 'til the Midnight Hour*, 71. My notion of the affective power of misfit energy

is in dialogue with Joseph's struggles to explain how Baldwin, an atheist and avowed interracialist who was also committed to sexual equality, ends up being charmed by Muhammad.

29. On Baraka at this time, see Marable, *Race, Reform, and Rebellion*, 132; Frazier, "Baraka, Brother Mao, and the Year of '74"; Woodard, *A Nation within a Nation*.

30. *Soul!* #306, "Baraka, the Artist," November 8, 1972.

31. All of the quotations in this paragraph are from the interview with Baraka. In addition to being roughly the same age, Baraka and Haizlip both grew up in supportive, middle-class households, and both attended—but did not graduate from—Howard University in the early 1950s.

32. Three of the poems that Baraka performs are from *Spirit Reach* (1972): "Snapshots of Everything," "The Spirit of Creation Is Blackness," and "Somebody's Slow Is Another Body's Fast (Preachment)."

33. It is unclear whether Amina Baraka is present in the audience, or whether the crying baby is Baraka's. Neither of the men on the stage registers an awareness of the baby's disruptive squalls.

34. Woodard, *A Nation within a Nation*, 181–82; Springer, "Black Feminists Respond to Black Power Masculinism."

35. R. Ferguson, *The Reorder of Things*, 114.

36. Baraka fondly recalls Haizlip's pronunciation of the "Imamu" honorific in his eulogy for the producer. See Baraka, "The Soul Brother," 147.

37. Interview with Grosvenor.

5. *The Racial State and the "Disappearance" of* Soul!

1. Interview with Yarbrough.

2. *Soul!* "Baldwin and Giovanni, part I," December 15, 1971.

3. CPB Board of Directors, Resolution, March 7, 1973, 1, folder 10, box 2, series 1, The Papers of Ralph B. Rogers, Archives of the CPB, National Public Broadcasting Archives, University of Maryland.

4. The Carnegie Commission on Educational Television was a fifteen-member body tasked with studying noncommercial television in the United States. In January 1967, it issued *Public Television: A Program for Action*, a report that influenced Congress's passage of the Public Broadcasting Act of 1967, which created the Corporation for Public Broadcasting as an independent, nonprofit corporation to foster the growth and development of public radio and television. The Carnegie Report also led to the creation of PBS as the primary system of station interconnection.

5. "Without the pressure of the riots" following Martin Luther King Jr.'s

assassination, writes Devorah Heitner, "Ford and other foundation and corporate sponsors became far less invested in funding" programs like *Soul!* and *Black Journal* as "'outlets' for Black discontent" (*Black Power TV*, 122). I agree with Heitner, although I find that the decline of such pressures was only one part of the larger picture of *Soul!*'s demise.

6. Omi and Winant, *Racial Formation in the United States*, 138–39.

7. For a trenchant critique of the trajectory of this focus on representation at the expense of other metrics for thinking about racial justice in the post–civil rights era, see Gray, "Subject(ed) to Recognition."

8. Day, *The Vanishing Vision*; Ledbetter, *Made Possible By—*; Barsamian, *The Decline and Fall of Public Broadcasting*; Ouellette, *Viewers Like You?*

9. Day, *The Vanishing Vision*, 212.

10. See, in particular, Ledbetter, *Made Possible By—*; Hoynes, *Public Television for Sale*; Barsamian, *The Decline and Fall of Public Broadcasting*; Ouellette, *Viewers Like You?* My account of public television's decline is also indebted to scores of documents contained in the various collections at the National Public Broadcasting Archives, University of Maryland, College Park, MD. See also Mary Russell, "Public Broadcasting: Under Fire Again," *Washington Post*, June 2, 1972; "The Public TV Bogey," *Christian Science Monitor*, July 7, 1972; Bill Greeley, "The Public (TV) Be Damned," *Variety*, January 19, 1972.

11. Dwight Newton, "Public TV Has Been Tamed," *Sunday* [San Francisco] *Examiner and Chronicle*, February 23, 1975.

12. Peter M. Flanigan, "Memorandum to the President," November 4, 1969, n.p., folder 4, box 1, series, The Papers of Ralph B. Rogers, Archives of the CPB.

13. Clay T. Whitehead, draft memorandum to the president, November 15, 1971, n.p., folder 13, box 1, series 1, The Papers of Ralph B. Rogers, Archives of the CPB.

14. Clay T. Whitehead, draft memorandum to the president, September 28, 1971, n.p., folder 11, box 1, series 1, The Papers of Ralph B. Rogers, Archives of the CPB.

15. Governor Mitt Romney's invocation of Big Bird in the first televised debate of the U.S. presidential campaign on October 3, 2012—during which he told debate moderator Jim Lehrer, "I'm sorry, Jim. I'm going to the stop the subsidy to PBS. I'm going to stop other things. I like PBS. I love Big Bird. I actually like you, too. But I'm not going to keep on spending money on things to borrow money from China to pay for it"—echoed Whitehead's private opinion from 1971. See Brian Stelter and Elizabeth Jensen, "Romney's Pledge Puts Focus on Public TV," *New York Times*, October 11, 2012. For a complete tran-

script of the debate, see http://www.debates.org/index.php?page=october-3 -2012-debate-transcript. Accessed July 24, 2014.

16. For the speech, see Clay T. Whitehead, "Local Autonomy and the Fourth Network: Striking a Balance," October 1971, folder 17, box 3, series 1:2–3, Papers of James Day, Archives of the CPB. For background on the Nixon strategy, see John Carmody, "Public TV Confrontation," *Washington Post*, April 15, 1972; "Whitehead Asserts Nixon Bill Does Not Seek to Curtail Television Freedom," *New York Times*, January 11, 1973; John J. O'Connor, "Can Public Television Be Bought?," *New York Times*, October 3, 1974.

17. Quoted in Ledbetter, *Made Possible By—*, 75. As Ledbetter notes, "this was an extraordinarily disingenuous statement."

18. Arlen, "Comment," 27.

19. Ledbetter, *Made Possible By—*, 77–78. Only by limiting public broadcasting's size and influence, Nixon essentially argued, could it effectively serve the public according to the Carnegie Commission's mandate.

20. Jay Iselin, "Re: Clay Whitehead," memorandum, June 8, 1972, folder 17, box 3, series 1:2–3, Papers of James Day, Archives of the CPB.

21. O'Connor, "Can Public Television Be Bought?"

22. In my research I found no White House memorandum that specifically mentions *Soul!*, although *Black Journal* is occasionally cited as a thorn in the administration's side.

23. Day, *The Vanishing Vision*, 236.

24. Alvin Snyder, untitled memorandum to Peter Flanigan, November 22, 1971, folder 13, box 1, series 1, Papers of Ralph B. Rogers, Archives of the CPB.

25. Briefly, PBS affiliates exercised authority over shows distributed through the cooperative. Hence, station managers could claim that people in their localities were uninterested in *Soul!* or *Black Journal* or that the shows were too expensive for them to carry, given what they deemed to be an inadequate number of black viewers in their station's area.

26. Quoted in "Program Evaluations 1971," folder 18, box 20, series 4, Papers of James Day, Archives of the CPB. The document refers to page 6 of a February 11, 1972, report submitted by Pepper Weiss, Research Associates, studying the fall (October–December) 1971 season. The report contained no evidence that station managers had ever studied or polled black households in their localities, suggesting that they were basing their conclusions on nothing more than anecdotal evidence, if not outright contempt.

27. Macy, *To Irrigate a Wasteland*, 62.

28. See my discussion of the Last Poets in chapter 2. Although the 1968 episode in which the Last Poets appeared was not aired nationally, it provides some insight into the use and reception of profane language in spoken poetry.

29. Ellis Haizlip to Kit Lukas, February 23, 1971, courtesy of Christopher "Kit" Lukas, from his personal collection, and quoted by permission.

30. Jack Gould, "TV's New 'Black Journal,'" *New York Times*, December 29, 1970. The authors of a late 1972 journal article made the point tactfully, praising *Soul!* and *Black Journal* but also noting that the latter faced "inherent limitations" in "the presentation primarily of one perspective" (Wareham and Bynoe, "The New Stereotypes Are No Better Than the Old," 18). WNET memoranda from 1972 and 1973 indicate anxieties about Brown on the part of station executives.

31. As noted in a letter from Ward B. Chamberlain Jr., executive vice president of WNET, to John W. Macy Jr., president of the CPB, May 5, 1971, 1, folder 24, box 27, series 3, Papers of Henry Loomis, Archives of the CPB.

32. Tony Brown, letter to Henry Loomis, November 29, 1972, 1, folder 38, box 37, series 4, Papers of Henry Loomis, Archives of the CPB. "Black affairs" was Brown's own category, meant to differentiate *Black Journal* from other threatened public-affairs programs. By the standard of "black affairs," Brown's show was unique on public television.

33. Henry Loomis, undated letter (probably December 1973) to Tony Brown, 1, folder 38, box 37, series 4, box 4: 4, series 1, Papers of Henry Loomis, Archives of the CPB.

34. Quoted in James P. Murray, "TV's Black Journal Is Hanging in the Balance," *New York Amsterdam News*, December 30, 1972. Heitner (*Black Power TV*, 117–22) notes that when *Black Journal* was eventually re-funded by the CPB, it was with a greatly reduced budget, owing to the loss of Ford money. In 1977 the show migrated to commercial television as *Tony Brown's Black Journal*, but its impact there was greatly diminished.

35. Betty Lawson, undated letter to Ellis Haizlip, n.p., folder 7, box 5, Ellis B. Haizlip Papers, Anacostia Community Museum Archives, Smithsonian Institution, Washington, DC.

36. Interview with Willis.

37. Quoted in Tom Shales, "A Lost 'Soul'?" *Washington Post*, May 17, 1973.

38. Henry Loomis, letter to Hon. Ralph H. Metcalfe, House of Representatives, July 9, 1973, 1, folder 4, box 4, series 1, Papers of Henry Loomis, Archives of the CPB. The Congressional Black Caucus was formed in 1971. In March 1972 it held a two-day hearing into the problems of black journalists in the mass media (including print journalism). When conflict between the CPB and *Black Journal* and *Soul!* erupted, members of the caucus were recruited to put political pressure on the CPB board. On the 1972 hearings, see Efron, "What Is Happening to Blacks in Broadcasting?"

39. Hartford N. Gunn Jr., testimony before John O. Pastore, chairman, Senate Commerce Committee, Subcommittee on Communications, New Senate Office Building, Washington, DC, submitted as "Appendix B," 24, in "Long-Range Funding for Public Broadcasting," Report of the Senate Subcommittee on Commerce on S. 2584.

40. Lott, *The Invention of Race*, 94. *Freedomways* also covered commercial television, radio, and film.

41. Omi and Winant, *Racial Formation in the United States*, 78. "From the early 1970s of Richard Nixon to the early 1990s of Bill Clinton, the state has sought to absorb, to marginalize, and to transform ('rearticulate') the meaning of the reforms won in the earlier decade." Omi and Winant's analysis is heavily indebted to Gramsci, *Selections from the Prison Notebooks*.

42. Ellis Haizlip, "A Proposal to the Corporation for Public Broadcasting for a Series of Black Cultural Programs," February 15, 1975, 2, folder 2, box 19, Ellis B. Haizlip papers, Anacostia Community Museum Archives, Smithsonian Institution, Washington, DC.

43. Quoted in "Cancellation of SOUL TV Show Termed 'An Insult,'" 45.

44. Quoted in Joel Dreyfuss, "CPB's Minority Funding," *Washington Post*, November 9, 1973.

45. National Friends of *Black Journal*, "Soul! Cancelled, Black Journal in Danger: A Blackgate in Public Broadcasting," undated statement from spring 1973, 5, attached to letter from Rep. Ralph H. Metcalfe, Illinois, to Henry Loomis, president of the CPB, June 19, 1973, folder 4, box 4, series 1, Papers of Henry Loomis, Archives of the CPB.

46. National Friends of *Black Journal*, "Soul! Cancelled, Black Journal in Danger: A Blackgate in Public Broadcasting," 4, Archives of the CPB.

47. Quoted in Tom Shales, "A Lost 'Soul'?," *Washington Post*, May 17, 1973.

48. Quoted in "Cancellation of SOUL TV Show Termed 'An Insult,'" 45. In erroneously calling PBS a "network" in the statement, Haizlip inadvertently gave credence to White House critics of public broadcasters' aspirations to become a U.S. version of the BBC.

49. Quoted in "WNET Vows Fight to Get CPB Funding for Black Series," *Broadcasting*, 46.

50. In a subsection of its annual report for fiscal 1974 titled "Special Concerns: Education, Minorities, Women," WNET noted that although the CPB stood behind the principle of the autonomy of local stations, it had also deemed "the case of minorities . . . a special one." The report quoted Loomis: "The need is for concerted, nationwide effort to correct a systematic inadequacy in serving that audience" ("WNET Annual Report, National and Local

Broadcasting, July 1, 1974–June 30, 1975," folder 23, box 6, WNET Archive Collection, National Public Broadcasting Archives, University of Maryland, College Park, MD).

51. Interview with Brown.

52. "WNET Vows Fight to Get CPB Funding for Black Series," *Broadcasting*, 46. The estimate of 100,000 expressions of support is quoted in Tom Shales, "A Lost 'Soul'?" *Washington Post*, May 17, 1973.

53. On the implied threat of viewer picketing, see "WNET Vows Fight to Get CPB Funding for Black Series," *Broadcasting*, 46. Although such pickets never materialized, viewer support may have played a role in the CPB's July announcement of a one-time grant of $175,000 to WNET to produce two one-hour programs, one on gospel music and the other on Alvin Ailey's dance troupe, for the 1973–74 season. Although not presented under the *Soul!* banner, these programs kept Haizlip and other core employees of the program on Channel 13's payroll into 1974. See "'Soul!' Kept Alive by Two-Show Grant."

54. Moten and Harney, "The University and the Undercommons," 102–4. Moten and Harney were speaking of the university, but insofar as they see the university as an extension of the state (and in that sense not opposed to the prison but on a continuum with it), their theorizations are relevant to my thinking here. Their concept of the undercommons has more recently been explored in *The Undercommons: Fugitive Planning and Black Study*.

55. *Soul!*, "To the People, Thank You," March 7, 1973. My understanding of Haizlip's words leads me to think that he saw the last *Soul!* episode as beginning "the root of documenting our own history," but it is also possible to hear the word "route" in his phrase.

56. The quotes from the letter are my own transcription from a tape of the episode. I cannot vouch for the spelling of the writer's name.

57. In using the term *disidentification*, of course I am referring to Muñoz, *Disidentifications*.

58. I discuss this scene from the episode with Carmichael at greater length in the introduction.

59. In Ellison's novel, of course, the *Invisible Man* narrates from an underground location. The speaker of Hughes's "I, Too" notes that although in the present he is relegated to the kitchen, he will laugh and grow strong there, preparing for a different tomorrow.

60. Watts and Wickham, "Hooray for that Sweet Soul Music."

61. For a fuller account of the work of Cage and Ra regarding vibrations, see Wald, "Soul Vibrations."

62. Dede Compagno, "The Ellis 'n' Alice Show," *Image: Channel 13 Program Guide* 7, 8 (June 1970): 12.

63. Quoted in Les Ledbetter, "Sunday Is Soul Day at Lincoln Center," *New York Times*, July 21, 1972.

64. Ellis B. Haizlip, "Note from the Producer," n.p., Lincoln Center Presents Soul at the Center program, July 23 through August 5, Lincoln Center for the Performing Arts Archives, New York, NY.

Conclusion

1. "Why This Issue?," *Freedomways* 14, no. 3 (1974): 181. The journal's associate editors at the time were John Henrik Clarke, Ernest Kaiser, and J. H. O'Dell.

2. Hobson, "The Rise and Fall of Blacks in Serious Television," 185.

3. Hobson, "The Rise and Fall of Blacks in Serious Television," 185. I distance myself from Hobson's critique of entertainment programming—including *Soul Train*, which she derided as "that boogalooing Black answer to Dick Clark's sedate *American Bandstand*" (191). The black community, she wrote, "has allowed itself to be too easily seduced by media forms that serve no immediate purpose other than to entertain" (197).

4. Baraka, "The Soul Brother," 148.

5. Quoted in "Soul at the Center: A Summary," unsigned and undated document, Lincoln Center for the Performing Arts Archives, New York, NY. A July 1973 display advertisement in the *New York Times* promises a lineup that includes *Soul!* veterans as well as Aretha Franklin, whom Haizlip wanted but was unable to get either for *Soul!* or the Lincoln Center festivals.

6. Aletti, "Paar-ty at the Lincoln Center"; David A. Andelman, "Suburbia: A New Jazz Constituency?" *New York Times*, July 9, 1973.

7. Baraka, "The Soul Brother," 148.

8. *Soul!*, "Wherever We May Be," February 7, 1973.

9. Interview with Haizlip.

10. Interview with Fields.

11. I attribute this observation to Thomas Harris, who noted that "*Soul!* was Haizlip's Factory—Factory and Spirit House together" (interview). Similarly, Haizlip's friend Carlos de Jesus described the producer as "an artist in getting people together" (interview).

Bibliography

A note on sources: an accurate and complete accounting of *Soul!* episodes from 1968 to 1973 is elusive. For this book, I have relied on a combination of sources, including Channel 13 (WNDT and WNET) press releases; TV listings from the *New York Times*; published previous or reviews of episodes; archival documents such as memoranda and letters; video archives at the Library of Congress, the University of Georgia, and the WPA Film Library; and a listing of *Soul!* episodes at http://www.thirteen.org/soul/about-soul/soul -episode-guide-1968-1973/. When necessary, I indicate my uncertainty about the reliability of these sources in the text. For example, press releases sent to print media do not necessarily reflect last-minute changes to the line-ups of episodes. Thus, while the Thirteen.org listing is the most definitive widely available source on *Soul!*, it has omissions and errors that this book addresses. For example, it contains no reference to Toni Morrison's appearance on *Soul!*, although Chester Himes's photograph, reproduced here, and other published sources provide evidence of her presence on a show featuring Junior Walker and the Allstars from April 1971. That said, I have not been able to locate footage of this episode.

Archives Consulted

Ellis B. Haizlip Papers (gift of Doris Sanders), Anacostia Community Museum Archives, Smithsonian Institution, Washington, DC.
Ford Foundation Archives, Rockefeller Archive Center, New York, NY.
Lincoln Center for the Performing Arts Archives, New York, NY.
National Public Broadcasting Archives, University of Maryland, College Park, MD.
WNET Archives, New York, NY.

WNET Collection; Motion Picture, Broadcast and Recorded Sound Division; Library of Congress, Washington, DC.

Interviews Cited

Amiri Baraka, phone, August 5, 2009.
Alonzo Brown Jr., Washington, DC, June 26, 2009.
Ivan Curry, phone, July 7, 2009.
Carlos de Jesus, New York City, August 13, 2009.
Walter Fields, phone, July 20, 2009.
Vertamae Grosvenor, Washington, DC, August 28, 2009.
Harold Haizlip, phone, August 31, 2009.
Thomas Allen Harris, phone, September 16, 2009.
Nona Hendryx, phone, June 24, 2009.
Anna Horsford, phone, November 14, 2007.
Al Johnson, phone, July 22, 2009.
Florence Ladd, phone, October 4, 2012.
Felipe Luciano, phone, June 2 and July 7, 2009.
Christopher "Kit" Lukas, phone, March 11, 2009.
Novella Nelson, New York City, June 29, 2009.
Valerie Patterson, phone, August 4, 2009.
Alvin Poussaint, phone, July 15, 2009.
Bobby Sanabria, phone, July 29, 2009.
Cheryl Sanders, Washington, August 12, 2009.
Sarah-Ann Shaw, phone, October 14, 2009.
Andrew Stern, phone, February 16, 2013.
Roland Washington, phone, July 12, 2009.
Jack Willis, phone, September 10, 2009.
Camille Yarbrough, phone, February 6, 2009.

Secondary Sources

Abdul, Raoul. *Famous Black Entertainers of Today*. New York: Dodd, Mead, 1974.
Acham, Christine. *Revolution Televised: Prime Time and the Struggle for Black Power*. Minneapolis: University of Minnesota Press, 2004.
Aletti, Vince. "Paar-ty at the Lincoln Center: Beige Is Beautiful." *Rolling Stone*, October 25, 1973, 20–22.
Allen, Robert L. *Black Awakening in Capitalist America: An Analytic History*. Garden City, NY: Doubleday, 1969.

Anderson, Telia U. "'Calling on the Spirit': The Performativity of Black Women's Faith in the Baptist Church Spiritual Traditions and Its Radical Possibilities for Resistance." In *African American Performance and Theater History: A Critical Reader*, edited by Harry J. Elam Jr. and David Krassner, 114–31. New York: Oxford University Press, 2001.

Ang, Ien. *Desperately Seeking the Audience*. New York: Routledge, 1991.

Appiah, Anthony, and Henry L. Gates. *Africana: Civil Rights: an A-to-Z Reference of the Movement That Changed America*. Philadelphia: Running Press, 2004.

Arlen, Michael J. "Comment." *New Yorker*, February 5, 1972, 27.

Arnold, Matthew, and Jane Garnett. *Culture and Anarchy*. Oxford: Oxford University Press, 2006. *eBook Collection (EBSCOhost)*. Web. July 18, 2014.

Austen, Jake. *TV A-Go-Go: Rock on TV from American Bandstand to American Idol*. Chicago: Chicago Review, 2005.

Baker, Houston, Jr. *Blues, Ideology, and Afro-American Literature: A Vernacular Theory*. Chicago: University of Chicago Press, 1984.

———. "Critical Memory and the Black Public Sphere." In *The Black Public Sphere*, edited by the Black Public Sphere Collective, 5–38. Chicago: University of Chicago Press, 1995.

Baldwin, James. "Freaks and the American Ideal of Manhood." 1985. In James Baldwin, *Collected Essays*. New York: Library of America, 1998, 814–29.

———. "Letter from a Region of My Mind." *New Yorker*, November 17, 1962.

———. "Sweet Lorraine." 1969. In *The Price of the Ticket: Collected Nonfiction, 1948–1985*, 443–47. New York: St. Martin's Press, 1985.

Baldwin, James, and Nikki Giovanni. *A Dialogue*. Philadelphia: Lippincott, 1973.

Baraka, Amiri. "The Changing Same (R&B and New Black Music)." In *The LeRoi Jones/Amiri Baraka Reader*, edited by William J. Harris, 186–209. New York: Thunder's Mouth, 1991.

———. *It's Nation Time*. Chicago: Third World Press, 1970.

———. "The Soul Brother." In Amiri Baraka, *Eulogies*, 147–49. New York: Marsilio, 1996.

———. *Spirit Reach*. Newark, NJ: Jihad Productions, 1972.

Barsamian, David. *The Decline and Fall of Public Broadcasting*. Cambridge, MA: South End, 2001.

Berlant, Lauren. *Cruel Optimism*. Durham, NC: Duke University Press, 2011.

Bernard, Emily. "A Familiar Strangeness: The Spectre of Whiteness in the Harlem Renaissance and the Black Arts Movement." In *New Thoughts on the Black Arts Movement*, edited by Lisa Gail Collins and Margo Natalie Crawford, 255–72. New Brunswick, NJ: Rutgers University Press, 2008.

Berrios-Miranda, Marisol. "Salsa Music as Expressive Liberation." *Centro Journal* 16, no. 2 (2004): 157–73.

Blue, Mary, and Vanessa Murphree. "'Stoke the Joke' and His 'Self-Appointed White Critics': A Clash of Values on Network Television News, 1966–70." *Media History* 15, no. 2 (2009): 205–20.

Bodroghkozy, Aniko. *Equal Time: Television and the Civil Rights Movement.* Urbana: University of Illinois Press, 2012.

———. *Groove Tube: Sixties Television and Youth Rebellion.* Durham, NC: Duke University Press, 2001.

———. "'Is This What You Mean by Color TV?': Race, Gender, and Contested Meanings in NBC's *Julia*." In *Private Screenings: Television and the Female Consumer*, edited by Lynn Spiegel and Denise Mann, 143–68. Minneapolis: University of Minnesota Press, 1992.

Bogle, Donald. *Primetime Blues: African Americans on Network Television.* New York: Farrar, Straus and Giroux, 2001.

Brennan, Teresa. *The Transmission of Affect.* Ithaca, NY: Cornell University Press, 2004.

Brooks, Daphne A. "'All That You Can't Leave Behind': Black Female Soul Singing and the Politics of Surrogation in the Age of Catastrophe." *Meridians* 8, no. 1 (2008): 180–204.

———. *Bodies in Dissent: Spectacular Performances of Race and Freedom, 1850–1910.* Durham, NC: Duke University Press, 2006.

———. "Nina Simone's Triple Play." *Callaloo* 34, no. 1 (2011): 176–97.

———. "'Sister, Can You Line It Out?': Zora Neale Hurston and the Sound of Angular Black Womanhood." *Amerikastudien / American Studies* 55, no. 4 (2010): 617–27.

Brown, H. Rap. *Die, Nigger, Die!* 1969. Reprint, Chicago: Lawrence Hill, 2002.

Brown, Jayna. *Babylon Girls: Black Women Performers and the Shaping of the Modern.* Durham, NC: Duke University Press, 2008.

Brown, Les. *Television: The Business behind the Box.* New York: Harcourt Brace Jovanovich, 1971.

"Cancellation of SOUL TV Show Termed an Insult." *Jet*, June 21, 1973, 45.

Carmichael, Stokely, and Charles V. Hamilton. *Black Power: The Politics of Liberation.* New York: Vintage Books, 1967.

Carnegie Commission on Educational Television. *Public Television, a Program for Action: The Report and Recommendations of the Carnegie Commission on Educational Television.* New York: Harper & Row, 1967.

Carson, Mina, Tisa Lewis, and Susan M. Shaw, *Girls Rock! Fifty Years of Women Making Music.* Lexington: University Press of Kentucky, 2004.

Childress, Alice. "The Soul Man." *Essence*, May 1971, 68–69, 94.

Clarke, Cheryl. *"After Mecca": Women Poets and the Black Arts Movement.* New Brunswick, NJ: Rutgers University Press, 2005.

Cleaver, Eldridge. *Soul on Ice.* New York: Random House, 1999.

Compagno, Dede. "The Ellis 'n' Alice Show." *Image: Channel 13 Program Guide,* June 1970, 12–15.

Day, James. *The Vanishing Vision: The Inside Story of Public Television.* Berkeley: University of California Press, 1995.

Delmont, Matthew F. *The Nicest Kids in Town:* American Bandstand, *Rock 'n' Roll, and the Struggle for Civil Rights in 1950s Philadelphia.* Berkeley: University of California Press, 2012.

Dolan, Jill. "Performance, Utopia, and the 'Utopian Performative.'" *Theater Journal* 53, no. 3 (2001): 455–79.

Du Bois, W. E. B. *The Souls of Black Folk.* New York: Penguin, 1996.

Edwards, Erica R. *Charisma and the Fictions of Black Leadership.* Minneapolis: University of Minnesota Press, 2012.

Efron, Edith. "What Is Happening to Blacks in Broadcasting?" *TV Guide,* August 26, 1972, 20–25.

Ellison, Ralph. *Invisible Man.* New York: Vintage, 1995.

Fanon, Frantz. *A Dying Colonialism.* Translated by Haakon Chevalier. New York: Grove, 1967.

Fearn-Banks, Kathleen, ed. *Historical Dictionary of African-American Television.* Lanham, MD: Scarecrow, 2006.

Ferguson, Karen. *Top Down: The Ford Foundation, Black Power, and the Reinvention of Racial Liberalism.* Philadelphia: University of Pennsylvania Press, 2013.

Ferguson, Roderick A. *The Reorder of Things: The University and Its Pedagogies of Minority Difference.* Minneapolis: University of Minnesota Press, 2012.

Ford Foundation. *Ford Foundation Activities in Noncommercial Broadcasting, 1951–1977.* New York: Ford Foundation, 1977.

Fowler, Virginia C. *Nikki Giovanni: A Literary Biography.* Santa Barbara, CA: Praeger, 2013.

Frazier, Taj P. "Baraka, Brother Mao, and the Year of '74." *Souls* 8, no. 3 (2006): 142–59.

Frith, Simon. "Look! Hear! The Uneasy Relationship of Music and Television." *Popular Music* 21, no. 3 (2002): 277–90.

Gates, Henry Louis, Jr. *Thirteen Ways of Looking at a Black Man.* New York: Random House, 1997.

Giovanni, Nikki. *Black Feeling Black Talk.* New York: Afro-Arts, 1968.

———. *Black Judgment.* Detroit: Broadside Press, 1968.

———. *Gemini: An Extended Autobiographical Statement on My First Twenty-Five Years as a Black Poet.* Indianapolis: Bobbs-Merrill, 1971.

Giovanni, Nikki, and the New York Community Choir. *Truth Is on Its Way.* New York: Right-On Records, 1971.

Gould, Deborah B. *Moving Politics: Emotion and ACT UP's Fight against AIDS.* Chicago: University of Chicago Press, 2009.

Gramsci, Antonio. *Selections from the Prison Notebook.* Edited and translated by Quintin Hoare and Geoffrey Nowell Smith. New York: International Publishers, 1971.

Gray, Herman. *Cultural Moves: African Americans and the Politics of Representation.* Berkeley: University of California Press, 2005.

———. "Subject(ed) to Recognition." *American Quarterly* 65, no. 4 (2013): 771–98.

———. *Watching Race: Television and the Struggle for "Blackness."* Minneapolis: University of Minnesota Press, 1995.

Greenlee, Sam. *The Spook Who Sat by the Door: A Novel.* New York: R. W. Baron, 1969.

Griffin, Farah Jasmine. "When Malindy Sings: A Meditation on Black Women's Vocality." In *Uptown Conversation: The New Jazz Studies*, edited by Robert G. O'Meally, Brent Hayes Edwards, and Farah Jasmine Griffin, 102–25. New York: Columbia University Press, 2004.

Hall, Jacquelyn Dowd. "The Long Civil Rights Movement and the Political Uses of the Past." *Journal of American History* 91, no. 4 (March 2005): 1233–63.

Hall, Stuart. "Encoding/Decoding." In *The Cultural Studies Reader*, edited by Simon During, 90–103. New York: Routledge, 1999.

Harper, Phillip Brian. "Extra-Special Effects: Televisual Representation and the Claims of 'the Black Experience.'" In *Living Color: Race and Television in the United States*, edited by Sasha Torres, 62–81. Durham, NC: Duke University Press, 1998.

Harney, Stefano, and Fred Moten. "The University and the Undercommons: Seven Theses." *Social Text* 79 (summer 2004): 101–15.

———. *The Undercommons: Fugitive Planning and Black Study.* Wivenhoe; New York; Port Watson: Minor Compositions, 2013.

Haskins, James. "New Black Images in the Mass Media—How Educational Is Educational TV?" *Freedomways* 14, no. 3 (1974): 200–208.

Heard, Nathan. *A Cold Fire Burning.* New York: Simon and Schuster, 1974.

Heilbut, Anthony. *The Fan Who Knew Too Much: Aretha Franklin, the Rise of the Soap Opera, the Children of the Gospel Church, and other Meditations.* New York: Alfred P. Knopf, 2012.

Heitner, Devorah. *Black Power TV.* Durham, NC: Duke University Press, 2013.

Henderson, Stephen. "The Forms of Things Unknown." In *Understanding the New Black Poetry: Black Speech and Black Music as Poetic References.* New York: Morrow, 1973.

Hernandez, Rod. "Latin Soul: Cross-Cultural Connections between the Black Arts Movement and Pocho-Che." In *New Thoughts on the Black Arts Movement*, edited by Lisa Gail Collins and Margo Natalie Crawford, 333–48. New Brunswick, NJ: Rutgers University Press, 2008.

Hickey, Neil. "Do TV Cameras Add Fuel to Riot Flames?" *TV Guide*, September 16, 1967, 6–12.

Hobson, Sheila Smith. "The Rise and Fall of Blacks in Serious Television." *Freedomways* 14, no. 3 (1974): 185–99.

Hoynes, William. *Public Television for Sale: Media, the Markets, and the Public Sphere*. Boulder, CO: Westview, 1994.

Iton, Richard. *In Search of the Black Fantastic: Politics and Popular Culture in the Post-Civil Rights Era*. New York: Oxford University Press, 2010.

Jefferson, Margo. "Different Drums." *Newsweek*, May 6, 1974, 86–87.

Johnson, E. Patrick. "Camp Revival: 'Quaring' Masculinity in the Black Church." Paper presented at the annual meeting of the American Studies Association, Oakland, CA, October 13, 2006.

———. "*From* Quare Studies, or Almost Everything I Know about Queer Studies I Learned from My Grandmother." *Callaloo* 23, no. 1 (2000): 120–21.

Johnson, Lyndon B. "The President's Address to the Nation on Civil Disorders." July 27, 1967. In *Public Papers of the Presidents of the United States: Lyndon B. Johnson*. Washington: GPO, 1968.

———. "Remarks upon Signing Order Establishing the National Advisory Commission on Civil Disorders." July 29, 1967. In *Public Papers of the Presidents of the United States: Lyndon B. Johnson*. Washington: G.P.O., 1968.

Jones, LeRoi. *Blues People: Negro Music in White America*. New York: W. Morrow, 1963.

———. "City of Harlem." In LeRoi Jones, *Home: Social Essays*, 107–14. New York: Akashic, 1966.

Joseph, Peniel E. *Waiting 'til the Midnight Hour: A Narrative History of Black Power in America*. New York: Henry Holt, 2006.

Jottar, Berta. "Central Park Rumba: Nuyorican Identity and the Return to African Roots." *Centro Journal* 23, no. 1 (2011): 4–29.

Keeling, Kara. *The Witch's Flight: The Cinematic, the Black Femme, and the Image of Common Sense*. Durham, NC: Duke University Press, 2007.

Kelley, Robin D. G. *Freedom Dreams: The Black Radical Imagination*. Boston: Beacon, 1992.

Killens, John O. *The Cotillion, or One Good Bull Is Half the Herd*. 1971. Reprint, Minneapolis, MN: Coffee House, 2002.

———. "'Our Struggle Is Not to Be White Men in Black Skin': A Writer's Observations of the State of Negroes in TV." *TV Guide*, July 25, 1970, 6–9.

King, Jason. "Toni Braxton, Disney, and Thermodynamics." *TDR: The Drama Review* 46, no. 3 (2002): 54–81.

Kruth, John. *Bright Moments: The Life & Legacy of Rahsaan Roland Kirk*. New York: Welcome Rain, 2000.

LaBelle, Patti, with Laura B. Randolph. *Don't Block the Blessings: Revelations of a Lifetime*. New York: Riverhead, 1996.

The Last Angel of History. Dir. John Amkofrah. First Run/Icarus Films, 1995. Film.

Ledbetter, James. *Made Possible By—: The Death of Public Broadcasting in the United States*. New York: Verso, 1997.

Lentz, Kirsten Marthe. "Quality versus Relevance: Feminism, Race, and the Politics of the Sign in 1970s Television." *Camera Obscura* 15, no. 1 (2000): 44–93.

Lorde, Audre. *Sister Outsider: Essays and Speeches*. Trumansburg, NY: Crossing Press, 1984.

———. *Zami: A New Spelling of My Name*. Watertown, MA: Persephone, 1982.

Lott, Tommy Lee. "Documenting Social Issues: Black Journal, 1968–1970." In *Struggles for Representation: African American Documentary Film and Video*, edited by Janet K. Cutler and Phyllis Rauch Klotman, 71–98. Bloomington: Indiana University Press, 1999.

———. *The Invention of Race: Black Culture and the Politics of Representation*. Oxford: Blackwell, 1999.

Lotz, Amanda D. *The Television Will Be Revolutionized*. New York: New York University Press, 2007.

Loza, Steven. *Tito Puente and the Making of Latin Music*. Urbana: University of Illinois Press, 1999.

Lukas, Christopher. "Memories of Ellis Haizlip and Enlightenment." Thirteen. Accessed June 8, 2014. http://www.thirteen.org/soul/about-soul/memories-of-ellis-haizlip-and-enlightenment-by-soul-producer-christopher-lukas.

MacDonald, J. Fred. *Blacks and White TV: Afro-Americans in Television since 1948*. Chicago: Nelson-Hall, 1983.

Macy, John, Jr. *To Irrigate a Wasteland: The Struggle to Shape a Public Television System in the United States*. Berkeley: University of California Press, 1974.

Marable, Manning. *Race, Reform, and Rebellion: The Second Reconstruction and Beyond in Black America, 1945–2006*. Jackson: University of Mississippi Press, 2007.

Mayfield, Curtis, and the Impressions. *Movin' on Up: The Music and Message of Curtis Mayfield and the Impressions*. DVD. San Diego: Reelin' in the Years Productions, 2008.

Medsger, Betty. *The Burglary: The Discovery of J. Edgar Hoover's FBI*. New York: Alfred A. Knopf, 2014.

Meyer, Richard J. "ETV and the Ghetto." *Educational Broadcasting Review* 2 (August 1968): 19–24.

Minow, Newton N. "Television and the Public Interest." *Federal Communications Law Journal* 55 (2002–3), 395–406.

Mitchell, Timothy. "Society, Economy, and the State Effect." In *State/Culture: State-Formation after the Cultural Turn*, edited by George Steinmetz, 76–97. Ithaca, NY: Cornell University Press, 1999.

Monson, Ingrid. *Freedom Sounds: Civil Rights Call Out to Jazz and to Africa*. New York: Oxford University Press, 2007.

Moten, Fred. "Blackness and Nothingness (Mysticism in the Flesh)." *South Atlantic Quarterly* 112, no. 4 (2013): 737–80.

———. *In the Break: The Aesthetics of the Black Radical Tradition*. Minneapolis: University of Minnesota Press, 2003.

Mumford, Kevin. "Harvesting the Crisis: The Newark Uprising, the Kerner Commission, and Writings on Riots." In *African American Urban History Since World War II*, edited by Kenneth L. Kusmer and Joe W. Trotter, 203–18. Chicago: University of Chicago Press, 2009.

Muñoz, José E. *Cruising Utopia: The Then and There of Queer Futurity*. New York: New York University Press, 2009.

———. *Disidentifications: Queers of Color and the Performance of Politics*. Minneapolis: University of Minnesota Press, 1999.

Neal, Mark Anthony. "Nickolas Ashford and the Cult of Black Manhood." NewBlackMan (in Exile), September 2, 2011. Accessed June 12, 2014. http://new blackman.blogspot.com/2011/09/nickolas-ashford-and-cult-of-black.html.

———. "Sold Out on Soul: The Corporate Annexation of Black Popular Music." *Popular Music and Society* 21, no. 3 (1997), 117–35.

———. *Songs in the Key of Black Life: A Rhythm and Blues Nation*. New York: Routledge, 2003.

Ogbar, Jeffrey O. G. "Puerto Rico en Mi Corazón: The Young Lords, Black Power and Puerto Rican Nationalism in the U.S., 1966–1972." *Centro Journal* 18, no. 1 (2006): 148–69.

Omi, Michael, and Howard Winant. *Racial Formation in the United States: From the 1960s to the 1990s*. 2nd edition, New York: Routledge, 1994.

Ongiri, Amy Abugo. *Spectacular Blackness: The Cultural Politics of the Black Power Movement and the Search for a Black Aesthetic*. Charlottesville: University of Virginia Press, 2010.

Ouellette, Laurie. *Viewers Like You? How Public TV Failed the People*. New York: Columbia University Press, 2002.

Ozersky, Josh. *Archie Bunker's America: TV in an Era of Change, 1968–1978*. Foreword by Mark Crispin Miller. Carbondale: Southern Illinois University Press, 2003.

Perlman, Allison. "Television, Racial Inequality, and 'Carpetbagger Justice': The Peculiar History of the Alabama Educational Television Commission." Paper presented at the annual meeting of the American Studies Association, San Juan, Puerto Rico, November 15, 2012.

Peterson, Carla L. "Eccentric Bodies." In *Recovering the Black Female Body: Self-Representations by African American Women*, edited by Michael Bennett and Vanessa D. Dickerson, ix–xvi. New Brunswick, NJ: Rutgers University Press, 2001.

Reed, Anthony. *Freedom Time: The Poetics and Politics of Black Experimental Writing*. Baltimore: Johns Hopkins University Press, 2014.

Retman, Sonnet. "Between Rock and a Hard Place: Narrating Nona Hendryx's Inscrutable Career." *Women and Performance* 16, no. 1 (2006): 107–18.

Rickford, Russell J. *Betty Shabazz: A Remarkable Story of Survival and Faith before and after Malcolm X*. Foreword by Myrlie Evers-Williams. Naperville, IL: Sourcebooks, 2003.

Rodgers, Carolyn. *A Long Rap: Commonly Known as a Poetic Essay*. Detroit: Broadside Press, 1971.

Rooks, Noliwe M. *White Money/Black Power: The Surprising History of African American Studies and the Crisis of Race in Higher Education*. Boston: Beacon, 2006.

Royster, Francesca T. *Sounding Like a No-No: Queer Sounds and Eccentric Acts in the Post-Soul Era*. Ann Arbor: University of Michigan Press, 2013.

Scott-Heron, Gil. *The Last Holiday: A Memoir*. New York: Grove, 2012.

Self, Robert O. *All in the Family: The Realignment of American Democracy since the 1960s*. New York: Hill and Wang, 2012.

Senate Subcommittee on Commerce. "Long Range Funding for Public Broadcasting." *Report of the Senate Subcommittee on Commerce on S. 2584: To Amend Certain Provisions of the Communications Act of 1934, as Amended, to Provide Long-Term Financing for the Corporation for Public Broadcasting, and for Other Purposes*. Washington: GPO, 1975.

Sexton, Jared. "The Social Life of Social Death: On Afro-Pessimism and Black Optimism." *Tensions* 5 (Fall/Winter 2011). Web. Accessed July 14, 2014.

Shaw, Sarah-Ann. "The History of *Say Brother*," *The Say Brother Collection*. Web. http://main.wgbh.org/saybrother/history.html. Accessed July 27, 2014.

Smart-Grosvenor, Vertamae. *Vibration Cooking; Or, the Travel Notes of a Geechee Girl*. Garden City, NY: Doubleday, 1970.

Smith, Arthur L. "Television and the Tactics of Black Revolution." In *Television and the New Persuasion*, edited by Donn W. Parson and Wil A. Linkugel, 49–69. Lawrence, KS: House of Usher, 1970.

"*Soul!* Kept Alive by Two-Show Grant." *Broadcasting*, July 16, 1973, 34.

Spiegel, Lynn, and Michael Curtin. *The Revolution Wasn't Televised: Sixties Television and Social Conflict*. New York: Routledge, 1997.

Springer, Kimberly. "Black Feminists Respond to Black Power Masculinism." In *The Black Power Movement: Rethinking the Civil Rights–Black Power Era*, edited by Peniel E. Joseph, 105–88. New York: Routledge, 2006.

Squires, Catherine R. "Rethinking the Black Public Sphere: An Alternative Vocabulary for Multiple Public Spheres." *Communication Theory* 12, no. 4 (2002): 446–68.

Staple Singers, *Be Altitude: Respect Yourself*. CD. Stax, 1989.

Stewart, Jacqueline. "Negroes Laughing at Themselves? Black Spectatorship and the Performance of Urban Modernity." *Critical Inquiry* 29, no. 4 (2003): 650–77.

Sutherland, Meghan. *The Flip Wilson Show*. Detroit: Wayne State University Press, 2008.

Torres, Sasha. *Black, White, and in Color: Television and Black Civil Rights*. Princeton, NJ: Princeton University Press, 2003.

———, ed. *Living Color: Race and Television in the United States*. Durham, NC: Duke University Press, 1998.

"TV and the Riots," Congressional Record, Senate, S14075, October 3, 1967.

Tynan, Kenneth. "Fifteen Years of the Salto Mortale." *New Yorker*, February 20, 1978. Web. http://www.newyorker.com/magazine/1978/02/20/fifteen-years -of-the-salto-mortale.

United States Department of Labor, Office of Policy Planning and Research. *The Negro Family: The Case for National Action*. Washington: GPO, 1965.

United States National Advisory Commission on Civil Disorders. *Report of the National Advisory Commission on Civil Disorders*. New York: Bantam Books, 1968.

Vazquez, Alexandra T. *Listening in Detail: Performances of Cuban Music*. Durham, NC: Duke University Press, 2013.

Vogel, Shane. *The Scene of Harlem Cabaret: Race, Sexuality, Performance*. Chicago: University of Chicago Press, 2009.

Wald, Gayle. "Soul Vibrations: Black Music and Black Freedom in Sound and Space." *American Quarterly* 63, no. 3 (2011): 673–96.

Wallace, Michele. *Black Macho and the Myth of the Superwoman*. 1979. Reprint, New York: Verso, 1999.

Ward, Stephen. "The Third World Women's Alliance: Black Feminist Radicalism and Black Power Politics." In *The Black Power Movement: Rethinking the Civil Rights–Black Power Era*, edited by Peniel E. Joseph, 119–44. New York: Routledge, 2006.

Wareham, Roger, and Peter C. Bynoe. "The New Stereotypes Are No Better Than the Old." *Urban Review* 6, no. 2 (1972): 14–18.

Warwick, Jacqueline. *Girl Groups, Girl Culture: Popular Music and Identity in the 1960s.* New York: Routledge, 2007.

Watts, Michael, and Vicki Wickham, "Hooray for That Sweet Soul Music." *Melody Maker*, March 3, 1973, 24.

Weingarten, Marc. *Station to Station: The History of Rock 'n' Roll on Television.* New York: Pocket, 2000.

Wilkinson, Michelle Joan. "'To Make a Poet Black': Canonizing Puerto Rican Poets in the Black Arts Movement." In *New Thoughts on the Black Arts Movement*, edited by Lisa Gail Collins and Margo Natalie Crawford, 317–32. New Brunswick, NJ: Rutgers University Press, 2008.

Williams, Raymond. *Marxism and Literature.* Oxford: Oxford University Press, 1977.

———. *Television: Technology and Cultural Form.* 3rd ed. New York: Routledge, 2003.

Wilson, Olly. "The Heterogeneous Sound Ideal in African-American Music." In *New Perspectives on Music: Essays in Honor of Eileen Southern*, edited by Josephine Wright with Samuel A. Floyd Jr., 326–37. Warren, MI: Harmonie Park, 1992.

Winston, Michael R. "Racial Consciousness and the Evolution of Mass Communications in the United States." *Daedalus* 111, no. 4 (1982): 179–81.

"WNET Vows Fight to Get CPB Funding for Black Series." *Broadcasting*, May 21, 1973, 46.

Woodard, Komozi. *A Nation within a Nation: Amiri Baraka (LeRoi Jones) and Black Power Politics.* Chapel Hill: University of North Carolina Press, 1999.

Zinn, Howard, and Anthony Arnove. *Voices of a People's History of the United States.* New York: Seven Stories Press, 2004.

Index

Acklin, Barbara, 77
Affective compact: affect theory, 72; black audiences, 42–43, 51, 72–73, 86–91; black counterpublic spaces, 25, 151, 173–74; Latino music on "Shades of Soul I," 127–33, 240n40; of *Soul!*, 20–25, 27–28, 70, 71, 72, 86–91; transmission of affect, 72. *See also* Vibrations
African American (use of term), 225n4
African American church: black cultural expression in, 23–24, 69, 91, 141; Church of God (Holiness congregations), 23, 228n44; communities in, 23–24; concerts compared to revival meetings, 122; sexual difference in, 24, 229n45, 243n14; as touchstone for *Soul!*, 23, 24, 69, 88, 91, 109–10, 164, 228n44; traditions of dissent in, 110; vibrations in, 23–24
Afro-Boricuan consciousness, 128, 130
Afro-Cuban percussion, 127, 131, 132, 135–36
Afrofuturism, 23, 139, 228n42
Afros, 8, 18, 53, 79, 104–5, *105*
Agnew, Spiro, 186
Ailey, Alvin, 150, 250n53
Alabama Educational Television Commission, 56
Allen, Debbie, 108

Allen, Robert, 61
"Alone Again," 206
American Bandstand, 13–14, 113, 116
Amos 'n' Andy, 12
Amsterdam News, 73, 99
Anderson, Gloria, 198, 200
Anderson, Marian, 22
Angelou, Maya, 92
Apollo Theater, 22, 76, 99–100
Arlen, Michael, 189
Arsenio Hall Show, 12, 218
Ashby, Dorothy, 23
Ashford, Nick, 1, 6, 104, *105*, 144
Atkins, Cholly, 115
Audience, black: black community reflected in, 10–11, 65–68, 69, 71, 74, 80–81; collective intimacy experienced by, 159–60, 164, 244n23; cultural practices of, 73–74; demographics of, 5, 42, 47, 50–51, 55, 58–59, 76, 192; development of programming for, 46, 54; identification of, 43–44; letters in support of *Soul!*, 99, 100, 102, 200–201, 204–6, 213–14, 238n50; polls of, 5, 97, 183, 192, 247n26; on provocative language in *Soul!*, 191

Baldwin, David, 156, 157, 162
Baldwin, James, *158*; black Left criticism of, 155; on black masculinity,

Baldwin, James (*continued*)
156, 159, 161–62; Giovanni dialogue
with, 154–57, 244nn22–23; on
misfittedness, 145, 151, 155, 161–62;
receptiveness to Elijah Muhammad,
168, 244n28; sexual identity of, 151,
155, 161–62; spiritual formation of,
228n44
Baldwin-Giovanni dialogue: on black
sexuality, 157, 161–62, 165; family in,
157, 159; Giovanni's feminist critique
of Baldwin, 154, 157–59; intimacy of,
159–60, 164, 244n23; staging for, 156,
161; weirdness, 160, 161
Bambara, Toni Cade, 206
Baraka, Amina, 172, 174, 176
Baraka, Amiri (LeRoi Jones), *170*;
background of, 23, 169; on black
music, 88, 106–7, 122; "The Changing Same" (Baraka), 106–7, 127, 151;
on family, 172–78; on Haizlip, 171,
213, 214, 234n12; on homosexuality,
174–75; plays of, 87; political work,
169, 172–73; on social change, 214; on
Soul!, 19, 92, 98; Spirit House, 75–76,
217–18; viewers' reaction to, 204; on
women's family roles, 172–73, 174
"Baraka, the Artist," 169, 171–80
Batten, Tony, 194, 198
BBC, 187, 188, 249n48
Beach Boys, 23, 209
Beautiful (use of term), 30, 32–33
Belafonte, Harry, 1, 9, 81–82, 115, *148*
Berlant, Lauren, 33
Bernard, Emily, 244n19
Berry, Gordy, 14
Big Bird, 187, 191, 246n15
Black (use of term), 225n4
Black Awakening in Capitalist America
(Allen), 61
Black community: as audience for *Soul!*,
10–11, 64–69, 71, 74, 81, 98; Haizlip
on, 23–24, 65–68, 69, 71, 74–76;
impact of civil rights movement on,
37; letters in support of *Soul!*, 99, 100,
102, 200–201, 204–6, 213–14, 238n50

Black consciousness, 2, 56, 70, 82, 87–91
Black employment: on television, 29,
40–41, 51, 59–60, 248n38
Black Experience Revival, 22
Black Feeling, Black Talk (Giovanni), 155
Black feminism, 12, 19, 79, 139–40, 154,
157–60, 228n33
"Black is beautiful," 7, 21, 30, 106, 142
Black Journal: audience for, 193; cancellation of, 182; as competition to *Soul!*,
192, 248n30, 248n38; criticism of, 60,
197, 248n30; format of, 39; funding
for, 54–55, 98, 183, 248n34; government opposition to, 190, 247n22;
political influence of Tony Brown,
191–93, 248n32; support for, 27, 198,
199; "Where It's At," 58, 59, 63–64, 65,
66, 69
Black Judgement (Giovanni), 155
Black Left, 154, 155
*Black Macho and the Myth of Super-
woman* (Wallace), 19, 155–56
Black masculinity, 86, 102, 126, 156, 157,
159–62, 166–67, 175
Black music: agency given to musicians,
112–13, 239n14; artistic value of, 106;
as central to *Soul!*, 68, 75–76, 80,
105–7; experimentation in, 87–88,
89, 136; Latino music linked with,
132–37; Motown, 14, 114, 115; pan-
Africanist roots of, 110–11, 133–34,
135; as privileged expression of black
consciousness, 106; as space of affective exchange and cultural cocreation,
108–9
Black musical aesthetic, 96
Black Muslims. *See* Malcolm X;
Shabazz, Betty
Black nationalism, 155, 175–77
"Blacknuss," 124, 141
Black Panthers, 31, 38, 130, 155, 163, 190.
See also Cleaver, Eldridge
Black performers: on commercial television, 5, 11–12, 60, 82, 87–90, 89, 92,
117–18, 161, 237n34; discrimination
against, 26–27, 148, 150; expanded

opportunities for, 215; performance
styles of, 34, 90–91, 119–23, 134–35,
141, 211–12, 240n32
Black performing art festivals. *See* Soul
at the Center (festival)
Black political expression, 56–57, 60,
81–82, 117–18, 123–27, 152–54
Black pop, 13–14, 27, 34, 84, 98, 112, 114,
115
Black Power, 2, 9, 16, 19, 30–32, 62, 90,
139, 217, 234n60. *See also* Carmichael,
Stokely
Black programming: authority over,
197–99; black self-determination in,
64–69, 72, 75; challenges of, 55–57;
commercial underwriting of, 98; corporate sponsorship of, 98; crossracial
dialogue on, 194; funding for, 54, 56,
57, 62–64, 73, 94–96; on local PBS
stations, 191, 247n25; meaningfulness
in, 64, 74–76; minority representation
in, 196; political expression, 56–57,
60, 81–82, 117–18, 123–27; polls of,
5, 97, 192, 247n26; provocative language used in, 191; reviews of, 56;
Talking Black, 56, 57; viewer support
for, 94–100, 102, 193, 199–201, 204,
250n53
Black revolutionary project: alternative
roles in, 176–77
Black seeds, 9, 203, 207, 227n20
Black viewers: identification with *Soul!*,
99–102; influence of TV news on, 46;
Kerner Report on, 43, 46–48, 51, 66;
support for *Soul!*, 99–100, 199–201,
204–6; TV representations of vio-
lence, 46
Bledsoe, Gerry, 27, 134, 135, 136, 215
Blindness, 120, 125, 126
Bluest Eye (Morrison), 1, *3*
Bond, Julian, 77, 79
Bourne, St. Claire, 196
Bradford, Alex, 116
British boy bands, 115
Broadcasting and Social Action, 50–51, 52
Brooks, Daphne, 81, 227n32, 243n11

Brown, Alonzo, Jr., 67, 118, 239n6
Brown, H. Rap, 62
Brown, James, 107
Brown, Jayna, 243n11
Brown, Lynn, 176
Brown, Tony. See *Black Journal*
Bullins, Ed, 236n23

Cage, John, 23, 209
Call and response, 23, 88, 164
Camera focus: on audience enthusiasm,
91, 141; of children, 173, *174*; of dancers, 14, 127–28; "Farrakhan the Minister," 166; on gestures, 88, 105, 113,
159, 167–68, 179; gestures caught in,
88, 105, 113, 159, 167–68, 179; intimacy
caught in, 159–60, 164, 244n23; on
Kirk's chair act, 123–25; on Labelle,
140–41; on Latino musicians, 131;
montages, 128; on "Nigga" repeated
by David Nelson, 91; on performers,
8, 91, 124–25; of studio audience, 1, *53*,
86, 88, 105, 108, 125, 141, 167
Cancellation of *Soul!*: challenges to, 185;
Corporation for Public Broadcasting
(CPB), 29–31, 43, 94–95, 182, 194–95,
200, 250n53; Ford Foundation, 94,
101; funding cutbacks and, 95–98, 101;
Haizlip on, 181, 208, 249n48; "it's been
beautiful," 32–34, 43, 206; rejections
of refunding, 94, 95–98, 189; "To the
People, Thank You" (final *Soul!* episode), 182, 202–7
Capitalism, 61–63, 68, 107, 122, 160, 205
Carmichael, Stokely: estrangement from
SNCC, 31–32; Haizlip interview with,
30–34, 43; Miriam Makeba and, 2, 31,
110, *111*, 147, 176; nonviolence rejected
by, 31–32; *Soul!* appearance by, 1,
30–34, 142, 206
Carnegie Commission, 183, 245n4
Carroll, Diahann, 87, 89, 161
Carroll, Vinnette, 94, 148
Carson, Johnny, 11–12, 13, 26, 84, 117, 118
Carter, Betty, 118
CFUN (Committee for a Unified New-
ark), 169, 172–73, 178

Chair act (Rahsaan Roland Kirk), 123–27
"The Changing Same" (Baraka), 106–7, 127, 151
Channel 13 (WNDT), 40, 54, 56; black workers at, 40, 51; formation of, 225n1; funding for black programming, 56, 57, 62–64, 73, 94–96; language alerts, 191; on-air appeals for *Soul!*, 99, 201, 238n50; support for *Soul!*, 73–74, 94–100, 182, 199–201, 250n53; viewer support for, 99–101
Charles, Ray, 64
Children, 6, 173, 174, 175–76
Childress, Alice, 110
Chisholm, Shirley, 9, 153
"Choice of Colors" (Mayfield and the Impressions), 116
Church, black: audiences' experience of, 88, 91, 141, 164; cultural expression in, 23–24, 69, 91, 141; musical traditions of, 122, 141; sexual difference in, 24, 229n45, 243n14; as touchstone for *Soul!*, 23, 24, 69, 88, 91, 109–10, 164, 228n44; traditions of dissent in, 110; vibrations in, 23–24, 164
Church of God (Holiness congregations), 23, 228n44
Citizenship, 38, 47–50, 198
Civil rights movement, 10, 16, 36–40, 90, 228n33
Clarke, Cheryl, 226n16
Cleaver, Eldridge, 64, 76, 142, 155, 190
Cleaver, Kathleen, 1, 2, 153, 176t
Club Soul, 7, 27, 119, 123, 164
Cohambee River Collective, 160
COINTEPRO (Counter Intelligence Program), 28, 229n55
A Cold Fire Burning (Heard), 62
Colón, Willie, 6, 108, 112, 127, 131, 132–33, 241n54
Commercial television: black programming on, 5, 60, 63, 87, 88, 89, 248n34; black visibility on, 12, 13, 29, 39, 56, 117–19, 161, 205, 214; corporate sponsorship of, 60–61; government intervention in, 186; *Julia*, 5, 56, 60,

87, 88, 89–90, 92; Latino music on, 117; political expression in, 56–57, 60, 81–82, 117–18, 152–54
Committee for a Unified Newark (CFUN), 169, 172–73, 178
Congressional Black Caucus, 248n38
Congress of African Peoples, 163, 169
Cornelius, Don, 13, 84, 98
Corporate sponsorship, 13, 14, 24, 60–61, 98, 238n46
Corporation for Public Broadcasting (CPB): cancellation of *Soul!*, 29–31, 43, 94–95, 182, 194–95, 200, 250n53; government intervention in, 185–90, 246n15; *Interface* funded by, 182, 184, 189, 194, 195; racial-state reasoning of, 195, 196–99, 202, 205; "Sesame Street," 187, 191, 246n15; viewer support for *Soul!*, 99, 100, 102, 193, 199–201, 250n53
Counter Intelligence Program (COINTELPRO), 28, 229n55
Counterpublic spaces, black, 25, 151, 173–74
CPB (Corporation for Public Broadcasting): cancellation of *Soul!*, 29–31, 43, 94–95, 182, 194–95, 200, 250n53; Ford Foundation and, 54; government interest in, 185–90, 245n4, 246n15; inquiry into serving minority audiences, 200; *Interface* funded by, 182, 184, 189, 194, 195; political influences on, 31, 183; process of evaluation of, 194–96; racial-state reasoning, 195, 196–99, 202, 205; "Sesame Street," 187, 191, 246n15; viewer support for *Soul!*, 99, 100, 102, 193, 199–201, 250n53. See also WNDT (Channel 13)
Cruz, Victor Hernandez, 241n43
Curry, Ivan, 10, 112–13, 203, 239n14
Curtis, King, 110, 118

Dance, 2, 13–14, 117, 127, 131, 241n40
Dash, Sarah, 136, 137, *138*, 140
Davis, David, 69, 73–74, 95, 96, 101, 234n66, 235n4

Delatiner, Barbara, 77, 79
Delfonics, 6, 94, 162
Detroit uprisings, 39, 40
Dick Cavett Show, 118
"Die Nigga!!!" (Last Poets): audience reaction to, 87, 91, 99, 102; language of, 27, 89, 247n28; performance of, 90–91
Die Nigger, Die! (Brown), 62
Disappearance: in the evolutionary process, 181, 206, 207, 208, 214; historical necessity of, 202–3, 207–8, 211–12, 214, 250n55; as strategy of regeneration, 207–8, 211–12, 250n59
Domesticity, 173, 174, 175–76
"Don't Let Me Be Lonely Tonight" (Taylor), 2
Douglas, Alan, 83
Douglass, Frederick, 72, 106
Du Bois, W. E. B., 64
Duke & Leonard, 83, 88, 92
Dunbar, Paul, 80
Dutchman (Baraka), 87
A Dying Colonialism (Fanon), 37–38

Early, Jackie, 147, *149*
Earth, Wind and Fire, 2, 9, 134, 194
East Wind performance loft, 76, 83, 92
Ebony, 67, 68
Ed Sullivan, 118, 119
Edwards, Armistead, 203, 207, 227n20
Ellison, Ralph, 63, 125, 208, 234n66, 250n59
Equity Library Theater, 148, 150
ETV (educational television), 13, 49–51, 56, 96–97, 233n44
Evers, Myrlie, 176

The Factory, 218
Family life: alternatives to, 176–77; on commercial television, 161; family reproductive economy, 175–77; nuclear family, 172–75, 176–77, 178; polygamy, 175, 176; women as mothers, 172–73, 174, 175–76; women in the nationalist family, 175–76
Fania All-Stars, 131
Fanon, Franz, 37–38

Farrakhan, Louis: audience reaction to, 164, 166–67, 218; emotional appeal of, 166–67; Haizlip's reaction to, 167–68; on homosexuality, 165–67, 166–67, 168–69; reception on *Soul!*, 19, 154, 162–64
"Farrakhan the Minister," 162–65
Fashion styles, *53*, *111*; Afros, 8, 18, *53*, 79, 104–5, *105*; of Baraka, 169, 173; black femininity expressed through, 137–38; Farrakhan's military suit, 164; individuality expressed through, 8, 136, 137, 226n15; matching gowns, 203
Feather, Leonard, 118
Feminism, black, 160, 243n11
Ferguson, Karen, 234n60
Ferguson, Roderick, 177
Fields, Walter, 6, 217
Fifth episode of *Soul!*: black unity expressed, 88; church moment on, 88; on commercial television, 87; Haizlip as skilled conversationalist, 84–89, 163–66, 171, 172; *Julia* discussion, 88, 89–90; Last Poets debut, 83, 86; performativity on, 89–90; radical black theater, 85–86; reaction to "Die Nigga!," 91; stage set, 86, 91; vibrations in, 91–92
Final episode of *Soul!*, 182, 202–7
Flack, Roberta, 9, *10*, 94, 204, 215
Flip Wilson Show, 12, 13, 205, 215
Fonda, Jane, 64, 76, 142, 155, 190
Ford Foundation, 15, 28, 40, 43; in black fiction, 61–62; Black Power movement, 62, 234n60; black programming funded by, 56, 57, 62–64, 87, 88, 89; black studies supported by, 96, 183, 234n60; funding request from Channel 13, 94–96; Project for New Television Programming, 54–55, 61, 94, 97, 101, 200, 234n66; public television funded by, 52, 54; rejection of refunding application for *Soul!*, 94, 95–98, 101; *Soul!* supported by, 15, 54, 62, 68–69, 74, 82, 87–89, 94, 101, 214; television audiences identified by, 43, 55, 66

"Four Women" (Simone), 137, 139–40
Fowler, Virginia, 156, 242n3
Foxx, Redd, 12, 161
Fragile alliance (term), 42
Franklin, Aretha, 64, 142, 215
"Freaks and the American Ideal of Manhood" (Baldwin), 151, 160, 162
Freedomways, 196, 213, 214
Freeman, Dan (*The Spook Who Sat by the Door* [Greenlee]), 61–62, 141–42
Friendly, Fred, 73, 97–98
Friends of Black Journal, 198, 199
Frith, Simon, 125, 239n19
Funding: *for Black Journal*, 54–55, 98, 183, 248n34; for black programming, 54, 56, 57, 62–64, 73, 94–96; challenges of, 55–56; of children's programming, 199; complexities of, 41–42; corporate sponsorship, 13, 24, 98, 184, 238n46; for *Interface*, 182, 184, 189, 194, 195; racial-state reasoning, 195, 196–99, 202, 205; rejection of refunding application for *Soul!*, 94, 95–98, 101; viewer support for programming, 94–100, 193, 199–201, 204, 250n53

Gates, Henry Louis, Jr., 244n19
Gay visibility, 151–52, 243n14
Gent, George, 56, 57
Gerry B, 27, 134
Gestures: body positions, 172; camera shots of, 88, 105, 113, 159, 167–68, 179; handshake between Haizlip and Farrakhan, 167–68, 179; putting on a bow, 88, 167; of resignation, 159–60
Gillespie, Dizzy, 135
Giovanni, Nikki, *149, 157*; Baldwin dialogue with, 154–62, 244n22; Betty Shabazz as friend of, 147; in black arts movement, 155; on black heterosexuality, 157; criticism of, 19, 155–56; cultural nationalism and, 155; feminist critique by, 154, 157–60; on Haizlip's circle of friends, 242n3; on male dominance, 157, 175, 176; on masculine

authority, 159; New York Community Choir, *24*, 155, 194; popularity of, 155, 204, 216, 218; as *Soul!* host, 27, *111*, 147
Giovanni's Room (Baldwin), 161
Girl groups. *See* Labelle
"God Bless the Child" (Holliday/ Hertzog), 2, 6, 27, 87, 91, 206
Gospel music, 64, 77, 229n45. *See also* Williams, Marion
Gould, Deborah, 46
Gray, Herman, 226n18
"Grazing in the Grass" (Union of South Africa), 110
Great American Dream Machine, 190
Green, Al, 9, *143*, 144, 194
Greenlee, Sam, 61–62, 141–42
Grosvenor, Vertamae, 2, 179, 209, *210*, 218
Gunn, Hartford N., Jr., 195–96, 197

Hair styles, 8, 18, *53*, 79, 104–5, *105*, 115, 203
"Haitian Fight Song," 118, 124
Haizlip, Ellis, 2, *85, 212, 219*; background of, 6, 14, 23, 41, 84, 110, 147–48, 150, 228n44; Betty Shabazz as friend of, 147; on black community, 23–24, 65–68, 69, 71, 74–76; on black cultural expression, 1, 5, 12–13, 20–21, 38, 51, 52, 66–69, 92–93; on the black experience revival, 22; black performers, 66–67, 68; church tradition of, 23–25, 110, 228n44; conversation skills of, 84–89, 152, 163–66, 171, 172, 237n30, 243n12; disappearance as strategy of regeneration, 207–8, 211–12, 214, 250n55; on educational television, 13, 96–97; family conventions challenged by, 174–75; founding of *Soul!*, 20–21, 52, 64–65, 66, 217; on government's commitment to black programming, 197–98; influence of, 4, 8–9, 62, 191–92, 202, 217–18, 251n11; interviewing style of, 30–32, 40, 84–86, 237n30; "it's been beautiful" used by, 32–33, 206; on

music, 68, 75–76, 80, 105–7; on NOI's view of homosexuality, 165–66; on public broadcasting, 35; reaction to "Die Nigga!," 91; sexual identity of, 19, 24, 84, 110, 147, 151–52, 165–66, 218, 237n30; social network of, 64, 66, 147–48, 150–51, 217–18; survival, 204–6; vibrations, term used by, 21–23, 34, 81, 92, 107, 209, 210–11; "Where It's At," 58, 59, 63–64, 65, 66, 69, 234n66. *See also* Lukas, Christopher "Kit"

Haizlip, Harold, 27, 67, 84, 85, 215

Hall, Arsenio, *12*, 34, 218

Hancock, Herbie, 9, 118, 128

Handshake between Haizlip and Farrakhan, 167–68, 179

Hansberry, Lorraine, 60, 151

Harlem, 76, 83, 162

Harney, Stefano, 202, 250n54

Harper, Phillip Brian, 234n54

Harris Poll, 5, 97

Haskins, James, 226n7

Hathaway, Donna, 9, 215

Heard, Nathan, 62, 95

Heilbut, Anthony, 229n45

Heitner, Devorah, 4, 229n54, 244n23, 245n5

Henderson, Stephen, 21

Hendrix, Jimi, 126

Hendryx, Nona, 70, 88, 113, 136, 137, *138*, 140. *See also* Labelle

Hertzog, Arthur, 206

Hickey, Neil, 232n24

Hille, Alice, 24, 92, *93*, 114

Himes, Chester, 147

Historical documentation of *Soul!*, 203–8

Hobson, Charles, 5, 225n7

Hobson, Sheila Smith, 213, 214, 251n3

Holiness congregations, 23, 228n44

Holliday, Billie, 2, 6, 27, 160, 206

Holt, Samuel, 192

"Home Is Where the Hatred Is" (Scott-Heron), 206

Homosexuality: black Left homophobia, 155; of Ellis Haizlip, 19, 24, 84, 110, 147, 151–52, 165–66, 218, 237n30; family reproductive economy, 175–77; of James Baldwin, 151, 155, 161–62; Nation of Islam's view on, 165–66

Horne, Lena, 115

Horsford, Anna, *17*, 18, 52, *53*, 108, 147, 150, 239n6

Howard Street (Heard), 95

Howard University, 14, 23, 84, 147–48, 191–92

Howe, Harold, 49

"How I Got Over," 88

Hughes, Langston, 203–4, 208, 250n59

Humphrey, Hubert, 49

Hurston, Zora Neale, 106

"I, Too" (Ellison), 208, 250n59

"I Believe That I've Finally Made It Home" (Hendryx), 137

the Impressions, 13, 76, 94, 115

Inside Bedford-Stuyvesant, 39, 225n7

Integrationist cultural productions: *Julia* as, 5, 60, 87, 88, 89–90, 92

Interface, 31, 182, 184, 189, 194, 195, 198–99; white viewers of, 198–99

Intimacy, 159–60, 164–68, 171–72, 244n23

Invisible Man (Ellison), 125, 208, 250n59

Iselin, John Jay, 199, 201

"It's been beautiful," 32–34, 43, 206

"I Wish I Knew How It Feels to Be Free" (Billy Taylor), 79, 80–81, 82

Jackson, George, 85

Jackson, Georgia, *85*

Jackson, Jesse, 153, 198

Jazz: of Bobby Sanabria, 5–6, 133–34, 226n9; intellectual appeal of, 67; Max Roach, 15, *120*; Nuyorican influences on, 132

Jazz and People's Movement, 117–18

Jefferson, Margo, 150

Joey Bishop Show, 116

"Johnny I Hardly Knew You," 79, 80–81, 82, 236n15

Johnson, Al, 113

Johnson, E. Patrick, 243n11, 243n14

Johnson, Lyndon: on affirmative action, 41; integration of television, 28; on media coverage of 1967 riots, 46–47; National Advisory Commission on Civil Disorders, 40, 231n18. *See also* Kerner Report

"The Johnson Girls" (Bambara), 206

Jones, LeRoi (Amiri Baraka), 92, 96, 98, 99, 145

Jones, Lisa, 8, 226n16

Joseph, Peniel, 244n28

Julia, 5, 56, 60, 87–90, 92, 161, 237n34

"Just Do the Best You Can," 92

Kain, Gylan, 86, 91

Karenga, Maulana, 169

Kawaida philosophy, 169

Kerner Report: on black audiences, 43, 46–48, 51, 66; impact of mass media on riots examined by, 45; Martin Luther King on, 44; public broadcasting's mission defined by, 39, 52, 58, 193; on racially biased representations in mass media, 46–47, 183; on violence, 44–45, 231n16; on white racism, 44; WNDT proposal for black programming, 57

Kgositsile, Keorapetse, 2

Kiermaier, John W., 63, 69, 74, 95–98, 234n66

Killens, John, 12, 29, 60, 92, 145, 234n54

King, B. B., 94, 116

King, Coretta Scott, 176

King, Jason, 32

King, Martin Luther, Jr.: anticolonial critiques of, 80; assassination of, 16, 28, 101; on black repression, 38, 68; on Kerner Report, 44–45

Kirk, Andy, 77

Kirk, Rahsaan Roland, *121*; "Black-nuss," 124, 141; blindness of, 120, 125, 240n32; chair act, 18, 123–27; conch shell blown by, 124; Jazz and People's Movement, 117–18; Newport festival appearance, 215; performance style of, 119–23, 240n32

Knight, Gladys, 6, *7*, 144, 147

Kruth, John, 118

Labelle, *138*; appearances on *Soul!*, 135, 136–40; evolution of, 18, 136–41; "Four Women" sung by, 139–40; "Lady Marmalade" sung by, 139; Mongo Santamaría appearance with, 112, 114, 134, 135; Patti LaBelle and the Bluebelles, 77, 79, 112, 113, 139, 203; performance style of, 141; "Won't Get Fooled Again" sung by, 137, 141

LaBelle, Patti, *138*; black seeds, 9, 203, 207, 227n20; "Four Women" performance, 140; as Patti LaBelle and the Bluebelles, 77, 79, 112, 113, 139, 203; "To the People, Thank You," reprise of performance, 203. *See also* Labelle

"Lady Black" (Last Poets), 86, 88, 154

"Lady Marmalade" (Labelle), 139

Landwehr, Michael, 64, 74, 77

The Last Holiday (Scott-Heron), 124

Last Poets: African American culture explored by, 88; audience reaction to, 91, 99, 102, 204; critical acclaim for, 92; fifth episode of *Soul!* appearance, 87, 88, 89; "Lady Black" performed by, 86, 88, 154; performance style of, 90–91; profanity used by, 247n28. *See also* "Die Nigga!!!"

Lathan, Stan, 10, *94*, 128, 203, 218

Latino community: alternatives to whiteness explored by, 71, 111, 128–29; Felipe Luciano, 111–13, 128–34, *129*; Nuyoricans, 127–28, 130; programming for, 117, 130, 241n47; promotional campaign for *Soul!* in, 73. *See also* Puerto Rican community

Latino music and musicians: African roots of, 128, 130, 133; black music linked with, 132–37; dance styles introduced by, 117; generational differences between, 132–33; instrumentation for, 91, 112, 127, 131–32, 134, 135; Mongo Santamaría, 2, 112, 133, 134, 135, 136, *137*; sonic explorations and expressions of, 127, 131, 132; *Soul!* performances of, 127–34, 240n40, 241n43; on television, 117, 130–31, 215. *See also* Colón, Willie; Lavoe, Héctor; "Shades of Soul I"

Latin Roots, 130, 241n47

"Latin Soul Beat and Music" (*Soul!* episode), 241n43

Lavoe, Héctor, 112, 127

Lawson, Betty, 192

Lerner, Max, 232n24

"Letters from a Region of My Mind" (Baldwin), 168

Letters in support of *Soul!*, 99, 100, 102, 200–201, 204–6, 213–14, 238n50

Liberator, 83, 87, 92

Like It Is, 5, 34, 214, 226n7

Lincoln Center, 21, 22, 112, 134–35

Lip-synching, 113

Local PBS stations, black programming on, 191, 247n25, 249n50

London, Frank, 123, 124

Long, Loretta, 77, 79, 84, 85, 86, 88, 154

Long, Peter, 99–100

A Long Rap: Commonly Known as a Poetic Essay (Rodgers), 12

Loomis, Henry, 192, 195, 196, 200

Lorde, Audre, 160, 243n11

Los Pleneros, 241n43

Lott, Tommy Lee, 4, 196

Luciano, Felipe, 111–13, 128–34, *129*

Lukas, Christopher "Kit": on black culture, 68, 76, 233n44; *Black Journal* as competition for *Soul!*, 192; on black representation on television, 57–60; funding for *Soul!*, 59–60, 74, 98, 183, 214–15, 238n46; "Where It's At," 58, 59, 63–65, 66, 69

Makeba, Miriam, 2, 31, 110, *111*, 147, 176

Malcolm X, 16, *17*, 80, 145, 163, 166

el Malo (Willie Colón), 6, 108, 112, 127, 131, 132–33, 241n54

Mangonès, Albert, 124

Martinez, Cruz, 241n43

Masekela, Hugh, 2, 110, 118

Masterpiece Theatre, 135, 188, 191, 199, 238n46

Mayfield, Curtis, 5, 13, 27, 76, 106, 114, 115

M'Boom, 11

Mbulu, Letta, 2

McCoy Tyner Quartet, 118

McLean, Ruth, 204–6, 213–14

Meaningfulness: in black television programming, 64, 74–76

Media: African American press, 39, 67, 68, 196, 213, 214, 225n7; black employment in, 29, 39, 40–41, 51, 59–60, 196, 213–14, 225n7, 248n38; on development of public television, 56; Haizlip on black cultural self-expression, 20–21; Kerner Report on, 45, 46–48; spectacles of violence in, 38–39, 57; *Variety*, 56, 92; women performers praised in, 77, 79

Melody Maker, 208

Mendelsohn, Harold, 233n49

Merv Griffin, 117

Meyer, Richard, 50, 59, 232n34, 242n34

Mingus, Charles, 118, 124

Minow, Newton N., 9

Misfittedness: of Ellis Haizlip, 19, 24, 84, 151–52, 165–66, 218, 237n30; homosexuality, 19, 24, 84, 151, 165–69; queerness, 19, 24, 84, 110, 139, 151–52, 161–62, 229n45, 243n14

The Mod Squad, 34, 60

Monk, Thelonious, 118, *119*

Moon Shadow (Labelle), 137

Moore, Melba, 9, 94

Moore, Queen Mother Audley, 9, 153

Morrison, Toni, 1, *3*

Moten, Fred, 202, 250n54

Motown, 14, 114, 115

Moynihan Report (*The Negro Family: The Case for National Action*), 160, 177

Muhammad, Elijah, 162, 164, 166, 168

Muhammad Ali, 110–11, 147

Muhammad Speaks, 73

El Mundo de Tito Puente, 117

Muñoz, José, 33, 228n42, 243n11

National Advisory Commission on Civil Disorders, 40

National Association of Educational Broadcasters, 50–51

National Black Political Conventions, 163

National Black Theater, 83, 92

Nationalism, 153–54

Nation of Islam (NOI), 154, 162–64, 165–69, 174, 244n26. *See also* Farrakhan, Louis

The Nat "King" Cole Show, 60–61

Neal, Evelyn, 145

Neal, Larry, 145

Le Nègre Marron (Mangonès), 124

The Negro Family: The Case for National Action (Moynihan Report), 160, 177

Nelson, David, 86, 90–91

Nelson, Novella, *37, 78, 148*; Betty Shabazz as friend of, 147; as the face of *Soul!*, 79, 147; Haizlip remembered by, 9, 36, 40–41, 80, 237n30; "I Wish I Knew How It Feels to Be Free" (Billy Taylor), 79, 80–81, 82; "Johnny I Hardly Knew You" sung by, 79, 80–81, 82, 236n15; performances of, 18, 37, 79, 80–81, 82, 98, 147, 236n15; on self-expression, 150

NET (New York). See *Black Journal*; WNDT (Channel 13)

New Negro era, 204

Newport Jazz Festival, 215

News programming: black audience for, 45–47; black political expression on, 152–54; black production crews for, 41; Nixon administration opposition to, 188–90, 247n22; opposition to, 184–88, 188–90, 197, 247n22; riots reported by, 38–39, 45–48 , 232n24

Newton, Huey, 192

New York City. *See* New York Community Choir; Puerto Rican community; WNDT (Channel 13)

New York Community Choir, *24*, 155, 194

"New York Television Theater," 95

Nixon administration (Richard Nixon): COINTELPRO (Counter Intelligence Program), 28, 229n55; federal authority over television under, 28; local autonomy over public broadcasting programming, 191; on news programming, 184–88, 188–89, 197, 201

NOI (Nation of Islam), 154, 162–64, 165–69, 174, 244n26

"Notes from the Producer" (Haizlip), 211

Nuclear family, 172–75, 176–77, 178

Nuyoricans, 127–28, 130. *See also* Colón, Willie; Lavoe, Héctor; Luciano, Felipe

Odetta, 9, *11*

Office of Public Broadcasting (Ford Foundation), 54

Office of Telecommunications (OTP), 187, 188–89, 190, 246n15

"Old Rugged Cross," 18, 122

Omi, Michael, 184, 197, 249n41

Ouellette, Laurie, 4, 49

"Oye como va" (Puente), 117

Oyewole, Abiodun, 86, 91

Ozersky, Josh, 236n22

Pan-Africanism, 110, 133–34, 135

Patti LaBelle and the Bluebelles, 77, 79, 112, 113, 139, 203

PBS, 28, 41

Peabody Award, 27, 83

Peaches and Herb, 94, 239n14

Pearson, Pete, 119

Peck, David, 238n46

"People Get Ready" (Mayfield and the Impressions), 116

Pharoah Sanders Quintet, 98, 116

Phillips, Esther, 206, *207*

Phillips, Reuben, 77, 84, 118

Pickett, Wilson, 2, 204

Pinza, Carla, 241n43

Pitchford, Russell, 86, 92

Poetry readings, 12, 13, 128, *129*, 147, *149*, 218. *See also* Giovanni, Nikki; Last Poets

Poitier, Sidney, 1, 87, *148*

Polygamy, 175, 176
Poussaint, Alvin, 27, 77, 79, 84, 85
Powell, Maxine, 115
Pozo, Chano, 135
Prisoners recruitment for Nation of
    Islam, 165
Project for New Television Program-
    ming, 54–55, 61, 94, 97, 101, 200,
    234n66
Public Broadcasting Act (1967), 49, 183,
    245n4
Public television: African Americans
    in, 51; black self-empowerment and
    self-definition in, 51; funding for, 41,
    52, 54–56; government support of,
    188; identifying audiences for, 56;
    opposition to news programming on,
    188–90, 247n22; racism, 56; urban
    production centers for, 52
Puente, Tito, 6, 15, 112, 117, 130, 131–33,
    215
Puerto Rican community: Afro-
    Boricuan consciousness in, 128, 130;
    Felipe Luciano, 111–13, 128–34, 129,
    130; music as generational bridge,
    130–33; Nuyoricans, 127–28, 130;
    promotional campaign for Soul!, 73;
    "Shades of Soul I," 127–28, 240n40;
    space mediated by music, 127, 241n43;
    television representations of, 131
"Puerto Rican Rhythms" (Luciano), 130

Queerness, 19, 24, 84, 110, 139, 151–52,
    161, 229n45, 243n14

Ra, Sun, 23, 106, 209–10, 228n42
Racial-state reasoning, 184–85, 195,
    196–99, 202, 205
Radical black theater, 85–86
R&B, 106–7
"Reach Out and Touch (Somebody's
    Hand)," 2
Realidades (Latino public affairs pro-
    gram), 130
Redding, Otis, 64
Red Skelton Show, 115
Relaxation (use of term), 86, 102

Representational paradigms, 8–9,
    226n18
"The Revolution Will Not Be Televised"
    (Scott-Heron), 29, 230n58
el Rey del Timbal (Tito Puente), 6, 15,
    112, 117, 130, 131–33, 215
Rickford, Russell, 145, 147, 155, 244n17
Riley, Clayton, 83, 86–87, 89, 104–5,
    236n23
Riots, 39, 40, 45–48, 82, 123–24, 126–27,
    232n24
Rituals of destruction, 123–27
Roach, Max, 15, 120
Rodgers, Carolyn, 12
Rolling Stones, 136
Rooks, Noliwe, 96–97
Room 222, 56
Royster, Francesca, 243n11
Russell Simmons Presents Def Poetry, 34

Salsa dance style, 117, 131, 241n40
"Salute to Black Women," 147, 149
Sanabria, Bobby, 5–6, 133–34, 226n9
Sanchez, Sonia, 1, 147, 149
Sanders, Cheryl, 228n44, 228n45
Sanford and Son, 5, 161
Santamaría, Mongo, 2, 112, 133, 134, 135,
    136, 137
Santana, 117
Santana, Carlos, 130
Saturation (Henderson), 21
Saturday Night Live, 18
Say Brother, 39
Scalia, Antonin, 187
Scott-Heron, Gil, 29, 104, 114, 124, 206,
    230n58
Seale, Bobby, 190
Sears, Roebuck and Company, 13, 98
"Sesame Street," 187, 191, 246n15
Sexual identity: of Ellis Haizlip, 19, 24,
    84, 151–52, 165–66, 218; of James
    Baldwin, 151, 155, 161–62
Shabazz, Betty, 16, 145, 146–47, 176,
    242n2
"Shades of Soul" (Soul! episodes), 5–6,
    108, 111–12

"Shades of Soul I," 111–12; Anglophone Latino audience of, 130; Felipe Luciano hosting, 128, *129*, 130, 131; Kirk's chair act, 123–27; Latin music on, 127–34, 240n40; young viewers influenced by, 123, 124, 133–34

"Shades of Soul II": English language introductions to music, 136; Labelle appearance on, 135, 136–40; Puerto Rican musicians on, 128; Santamaría on, 135, 136; Soul at the Center, 134–35

Shales, Tom, 195

Sharp, Saundra, 147, *149*

Shaw, Sarah-Ann, 57

Shepp, Archie, 117, 118

Simone, Nina, 79, 81, 139–40, 141

Simpson, Valerie, 1, 104, *105*, 144

"The Sixth Period," 152

Smith, Sheila (later, Sheila Smith Hobson), 5, 225n7

Smothers Brothers Comedy Hour, 81–82, 100, 112, 126

SNCC (Student Nonviolent Coordinating Committee), 31–32, 142, 206

Sonic explorations and expressions: audience involvement in, 135, 173–74; black church evoked by, 164; diasporan, 135; in John Cage's music, 209–10; in Kirk's chair performance, 124–25; of Latino musicians, 127, 131, 132; vibrations as, 34, 77, 104, 209–10, 211–12

Soul!: advertisements for, 24–25, 48, 73, 98; affective compact with viewers, 20–22, 71, 86–88; alternate hosts for, 27–28, 67, 77, 79, 84, 85, 215; Betty Shabazz appearance on, 147; as black community space, 10–11, 23–25, 74–76; black consciousness, 70, 82, 87–91; *Black Journal* as competition for, 192, 248nn30,38; black radicalism presented on, 16, 67–68, 152–54, 217; broadcast of, 1, 2, 228n36; the church as touchstone for, 23–25, 88, 91, 109–10, 164, 228n44; civil rights movement and the emergence of,

40–41; critical acclaim for, 5, 92, 116–17; criticism of, 100–101, 196, 197, 226n7; development of, 57–58, 64, 66, 68, 76, 79–80, 233n44; goals of, 13, 14–15, 20–21, 57, 64–66, 82–83, 216–17; influence of, 4–6, 8, 9–10, 123–24, 133–34, 217–18; intimacy experienced on, 159–60, 164–68, 171–72, 244n23; *Julia* compared with, 5, 60, 87, 88, 89–90, 92, 237n34; letters in support of, 99, 100, 102, 194, 200–201, 204–6, 213–14, 238n50; music on, 68, 77–81, 105–6, 114–15, 117–19; scholarly omission of, 4–5. *See also* Audience, black; Baldwin-Giovanni dialogue; Camera focus; Cancellation of *Soul!*; Fifth episode of *Soul!*; Ford Foundation; Last Poets; "Shades of Soul" episodes; Stage sets; WNDT (Channel 13)

Soul, use of term, 25, 64, 66, 104

Soul at the Center (festival), 21, 22, 112, 119, 134–35, 150, 211–12

Soul! episodes: chair act (Rahsaan Roland Kirk), 123–27; dance party, 127–28; Latin music on, 128–33, 241n43; "Malcolm X Memorial," 242n2; "Salute to Black Women," 147, *149*; "To the People, Thank You" (final *Soul!* episode), 182, 202–7. *See also* Fifth episode of *Soul!*; "Shades of Soul"

Soul on Ice (Cleaver), 64, 155

Soul '73, 215

The Souls of Black Folk (Du Bois), 64

Soul Train, 13–14, 27, 34, 84, 98, 112

The Spinners, 9, 194

Spirit House, 75–76, 217–18

The Spook Who Sat by the Door (Greenlee), 61–62, 141–42

Stage sets: audience seating, 7, 86, 91, 107–8, *111*, 119, 123, 139–40, 239n6; "Baraka, the Artist," 169, 171; Club Soul, 7, 27, 119, 123, 164; for "Farrakhan the Minister," 163–64, 171

Staple Singers, 107, *108*

Stern, Andrew, 64, 74, 84, 237n32
"Stop in the Name of Love" (Supremes), 141
Student Nonviolent Coordinating Committee (SNCC), 31–32, 142, 206
Studio audience: affective compact with, 88–90; applause of, 86, 88, 166–67; camera shots of, 1, *53* , 86, 88, 89, 105, 108, 123, 141, 167; children in, 173–74, *174*; church moments for, *24*, 88, 164; dance party, 127–28; Latin music familiar to, 131–32; performers' interactions with, 88–89, 91, 105–9, 112, 113, 119, 122–24, 141; reaction to "Die Nigga!," 91; reaction to Farrakhan, 164, 166–67; reaction to Kirk's chair act, 123–24, 127; seating for, *7*, 86, 91, 107–8, *111*, 119, 123, 125, 140, 239n6
Sullivan, Ed, 118, 119
Supremes, 113, 115–16, 141
"Sweet Lorraine" (Baldwin), 151
"Sympathy" (Dunbar), 80

Talking Black, 56, 57
Taylor, Billy, 79, 80–81
Taylor, James, 2
Teer, Barbara Ann: *Julia* criticized by, 87, 89; on Last Poets' performance, 86, 87, 88, 89, 91, 102, 154; National Black Theater founded by, 83, 92
Television: as an affective medium, 114; black employment on, 29, 40–41, 51, 59–60, 248n38; black male solidarity on, 167–68; black political expression on, 152–54; black visibility on, 34–35, 45–48; civil rights movement, 36–37, 38; as dominant form of domestic leisure, 114; Jazz and People's Movement, 117–18; Latin music on, 117, 130–32; Latino musicians on, 130–31; racial prejudice on, 56, 59–60, 115–16; riots reported by, 45–48 , 232n24; rock performances on, 125–26; sound quality of, 124; visual representations of musicians controlled by, 116; white ownership, 36
Thorpe, Sister Rosetta, 134

"Timberland" (Willie Collen y Si Conquest), 127, 131
The Tonight Show with Johnny Carson, 11–12, 13, 26, 117, 118
Tony Brown's Black Journal. See *Black Journal*
"To the People, Thank You" (final *Soul!* episode), 182, 202–7
Townsend, Pete, 126, 141
Truth Is on Its Way (Giovanni), 155
TV Guide, 29, 45, 60, 234n54
TV programming: black roles in, 47–48; black viewers, 45–48; social class reflected in, 45–47
Tyson, Cicely, 150

Umbra Poets Workshop, 241n43
Undercommons, 250n54
Unifics, 6, 94, 113
Union of South Africa, 110, 118
Up from the Roots, 135–36
U.S. government: support for racial integration, 184
US Organization, 169

Van Peebles, Melvin, 92, *94*
Van Vechten, Carl, 19
Vibration Cooking, or Travel Notes of a Geechee Girl (Smart-Grosvenor), 209
Vibrations: of black performance, 34, 211–12; creative solidarity, 104; defined, 21–23, 34; Haizlip's use of, 21–23, 34, 81, 92, 107, 209, 210–11; in music, 209–10; as sonic explorations and expressions, 77
Vibrations (Musical group), 94
Vibration Society, 119
Vietnam, 39, 80, 111, 190
Viewers: demographics of, 5, 42, 47, 50–51, 55, 58–59, 76, 192; empowerment of, 204–6, 216–17; letters in support of *Soul!*, 99, 100, 102, 194, 200–201, 204–6, 213–14, 238n50; on *Soul!*'s representation of black people, 204–5; support for black programming, 94–100, 193, 199–201, 204, 250n53

Vocal performance. *See individual headings (e.g. Nelson, Novella)*

Vogel, Shane, 243n11

Voting Rights Act (1965), 44, 228n33

Walker, Joe Tex, Jr., 94

Wallace, Michele, 19, 155–56

Warhol, Andy, 218

Warren, Calvin, 227n32

Washington, Roland, 6, 226n15

Watch Your Mouth, 152

"Watermelon Man" (Santamaría), 135

Watson, Irving, 12

Wein, George, 215

Wells, Mary, 94

"Where It's At," 58, 59, 63–64, 65, 66, 69, 234n66

Where the Action Is, 116

"Wherever We May Be" (*Soul!* episode with Stokely Carmichael), 1, 30–34, 142, 206

White, Maurice, 134

Whitehead, Clay, 187, 188–89, 190, 246n15

Whites and whiteness: black antipathy toward, 101, 102, 142, 161–62, 167, 168; black self-determination, 22, 25, 64–69, 71, 72, 75, 128; and European culture, 49–50, 68, 74–75, 126, 233n44; as *Interface* viewers, 198–99; *Julia* as assimilationist, 90; Latinos seeking alternatives to whiteness, 71, 111, 128–29, 217; patronage of black cultural projects, 41–42, 61–62, 89, 185, 202; racial inequality, 44–45, 47; as *Soul!* audience, 13, 25, 52, 65, 100–101, 191

the Who, 14, 18, 126, 136, 137

Wickham, Vicki, 136, 139, 208–9

Wild is the Wind, 139–40

Williams, Marion: appearance on fifth episode, 79, 83, 87–88, 204; on artistic freedom, 87–88, 89, 92; black identity, 87–88; critical acclaim for, 79; "God Bless the Child" (Holliday/Hertzog), 2, 6, 27, 87, 91, 206; "Prayer Changes

Things," 144; switch to country and western by, 87–88, 89

Williams, Martin, 118

Williams, Raymond, 6, 8

Williams-Jones, Pearl, 77

Willis, Jack, 193

Wilson, Brian, 23, 209

Wilson, Flip, 12, 13, 205

Winant, Howard, 184, 197, 240n41, 249n41

Withers, Bill, 9, 204

WNDT (Channel 13): campaign for *Soul!*, 73, 98, 182; formation of, 225n1; funding for black programming, 54, 56, 57, 62–64, 73, 94–96; language alerts, 191; support for *Soul!*, 82, 94–100, 199–201, 235n4, 250n53; "Where It's At," 58, 59, 63–64, 65, 66, 69. *See also* Lukas, Christopher "Kit"

WNET (formerly WNDT): autonomy of local stations, 249n50; founding of, 184; *Interface*, 182, 184, 189, 194; *Soul!* supported by, 31, 99, 199, 201, 238n50

Women: agency of, 87–88, 89, 115, 136–39, 176; black feminism, 12, 19, 79, 139–40, 154, 157–60, 228n33; *Julia*, 5, 56, 60, 87–90, 92, 237n34; motherhood, 172–73, 174, 175, 176–77; in NOI (Nation of Islam), 163, 167; political activism of, 9, 172–73, 174; reaction to "Lady Black," 86; reaction to *Soul!* programming, 88, 89; roles in black revolutionary project, 172–73, 174, 175, 176–77; "Salute to Black Women," 147, 149; as teachers of children, 173, 174, 175–76. *See also individual headings (e.g. Giovanni, Nikki)*

Women performers. *See individual headings (e.g. Nelson, Novella)*

Wonder, Stevie, 64, 104, 108, 114, 118, 144, 194, 215

"Won't Get Fooled Again" (the Who), 137, 141

Yarborough, Camille, 181

Young Lords Organization, 128, 130, 133